The Nature of Plants

THE
NATURE
OF PLANTS

Habitats, Challenges, and Adaptations

◆◆◆

JOHN DAWSON & ROB LUCAS

TIMBER PRESS

Portland • Cambridge

Frontispiece: *Eucalyptus macrocarpa.* Western Australia.

Right: A peaceful freshwater pond in a New Zealand forest, with sedges, long-leaved heads of *Carex secta,* and at center left, brownish spikes of *Eleocharis sphacelata.*

Page 6: A Mojave Desert scene with spring flowers.

Page 7: An alpine bog with tarns. New Zealand.

Drawings by Tim Galloway.

All photographs by Rob Lucas except those by Bob Chinnock (page 97), John Dawson (pages 25 left, 34, 48, 148, 149, 251, and 287), Tanguy Jaffré, Institut de Recherche pour le Développement (page 144 left), Pete Lowry, Missouri Botanical Garden (page 120), Andrew McEwen (page 200), Rudi Schmid (pages 6, 74, 80, 88, 111, 112, and 132), Barry Sneddon (page 26 right), Fanie Venter (pages 79, 98, 100, and 101), and John Whitehead (page 55).

Published in 2005 by

Timber Press, Inc.
The Haseltine Building
Suite 450
133 S.W. Second Avenue
Portland, Oregon 97204, U.S.A.

Timber Press
2 Station Road
Swavesey
Cambridge
CB4 5QJ, U.K.

www.timberpress.com

Designed by Susan Applegate
Printed in China

Library of Congress Cataloging-in-Publication Data

Dawson, John, 1928–
    The nature of plants: habitats, challenges, and adaptations / John Dawson and Rob Lucas.
        p. cm.
    Includes bibliographical references (p.   ).
    ISBN 0-88192-675-2 (hardback)
    1. Plants. 2. Botany. 3. Plant ecology. 4. Plant communities. I. Lucas, Rob, 1940– II. Title.
QK45.2.D39 2005
580–dc22   2004014251

A catalog record for this book is also available from the British Library.

Contents

♦ ♦ ♦

Preface

♦ ♦ ♦

With the exception of some bacteria, plants alone are able to manufacture their own food by harnessing the energy of light, using their chlorophyll in a process known as photosynthesis. Put simply, water from the soil is combined with carbon dioxide from the air, using light energy, to form sugars. Oxygen is a by-product. Essentially, the light energy is stored in the sugars or other foods such as the more complex starches, oils, and proteins built up from them. Plants, and the animals that eat them, later break down these foods to release the energy to maintain their living state. This process, known as respiration, requires oxygen and releases carbon dioxide.

Over evolutionary time, this special talent of plants for making energy-rich foods from simple molecules has subjected them to attack from the animals, fungi, and bacteria that feed on plants directly. Carnivorous animals, too, depend indirectly on plants, as they eat animals that eat plants, and so do fungi and bacteria that parasitize animals. If all plants became extinct, so would the animals, fungi, and most bacteria. If the situation were reversed and only plants remained, then those that depend partly on animals for their reproduction or on fungi and bacteria for some of their nutrients would be handicapped for a time at least, but many others would continue to flourish.

Plants have evolved means of preventing or reducing browsing damage from ani-

Aciphylla colensoi in flower. New Zealand. It is suggested that the spininess of *Aciphylla* would have dissuaded browsing by moas—large, flightless, extinct birds.

mals, and some exact a service for the food they provide. The most notable benefits provided by animals are pollinating flowers and dispersing fruits and seeds. Some fungi and bacteria pay their due by providing plants with certain important mineral nutrients.

Some plants make use of other plants. Vines climb trees to get to good light, and for the same reason epiphytes (perching plants) grow in tree crowns. Parasitic plants behave like animals and obtain some or all their nutrients from their cousins.

Except for some microscopic unicellular organisms, plants as well as fungi have the disadvantage that they cannot move around individually. Animals can move to where conditions are most suitable, and in the case of migratory birds this can involve journeys of thousands of kilometers or miles. Seeds germinate where they land—if conditions are not entirely suitable, they struggle, and if the conditions are totally unsuitable, they die. So plants and fungi produce large numbers of seeds or spores, to ensure that at least a small proportion will land in places where they can grow and reproduce.

Plants grow in many different habitats. Ideal conditions for most are probably to be found in the tropical rain forest. There, warm temperatures and abundant rainfall promote rapid growth. Moving away from this ideal, plants adapted to a wide range of more challenging habitats. Where rainfall is less, plants have evolved adaptations to locate, store, and conserve the limited and unreliable supplies of water, culminating in highly specialized desert plants. Where temperatures are lower, different adaptations have come into play with equally specialized results in the high mountains and Arctic tundra. Some plants have adapted to living with fires, to toxic soils, and to an excess of water. Some insectivorous plants have even turned the tables on smaller animals by trapping and digesting them.

There has always been interest in the ways animals live their lives. As animals ourselves, it is easy for us to identify with other animals. But plants, too, have many remarkable and fascinating stories that deserve to be told.

Acknowledgments

Several people greatly assisted us in the creation of this book. Barry Sneddon, botanist and friend, made a number of helpful suggestions about the text, particularly concerning some of the complexities in the reproduction of flowering plants. Jim Tyler, biologist, of northern Western Australia, also read the text. His special interest is in Australian plants of arid habitats, and he provided interesting information on adaptations to both drought and fire. The third reader was Damian Hewett, a young man with a keen interest in New Zealand forest plants, who assessed the book from the point of view of a generalist.

We would have liked to visit all the places in the world where plants with interesting adaptations are to be found, but as that was not possible we were fortunate in borrowing one or a few slides from several botanical photographers: Bob Chinnock, Tanguy Jaffré, Pete Lowry, Andrew McEwen, Rudi Schmid, Barry Sneddon, Fanie Venter, and John Whitehead.

We are also very grateful to Clive and Nicki Higgie for their hospitality and for access to their remarkable country garden, Paloma, with its array of succulent and other interesting plants. A number of photographs for the book were taken in their garden.

Finally, last but not least, we thank Timber Press for proposing the book to us and for much useful and encouraging advice.

CHAPTER ONE

The Freeloaders

◆ ◆ ◆

Plants Using Plants

The forests of the world, especially in the tropics, are probably the most complex of all the communities of plants and animals. In tropical forests the trees often support cable-like vines on their trunks, gardens of orchids and other epiphytes on their branches, and may also have parasitic plants plugged into the living tissues of their trunks or roots.

Vines start growing from the ground and usually remain connected to it, but their slender stems are not strong enough to carry their foliage to a height where there is sufficient light. So they hitch a ride on trees and shrubs, attaching themselves by a variety of means.

Epiphytes get the full light they need by germinating on the branches, or sometimes the trunks, of the trees. Apart from some large tree or shrub epiphytes that eventually send roots to the ground, however, most have no connection to the soil and rely on their capacity to store and conserve water to get through dry spells.

Parasitic plants draw water and nutrients via root-like structures called haustoria from trees, shrubs, and sometimes herbaceous plants. Some parasites, the mistletoes, have chlorophyll to manufacture most of their own food, deriving mainly water and minerals from their host. Others lack chlorophyll and depend completely on their hosts for sustenance.

The mistletoe *Peraxilla tetrapetala* (Loranthaceae)
in flower, with a network of runners attached to a
tree trunk by haustoria. New Zealand.

The plumbing system of plants

Before considering the adaptations of vines, epiphytes, and parasites, we need to have a basic understanding of the way in which water and nutrients are transported internally by plants. Trees gain a place in the sun for their foliage by building up tall trunks that, via a plumbing system just inside their bark, also convey water from the soil to the leaves through the xylem (wood), and sugars manufactured in the leaves down to the roots through the phloem. Smaller plants also have xylem and phloem, but to a more limited extent.

In vascular plants, water moves from the roots to the leaves through special, narrow and vertically elongated cells in the xylem tissue. These hard-walled xylem cells are dead and devoid of living contents at maturity. In one type of water-conducting cell, found in all vascular plants, the water moves from cell to cell through thin spots in the cell walls. Some xylem cells, the vessel elements, are joined end to end and have connecting walls with one or more holes in them, so each series of cells functions as a single pipe known as a vessel. This is believed to provide a more efficient means of water transport because the water meets less resistance moving through the open end walls;

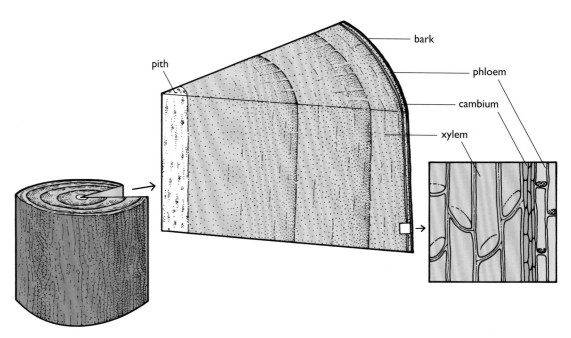

Diagrams of part of a tree trunk to show the water- (xylem) and sugar- (phloem) transporting cells, and the bark, which insulates the living tissues from cold and drought, and as it flakes away at the surface is replaced by a special cambium that forms in the older phloem. In the three-dimensional diagrams, three annual rings are seen in the wood (xylem). In the inset, the end walls of each cell of the xylem vessels have broken down, leaving circular openings. The phloem cells show the sieve-like end walls, but the protoplasm strands are not shown. Thin-walled cambium cells lie between the xylem and phloem.

some water also moves laterally through thin spots joining cells. The evolution of vessels is considered to be one of the many reasons flowering plants have been so successful in terms of their diversity. Conifers lack vessels, but they still manage to transport water to considerable heights. Some of the tallest trees in the world are conifers, including the tallest of all, the coast redwood (*Sequoia sempervirens*) of California and southwestern Oregon.

The sugar-conducting phloem is in a zone to the outside of the xylem. It, too, has conducting cells that are elongate and joined in linear series, but they are soft-walled and remain alive. Their usually transverse end walls are perforated like a sieve, and continuous strands of protoplasm, through which sugar in solution is conveyed, pass through the holes from cell to cell in each series.

Between the xylem and phloem in most trees and shrubs there is a layer of thin-walled, delicate cells known as the cambium. Cambial cells are able to divide, forming new xylem inwardly and new phloem outwardly throughout the life of the plant. In temperate regions a new layer of wood (xylem) and a thinner layer of phloem is formed each spring. Each layer of wood is known as an annual ring, and the rings can be counted to determine the age of a tree.

Climbing to the light—The vines

Some vines, particularly in tropical forests, have stout, woody, cable-like stems, though the quantity of water-conducting wood (xylem) is much less than that of trees of comparable height. These woody vines are often known as lianes. Vines are most abundant in tropical forests but are also present in temperate regions. Among woody vines native to Europe, ivy (*Hedera helix*) is widespread, as are species of *Clematis* and honeysuckle (*Lonicera*). The warmer Mediterranean area is the home of the grape vine (*Vitis vinifera*) and species of Dutchman's-pipe (*Aristolochia*) and greenbrier (*Smilax*). There are also nonwoody vines. Some are small annuals that climb on shrubs or perennial herbs, such as the wild pea and its relatives (*Pisum*); others are perennials, such as bindweed (*Convolvulus*), which dies down in winter, and periwinkle (*Vinca*), which is evergreen. Temperate North America shares a number of these genera, but there are others of tropical affinity, particularly in the warmer Southeast.

Most vines, though not all, need full light to flourish, so they are most abundant and often grow rampantly in damaged or regenerating forest. As the tree canopy gradually closes, the vines diminish as many of them cannot regenerate in shade. In a tall, mature tropical forest there may be few vines apart from the more shade-tolerant, mostly sub-canopy species. In some cases, vines are found in localized clusters in these tall forests. These mark the sites of former gaps in the canopy, resulting from the collapse of large, old trees.

Some of the larger woody vines, when they have reached the canopy, continue to

Massive woody cables of mature specimens of the liane *Metrosideros perforata*. A young plant, attached by roots, forms a leaf mosaic on the supporting trunk. New Zealand.

climb, or rather spread, from tree crown to tree crown. In fact, the total leaf area of such a vine can be at least as great as that of its supporting tree, if not several times greater. This is supported by studies in Venezuela, where lianes were found to make up 4.5% of the total aboveground biomass of the forest but 19% of its total leaf area, and Gabon, where 33–39% of the leaf litter in forests comes from vines (Putz and Mooney 1991, 127).

So to supply its extensive foliage with water, a vine clearly must have a more efficient system of transport through the limited amount of water-conducting tissue in its slender stems than a tree with the more extensive xylem in its large trunk. To find why this is so, we need to examine the cellular structure of the xylem of vine stems.

When a thin transverse section of a vine stem is examined microscopically, the most striking thing in many cases is the wide diameters of the vessels. Experiments with a woody vine of the pea family (Fabaceae) and an herbaceous vine of the pumpkin family (Cucurbitaceae) show that vines have a greater water-transporting capacity than trees. Water transport in the two vines was shown to be 60–120 times more efficient than in many trees (Putz and Mooney 1991, 150). Xylem vessels of vines can also be of considerable length, from 0.5 to 7 m (19 inches to 23 feet).

There is another way in which the stem anatomy of woody vines differs from that of trees. In trees, the wood or xylem, of which only the newest and outermost annual ring actually conducts water, is in the form of a solid cylinder whose rigidity is able to support large crowns of leaves and branches. Vines need to be more flexible to cope with the twists and turns of climbing or the stresses that result when they partly or completely slip away from their supports. Woody vines achieve flexibility by having a considerable amount of soft tissue as well as wood in their stems. In some, the cylinder of wood is divided into segments that alternate with soft tissue; in others, there are alternating cylinders of wood and soft tissue. Some woody vines also have flattened, ribbon-like stems to achieve greater flexibility. These are just a few of a number of patterns.

The scramblers

How do vines climb? They do so in a variety of ways. The scramblers are the least specialized with their weak, slender stems trailing through the foliage of shrubs and young trees. Those woody species that do not have a way to anchor their stems do not attain any great height because as their weight increases they tend to slip from their supports. In a number of species of oleaster (*Elaeagnus*), some anchorage is provided by short, stiff, backward-angled side branches. *Elaeagnus pungens* is sometimes grown as a hedge, but if not controlled it can quickly develop into an impenetrable thicket.

Many tropical species of *Gnetum* climb in a similar way by means of short, stiff side shoots. *Gnetum* belongs to an unusual, small group of plants (the Gnetales) that has some similarities to flowering seed plants but in fact are cone-bearing seed plants, along with conifers and cycads. The net-veined leaves of this genus look very similar to

An Australian rattan palm, *Calamus muelleri,* with daunting spines, and the bases of several whip-like climbing organs.

those of dicotyledonous flowering plants. Stems of climbing gnetums become large and woody and can attain considerable heights in the forest.

More specialized scramblers are beset with backward-curved prickles on their stems and leaves. The genus *Rubus* is conspicuous. In northern temperate regions the blackberry and its relatives mostly form scrambling thickets on the ground, but in the tropics and southern temperate latitudes some *Rubus* species are high-climbing lianes with stout stems. They get established in the low growth at forest margins or in canopy gaps, spread from support to support, anchored by their hooks, and keep pace with the growth of trees so that eventually their foliage spreads widely in the forest canopy.

The most spectacular of the scrambling vines are the rattan palms of the African and Asian tropics, although their anchorage is provided by backward-angled spine-like prickles. The tips of their compound leaves or, in some species, modified inflorescences (clusters of flowers) lengthen into barbed whips as long as 5 m (16 feet). The whips become almost thread-like toward the tips and can be quite a hazard to anyone pushing through the undergrowth. The prickles can hook into hair, nostrils, and ears, and it is unwise to try to pull free. Rather, one should stop and carefully disentangle. In Queensland, Australia, these climbing palms have the appropriate common name wait-a-while. Firmly anchored by the whips, the stems of rattans elongate rapidly, sometimes as much as 5 m (16 feet) a year, eventually reaching the forest canopy, where they form crowns of leaves in the full light. The relatively slender cane-like stems can be remarkably long, with a record of 171 m (561 feet). In Southeast Asia these slender but tough stems are used for making cane furniture and other items and are an important source of income.

The stem twiners

The largest group of both woody and nonwoody vines are the stem twiners. In these, the stems of seedlings, or sometimes the shoots from spreading or fallen stems of already established plants, are initially self-supporting up to an average height in tropical forests of 30–40 cm (12–16 inches) and a maximum height of 2 m (6½ feet). If no support is encountered, the shoot curves down to the ground, grows along it for a while, then turns up at the end to begin searching again. To increase the chances of encountering a support the stem tips undergo a spiraling movement that completes a circuit from a few centimeters or an inch or more to more than 1 m (39 inches) in diameter every hour or two. It is thought these circling movements result from alternating expansion and contraction of cells on opposite sides of the stems.

When a circling stem comes near a support it begins to swing closer and closer until contact is made. If the support is less than 30 cm (12 inches) in diameter, as a general rule, the vine will twine around it and grow rapidly upward. At the earlier freestanding stage, the vine stems have, like the seedling trees, a solid cylinder of wood. When climbing begins there can be quite an abrupt change to a more flexible form of stem structure.

In many species of stem twiners the leaves are reduced or absent during the rapid climbing phase. When the well-lit forest canopy is reached, lateral, generally non-climbing branches form, bearing fully functional leaves and eventually flowers and fruits.

As already noted, some twining vine stems do not derive directly from seedlings but from a range of prostrate stems both above and below ground, and sometimes from roots. Such later-formed climbing stems have the advantage that they can get their energy for growth from food reserves in the structures that bear them. These food reserves derive from the canopy foliage of older stems in the same cluster.

Stems also arise directly from seedlings, but this is a much slower process as the only food reserves at first are those stored in the seed. The general sequence of events following germination can be illustrated by the closely studied New Zealand monocotyledonous vine *Ripogonum scandens* (Macmillan 1973). This twining vine is common in some New Zealand forests, where its often almost black, cane-like stems sometimes form impenetrable thickets. The seedling stem is about 1 mm (1/32 inch) in diameter and grows to a height of 6–9 cm (2½–3½ inches), when the apex aborts. Most of the nodes (stem joints where one or more leaves are attached) bear pairs of small dry scales, but adjacent to the aborted apex, one broad green leaf forms. Later in this first season a short branch develops near the tip and forms a few more leaves. In the second season a branch develops at the base of the stem below the ground, forms a short horizontal stem (rhizome), then turns up at the end to form an upright stem similar to the first though it is about 2 mm (1/16 inch) in diameter and attains a height of 15–20 cm (6–8 inches) before a few leaves appear and its apex aborts. In the third season a new stem forms at the base of the second, first forming a somewhat swollen and tuberous rhizome segment before turning up into another but stouter stem, with

A cobra-like, woody, twining vine. The original support has long since died.

a few leaves at the top, that can reach a height 50 cm (19 inches) or more before growth ceases. The first three seasons' growth now resembles a small shrub. None of the stems exhibits any tendency to twine. Despite the dim light, the chlorophyll in the leaves and stems provides sufficient food reserves to support a more vigorous upright stem in the fourth season. This bears pairs of scales in place of leaves, and at about 50 cm (19 inches) the apex begins to make spiraling movements. If a support is encountered, the stem twines about it, and at about 2 m (6 ½ feet) above the ground the tip aborts and a few side shoots with a few leaves are formed.

In subsequent years, new twining stems attain the maximum diameter of 1.5–2 cm (5/8–3/4 inch). At this stage the tips look very like *Asparagus* except for the dark, sometimes black, coloration that masks the green of the chlorophyll. These stems are now able to reach the forest canopy where, in the full light, lateral, nontwining, wiry stems are produced. These may also branch several times and bear two rows of quite large leaves, and eventually flowers and berries. Sometimes the twining stems on a sapling

can extend into the crown of a canopy tree when the sapling grows into the latter's lower branches, and sometimes newer stems twine around older stems to form multistranded cables 10 cm (4 inches) or more in diameter.

About 95% of twining vines twine clockwise. Most of the rest twine counterclockwise, with a few switching from one mode to the other. Sometimes one encounters a tree whose trunk bears a helical scar caused by a twining vine when the tree was young. As the young trunk steadily increased in diameter, it stretched the vine until it broke.

Most climbing ferns have roots that attach to their support, but species of the mostly tropical genus *Lygodium* twine and can extend into the forest canopy. The climbing organ here is strictly a frond with compound leaflets, though the fact that it has indefinite growth is usually characteristic of a stem rather than a leaf. The true stems of the fern are relatively short rhizomes growing close to the ground.

A multistranded cable of twining stems of *Ripogonum scandens*. To the right are flowers and foliage of *Metrosideros fulgens*, a root climber.

A twining stem of *Ripogonum scandens* cutting into a tree trunk.
As the trunk continues to enlarge, the vine's stem will break.

The tendril climbers

Tendrils are slender, wiry organs that are sensitive to touch, coiling tightly around any slender support with which they make contact. The tendrils are modifications of a variety of plant parts, such as leaves, leaflets, leaf stalks, inflorescences, and lateral branches.

Tendrils may be branched or unbranched, and like twining main stems they make spiraling movements in search of suitable support. A tendril reacts to the lightest touch—even contact with the filament of a spider's web is sufficient to trigger a coiling movement. The mechanism for this is still a topic of speculation, but it is known that the cells of a tendril in contact with a support contract while those on the outer side expand, resulting in coiling growth. The part of the tendril in contact with the support enlarges and hardens, and in some species the part connecting to the vine stem forms closely spiraled coils, pulling vine and support closer together. The spirals in this case do not all turn in the same direction—sequences of clockwise and counterclockwise turns alternate on the same tendril. This, it is suggested, prevents damage from too much twisting in one direction. The coiling also forms a flexible connection that can accommodate independent movements of the vine and its support in windy weather.

As tendril climbers require slimmer supports than those of stem twiners, they are most common in open habitats, disturbed forests, and forest margins, where slender supports are in good supply. At forest margins or in canopy gaps, woody tendril vines

Two tendrils from the *Passiflora tetrandra* stem on the left have twined around another on the right. New Zealand.

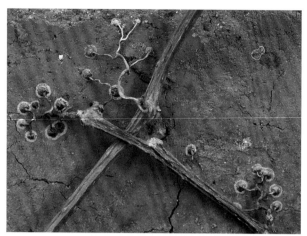

Dead winter stems of Virginia creeper, *Parthenocissus quinque-folia,* with tendril suckers still firmly fixed to a brick wall.

can reach the canopy. Of all the vines, tendril climbers are perhaps the most successful in spreading far and wide over the forest roof.

Well-known tendril climbers include a range of herbaceous species, mostly in temperate regions, such as the pea and its relatives in the Fabaceae, and pumpkins and melons in the Cucurbitaceae. Among woody species are the many species of passionflower (*Passiflora*), and the grape vine (*Vitis vinifera*) and its relatives. The species of *Clematis* stand somewhat apart from the rest of the tendril climbers in that their sensitive organs are the stalks of leaves and leaflets of otherwise normal leaves. These stalks are also sensitive to touch and coil around slender supports.

Rather different are some species with modifications of their tendrils that permit them to climb tree trunks and even cliffs. In the Virginia creeper (*Parthenocissus quinquefolia*), for example, the tips of the tendrils are expanded into small circular pads or suckers that adhere firmly to many kinds of surfaces, including tree trunks and walls of buildings. In other vines in the tropics, the tendril tips end in hard hooks that wedge into bark crevices of trunks or cling on to leaves and twigs.

The root climbers

The stems of some vines attach themselves to supports with clusters of roots, sometimes so strongly that if the stem is pulled away the roots are left behind. The roots may be quite short to very long, sometimes even extending right around the support several times. Root climbers are the most tolerant of shade and are best represented in closed-canopy forests. Some are slender, herbaceous, and low-climbing; others are stout, woody, and high-climbing. Among the former are ferns belonging to a number of genera, and species of aroids (arum lily family, Araceae). Woody species belong to a number of families, including the ivy family (Araliaceae, notably *Hedera helix*), the true pepper family (Piperaceae), the fig family (Moraceae, including *Ficus*), the *Hydrangea* family (Hydrangeaceae), and the myrtle family (Myrtaceae).

The stems of seedlings of vines that climb with attaching roots often spread, forming roots and branching over the forest floor in search of support to climb. In some, such as species of *Monstera* (Araceae), they grow consistently away from the light though their leaves are turned toward it. The stems in these cases are aiming toward larger dark objects in the forest, which are mostly large tree trunks, and especially those with wide buttresses in tropical forests. On encountering a tree trunk, the stems then grow steadily upward, though at a rather slower rate than those of the stem twiners, scramblers, and tendril climbers as the formation of attaching roots is not a rapid process.

Slender vines may extend into the lower branches of the tree crown; the woody vines generally reach full light at the top of the crown. In the crown, the branches that bear flowers and fruits extend away from the tree trunk and do not form roots. For this reason, vines that climb by their roots are generally unable to spread from tree crown to tree crown.

In many of the vines that are root climbers, the leaves on stems on the ground and the lower trunks are much smaller than those higher up. Ground and lower trunk fronds of the fern *Blechnum filiforme* in New Zealand are about 10 cm (4 inches) long with leaflets, in two rows, about 1 cm (3/8 inch) long. As the stem grows up the tree trunk, successive fronds become larger and larger until they reach a maximum of about 60 cm (24 inches) long with leaflets 15 cm (6 inches) long. It is among these largest fronds that the fertile fronds with their string-like leaflets are formed. In *Microsorum scandens* the fronds near the ground are simple; those higher up are compound.

A *Philodendron* (Araceae) with long, attaching roots.

Metrosideros fulgens (Myrtaceae) with short, attaching roots. New Zealand.

Microsorum scandens with simple fronds near the ground and compound fronds above. New Zealand.

Young climbing stems of *Metrosideros perforata* with the leaves forming a mosaic. New Zealand.

In some species of *Monstera*, stems on the ground bear scale leaves or small, saucer-shaped leaves with long stalks. Going up the tree trunk, the long-stalked, saucer-shaped leaves become progressively larger until the very large, often lobed, distinctively perforated adult leaves are attained.

As well as forming attaching roots, some slender vines also produce long roots that descend to the ground. These are termed feeding roots, and they are found in a number of the aroids and in *Freycinetia*, a genus of the screw pine family (Pandanaceae). Although having no true wood, stems of some of these slender vines can be quite hard. Those of a softer texture may die in their lower parts and lose contact with the ground, but some at least still have access to soil water and nutrients via feeding roots.

Stems of woody vines that climb by their roots can become massive, and when their attaching roots die they swing away from their supporting tree trunk, as shown on page 16. Leaves on the climbing stems in the shade are generally much smaller than the adult leaves in the good light of the canopy. The shade leaves press close to the tree trunk, forming a mosaic and ensuring that the leaves do not shade each other and can fully utilize the light available.

Juvenile forms of vines and other plants

We have seen that some vines that climb by roots that attach to supports have very small leaves when growing in the shade of the forest floor and on the lower parts of tree trunks, and much larger leaves when they reach higher, better-lit levels. Some vines that climb by scrambling, stem twining, and tendrils also exhibit this phenomenon (Dawson 1988).

A minority of trees also produce very small leaves during a juvenile phase, which may last 10 or more years. On the islands of Réunion and Mauritius in the Indian Ocean, there are 48 tree species in 43 genera, representing 35 families, that have very small-leaved juveniles (Friedmann and Cadet 1976). In some, the juvenile leaves are similar in shape to those of the adults but much smaller, or about the same length but much narrower. These species all grow on the drier sides of the islands, similar to a phenomenon observed in New Zealand in which trees with small-leaved juveniles are most conspicuous on the drier sides of the two main islands. It was suggested that the small leaves of the juveniles lose less moisture than larger leaves, enabling the juveniles to sur-

vive until they develop deep root systems to tap water at depth. Then, the change to the adult form with larger, more efficient leaves could take place (Wardle 1963). It should be noted, however, that a study in New Zealand shows that the juveniles of some of these species actually lose more water than the adults (Darrow et al. 2002), so the question is still open.

As well as having very small leaves, the juveniles in New Zealand often have densely branched, interlaced twigs, that is, a divaricate growth habit. In addition, more than 60 shrub species, distributed among a number of unrelated families, also have the divaricate, small-leaved form. Increasing aridity (and perhaps cold) during a glacial period may have brought divaricate shrubs into existence through the flowering and fruiting of divaricate juveniles that no longer changed into larger-leaved, adult-foliage trees (Wardle 1963). So some of these shrubs could be said to do without an adult-foliage phase.

Myrsine divaricata, a striking example of a divaricate shrub.

Most divaricate shrubs belong to genera such as *Pittosporum* and *Coprosma* that also include normally branched, large-leaved, forest species. In a number of such genera, when a large-leaved species meets a small-leaved species in nature, hybrids and sometimes hybrid swarms result. This supports the idea that some less hardy, large-leaved, forest species gave rise to smaller-leaved, hardier species of mostly open habitats in relatively recent Ice Age times.

An opposing view is that the divaricate habit was an adaptation to prevent or reduce browsing by the large, flightless New Zealand birds known as moas, which only became extinct in historical times (Greenwood and Atkinson 1977). There were a number of moa species, some of which were larger than the Australian emu. It was suggested that the small leaves, entangled twigs, and the sometimes brownish, dead appearance of the shrubs would have made them seem unpalatable to the moas. The proponents of this theory suggest that in the case of trees with divaricate juveniles, the switch to larger, more efficient, more palatable foliage takes place above moa reach. A different interpretation proposes that the changeover occurs above the level of ground frost (Mc-Glone and Webb 1981). Divaricate shrubs are unusually conspicuous in New Zealand, but they are also found elsewhere, mostly in deserts and seasonally arid habitats.

In most trees with juvenile foliage, the leaves of the juveniles are much larger than those of the adults. The juveniles grow in forest shade, and it has been suggested that their large leaves are designed to capture as much of the limited light as possible. If this is so, however, then how can the equally shaded, small, juvenile leaves of other trees and many vines be explained?

Large juvenile leaves are often similar in shape to the smaller adult leaves, but in some they are narrower but much longer. A New Zealand example of the latter, *Pseudopanax crassifolius*, is one of the most remarkable of the juvenile–adult contrasts. The two stages are so different that they were at first considered different species. The juvenile stage, which can last 15–20 years, has a slender but woody, unbranched trunk with a terminal cluster of tough, extremely long and narrow, strongly deflexed leaves that have been likened in appearance to the ribs of a broken umbrella. These leaves are as long as 1 m (39 inches) or more but only about 1 cm (3/8 inch) wide. When the change to the adult stage begins, the tip of the stem branches freely, forming a rounded crown with dark green, upward-angled leaves that are only 10–20 cm (4–8 inches) long and 2–3 cm (3/4–1 1/4 inches) wide.

Several juveniles and one adult of *Pseudopanax crassifolius*. The long, narrow leaves of the juveniles hang downward. Just to the right of the crown of the tallest juvenile at the center is the much-branched crown of a young adult tree with much shorter, more or less erect, dark green leaves.

Living in the treetops—The epiphytes

Long before the great era of exploration, primitive maps from earlier times showed the known world—Europe, northern Africa, and parts of Asia—surrounded by unknown territory, sometimes dauntingly annotated "Here be dragons." No dragons were reliably encountered, but when explorers penetrated beyond the Sahara in Africa they brought back accounts of animals that were strange enough, including giraffes, rhinoceroses, and zebras. Without proof, such accounts were often disbelieved.

Strange plants were discovered, too, in the tropical forests of Africa and elsewhere, and the most eye-catching were those that grow, often in great profusion, up in the crowns of tall trees. To the European visitor the only similar plants back home were mistletoes, which form large clumps in tree crowns. Mistletoes, however, are parasites, drawing water and nutrients from their host tree via root-like suckers. There are plant parasites, too, in tropical forests, but most of the plants in tree crowns there are better termed perching plants or, botanically, epiphytes. They do not parasitize their hosts. The advantage of the parasitic way of life is obvious, but what do epiphytes gain from their unusual habitat? They are mostly light-demanding plants, requiring quite high levels of light to grow and reproduce. The light that reaches the forest floor, often only about 1% of that in the open, is insufficient for their needs, but the tree crowns can provide them with almost the intensity that is available to plants of open habitats (Benzing 1989, 1990).

Most of the light-demanding epiphytes can sometimes be observed growing terrestrially, especially on rocky outcrops in the open, which offer conditions similar to those of tree branches. If some of the smaller epiphytes are dislodged and fall to the forest floor, they usually die from lack of light, unless a storm has opened a gap in the forest canopy.

Some lichens and mosses can be found as epiphytes in both temperate and tropical forests. These are small, relatively unspecialized plants, and as well as the many species growing on trunks and branches, there are some that hang curtain-like from twigs in cloud forests. In a more unusual case, in the undergrowth of tropical forests, the leaves of shrubs, young trees, and vines are often colonized by small lichens, mosses, and liverworts, some of which grow nowhere else. Other small shade epiphytes grow on the lower trunks of trees or on tree fern trunks. Again, they include mosses, liverworts, and lichens but also small ferns and related plants, and a few small flowering plants. The light these plants obtain can only be a little more than that reaching the forest floor, but perhaps the advantage they gain is escaping the smothering effect of leaf litter and the shade of the larger ground plants.

The generally much larger fern and flowering plant epiphytes belong to a plant group known collectively as vascular plants. These are specialized in a number of ways and are most notable for their efficient water- and nutrient-conducting systems, the xylem and phloem. In moist tropical forests, drought and cold are not a problem, as they can be in temperate forests, and vascular epiphytes are often conspicuous. They comprise many thousands of species, ranging in form from small orchids to trees that begin their lives as seedlings in tree crowns. Unexpectedly, vascular epiphytes, as individuals if not species, are often more abundant and conspicuous in tropical mountain and subtropical forests than in lowland tropical forest. Perhaps this is due to the lower rate of evaporation in the cooler forests, allowing epiphytes to grow more luxuriantly.

Sometimes one reads, in books written in the northern hemisphere, that vascular epiphytes are restricted to the tropics, but this is certainly not true in the southern hemisphere. In New Zealand particularly, such epiphytes are conspicuous in many forests (Dawson and Lucas 1993, 2000). The same is true, in lesser degree, of similar forests in Chile and eastern Australia. This probably results from the fact that oceans predominate in middle southern latitudes, with only limited and sometimes narrow areas of land. The oceans retain summer heat more efficiently than the land, and their influence greatly reduces the severity of winters near the sea in these latitudes.

Plenty of light but some problems

By exploiting tree crowns, epiphytes obtain the good light they require, but to survive they have to overcome several problems not faced by forest plants rooted in the ground. Even in forests with abundant rainfall, the treetops can sometimes be quite dry. Wind and sun induce high evaporation, there is little or no soil to absorb and retain moisture, and gravity ensures that rainwater rapidly drains away to the ground. Epiphytes growing in monsoon forests, where there is a marked dry season, are at an even greater disadvantage.

Another major problem is that essential mineral nutrients, readily available in the soil for most plants, are in short supply on the surfaces of leaves and tree limbs. As we shall see, epiphytes have evolved modifications to solve or at least minimize these problems.

How many epiphytes are there?

For vascular plants, estimates have been made of the total number of epiphyte species, but because tropical forest floras are still not fully known, these estimates can only be approximate. Also, there is some disagreement about how epiphytes should be defined relative to vines, and this results in somewhat different assessments. Vines with woody stems retain their connection with the soil throughout their lives, but in some slender ferns and aroids the part of the stem near the ground dies and the remaining stem continues to climb, deriving sufficient water for its needs through the attaching roots or by sending feeder roots to the ground. Some botanists classify such plants as secondary epiphytes; others, including us, prefer to consider them vines.

An abundance of epiphytes in the crown of a *Metrosideros robusta* tree, itself initially epiphytic. There are two nest epiphytes, *Collospermum hastatum* (leaves in fans) and *Astelia solandri*, and one abundant fern, *Asplenium polyodon*. At center left is a small shrub, *Pittosporum cornifolium*, and at center top an eventually large shrub, *Griselinia lucida*. New Zealand.

Despite such uncertainties, however, it is estimated that about 24,000 mostly tropical species of vascular plants are epiphytes (Benzing 1990). Of these, more than half, about 14,000, are orchids. Other flowering epiphytes constitute about 7,000 species. They exhibit a wide range of forms and belong to many families. There are no conifer epiphytes and only one cycad, a species of *Zamia*. Of the approximately 10,000 species of ferns and allied plants, about 3,000 are considered epiphytes, though this number includes vines that lose contact with the ground.

Bromeliads, bird's-nest ferns, and the like

Nest epiphytes, as bromeliads, bird's-nest ferns, and similar plants are collectively termed, have very short stems, so their mostly long and narrow leaves are arranged in rosettes or dense clumps. In the Asian and African tropics they are mostly ferns, while in the Central and South American tropics the highly specialized and diverse bromeliads predominate. A third and smaller group of nest epiphytes, comprising species of *Astelia* and *Collospermum*, belonging to the lily group of families, is found in the Pacific from New Zealand and New Caledonia to Hawaii.

The bird's-nest ferns are species of *Asplenium* whose sometimes large rosettes of fronds are shallowly bowl-like in form and could be mistaken for nests of rather large birds. Twigs, leaves, spent flowers, fruits, and bark flakes from trees are caught in these nests and gradually decay into a coarse humus around the bases of the fronds. This humus absorbs and retains water like a sponge. Roots from the fern grow into it to obtain water and also nutrients, which ultimately derive from the ground via the trees that produce the debris.

Other ferns that trap debris are more specialized and are sometimes known as bracket epiphytes. The staghorn ferns (*Platycerium*) have sterile fronds that are plate-like and extend upward, close to each other and to the tree trunk. Debris is trapped between these special fronds and again provides a source of water and nutrients. The fertile fronds are quite different. They fork several times in an antler-like fashion and extend outward or hang downward. On their undersides they are densely covered with very small, spore-producing organs called sporangia. Some of these ferns are massive, 1 m (39 inches) or more wide. Species of *Drynaria* also have two types of fronds. Their erect, sterile fronds become dry and brown, and the fertile fronds are also more or less erect and have the more usual fern pattern of an axis and pairs of leaflets.

The bromeliads (Bromeliaceae) are a remarkable family of plants. Only one species, *Ananas comosus*, provides an edible fruit, the pineapple, but many others are prized horticulturally for their unusual forms and for the striking and sometimes strange coloring of their leaves and flowers. They are not to everyone's taste, however, as many of them are very prickly, and some plant lovers consider their flowers gaudy rather than beautiful. About half the 2,500 species of this family are epiphytes.

Bird's-nest ferns, *Asplenium nidus*. Singapore.

Australian staghorn ferns, *Platycerium superbum*. The large shell-like structures are the sterile, debris-collecting fronds. Branching, spore-bearing fronds hang below some of them.

Flowers of the bromeliad *Billbergia* with bright red bracts.

Bromeliads are abundant and diverse in the rain forests of Central America and northern South America, but there are also a few species as far south as Patagonia and as far north as the southeastern United States. The only bromeliad outside the Americas is *Pitcairnia feliciana,* in West African forests, but it may be an introduction.

As well as storing water in various ways, those bromeliad epiphytes that occupy the driest sites in tree crowns reduce water loss through evaporation by a special mode of photosynthesis—the formation of sugars by chlorophyll using the energy of sunlight—that they share with epiphytic orchids of similar habitats, and also a number of desert plants. In all vascular plants the carbon dioxide and oxygen required for energy-storing photosynthesis and energy-releasing respiration have to dissolve in moisture on the surfaces of special cells. These cells are enclosed in the interior of leaves, preventing them from losing too much water vapor through evaporation. Air enters the leaves through minute pores known as stomata, mostly found on the shady leaf undersides. As air containing carbon dioxide and oxygen comes in, water inevitably goes out, but the stomata are able to exercise some control over water loss by opening and closing in accordance with water availability. In plants of moist habitats, stomata are open during the day when light is available for photosynthesis, and closed at night when photosynthesis ceases. This is the common or C_3 mode of photosynthesis.

In some plants of arid habitats and high daytime temperatures, this sequence is reversed—the stomata are closed during the day when evaporation is excessive, and open at night when evaporation is much less. What about photosynthesis in such plants? Well, the carbon dioxide taken in at night is converted to malic acid and stored until daytime. Next day, the acid is broken down to release carbon dioxide, and photosynthesis proceeds with the stomata firmly closed. This water-conserving process was first discovered in succulent species of the stonecrop family (Crassulaceae); it is known by the acronym CAM (crassulacean acid metabolism).

A third mode of photosynthesis is known as C_4, which is able to function at high temperatures such as those experienced by short-lived ephemeral plants in hot deserts. Unlike C_3 photosynthesis, one of the first products in the reaction chain is a four-carbon rather than three-carbon molecule.

Bromeliads are most conspicuous as epiphytes in rain forests, but there are also species in deep shade on the forest floor, others in deserts, and some of the largest specimens of all grow in the cold climates of the high Andes.

The *Pitcairnia* subfamily is the least specialized of the bromeliads and overwhelmingly terrestrial rather than epiphytic. Water and nutrients are obtained by roots from the soil in the normal fashion. The exposed plant surfaces are often densely covered with overlapping scales that presumably reduce water loss in arid habitats and insulate against cold and intense solar radiation at high elevations.

The *Bromelia* subfamily is much more specialized. In the terrestrial species, the one to several leaf rosettes of each plant are arranged so that the broad leaf bases overlap, trapping and retaining water and debris in spaces referred to as tanks. Special roots grow upward into the tank to absorb water and nutrients, but they supply only part of the plant's needs. The remainder is obtained by normal roots in the soil. The epiphytic members of this subfamily are more specialized still. The leaves in each rosette overlap closely, forming a single, narrow, tube-like tank capable of holding a considerable quantity of water and plant debris. It also provides a home for a wide range of insects or their larvae as well as some small species of frogs. The excreta of these animals and

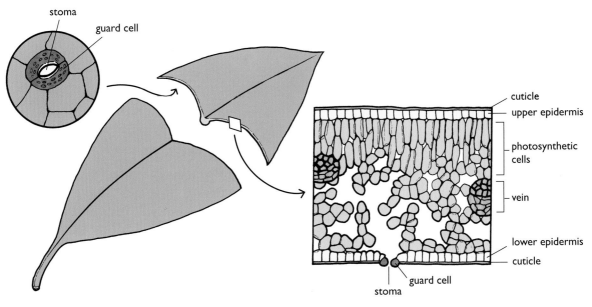

Diagram of a leaf.

their decayed bodies are an important source of nutrients for the plant. In these specialized epiphytes, water and nutrients are exclusively absorbed by specialized scales on the inner leaf surfaces. The roots do not absorb water and serve for attachment only. The seeds in this subfamily are contained in fleshy berries and are distributed by birds.

Almost all the members of the *Tillandsia* subfamily are epiphytic. The exceptions are a number of thin-leaved species that grow on the forest floor. The epiphytic species mostly have well-developed tanks that function in the same way as those of the epiphytes of the *Bromelia* subfamily, and once again the roots are for attachment only. Some species of *Tillandsia* have much-reduced tanks, but Spanish moss (*T. usneoides*) has gone to the extreme and given them up entirely. It has also given up roots and, with its small leaves and many branches, drapes itself over twigs and branches like some lichens. The surfaces of this curious plant are densely covered with overlapping scales that avidly absorb water when it rains and slow water loss during drought. At times, this *Tillandsia* dries up almost completely but revives when it rains, so it is a res-

Water-storing, leaf-rosette tubes of the bromeliad *Billbergia*.

A tufted *Tillandsia* in flower. Hanging at lower left is a small specimen of Spanish moss, *T. usneoides*.

urrection plant. For mineral nutrients, Spanish moss has to depend on the lean input of dust. The small seeds of this subfamily bear plumes of hairs and are wind-dispersed.

Bromeliad flowers are pollinated by hummingbirds, and like the leaves of some species, they, too, are tubular and contain a considerable quantity of nectar. The flowers are often very strikingly colored, sometimes in shades rarely encountered elsewhere in plants. Bright red is common and also bright blue, sometimes in combination, but there are other shades, including a strange, dark, slaty blue. The bracts associated with the flowers can be pink or red, so some inflorescences are decidedly multicolored. Sometimes the flowers, though crowded and numerous, are not so conspicuous. In these, the leaves surrounding the inflorescence simulate a large flower with their bright, often red coloration.

The closely related *Astelia* and *Collospermum* have long, narrow leaves often densely covered with overlapping scales similar to those of the bromeliads. *Astelia* has about 25 species, mostly in the Pacific region, but there are also representatives in the Falklands and on Mauritius and Réunion. Only a few of the species are consistently epiphytic—one in New Zealand and one on New Caledonia. The other species grow on the forest floor, in swamps, and in low alpine vegetation.

Epiphytic astelias have three-ranked groups of narrow, silver-green leaves aggregated into large clumps. The leaves are tightly folded at their bases, so there are no spaces where water can be stored. Humus gradually builds up below each nest from the dead roots and leaves of the epiphyte itself with the addition of debris from the trees. The humus is a source of moisture and of nutrients from the tree fragments and the invertebrate inhabitants.

Collospermums are more specialized as epiphytes. There are two species in New Zealand and one each in Samoa and Fiji. The form of the nests is similar to those of the astelias, but the leaves are different. They are broadly rounded at the base and arranged in wide fans with enclosed spaces between them that function as water tanks.

Flowers of the bromeliad *Puya*.

An epiphytic clump of *Collospermum hastatum* with berries. New Zealand.

Debris can also sift into the tanks, and in New Zealand there is at least one native mosquito whose larvae develop in them. Roots grow upward into the tanks to absorb water, and it has been suggested that scales on the inner leaf surfaces may also absorb water after the fashion of the bromeliads, but this has not been proved. Roots also obtain water and nutrients from the humus below the *Collospermum* nests, built up in the same way as in the epiphytic astelias but even more extensively. These *Astelia* and *Collospermum* nests, by branching over many years, form massive clumps with equally massive accumulations of humus. Their weight becomes considerable, especially after rain, and when strong winds blow they can crash to the ground, sometimes taking a tree branch with them. In early tree-felling days in New Zealand, such falling nests were sometimes called "widow makers." The humus below these epiphytes is a favored site for the establishment of other epiphytes, including a number of ferns, a *Lycopodium,* and several shrubs.

Collospermum hastatum leaf fan with water in its tanks.

Epiphytic ferns and fern allies that do not form nests

A number of ferns and so-called fern allies, the latter mostly species of *Lycopodium,* are consistently epiphytic but not as specialized as bird's-nest ferns. Their stems and roots attach into the humus of nest epiphytes, or into the similarly fibrous trunks of tree ferns, or into moss cushions. The fern fronds generally hang downward, and the lycopodiums, with their small, undivided leaves, branch freely by equal forkings to form hanging tassels that sway in the lightest breeze. Another, more restricted genus, *Tmesipteris,* more closely related to true ferns, is represented by species in Australasia and on a number of Pacific islands. It and its sister genus *Psilotum* are of particular interest because they are considered to be descendants of one of the earliest groups of land plants. Epiphytic species of *Tmesipteris* sometimes grow from the humus of nest epiphytes but more often hang from tree fern trunks. Their small leaves are similar to those of *Ly-*

Branching tassels of *Lycopodium varium*. The hanging fern at top is *Asplenium flaccidum*, and the large-leaved shrub is *Griselinia lucida*, which eventually becomes a large shrub in the tree's crown with a root connecting to the ground. New Zealand.

copodium, but the stems branch little or not at all. The sporangia of *Tmesipteris* have two compartments and are attached to leaves that fork into two. Some species of *Psilotum* are epiphytes, others terrestrial. They are much-branched, have scale leaves, and sporangia with three compartments.

The filmy ferns *Hymenophyllum* and *Trichomanes* can also be abundant as epiphytes, particularly in very wet and misty cloud forests. There, in company with mosses, liverworts, and lichens, they can form thick sleeves of growth over tree trunks and branches. In this habitat the small filmy ferns appear very delicate, but like the liverworts they resemble, they are able to dry out and later revive.

Added to the truly epiphytic ferns are root climbers that may lose their ground attachment or become established on tree trunks above the ground and grow upward from there. Notable here is the genus *Pyrrosia,* whose species have undivided fronds that are often somewhat fleshy and water storing. The surfaces of the fronds are covered with round, overlapping scales that help reduce water loss.

Tmesipteris tannensis, showing the sporangia with two compartments. New Zealand.

Kidney fern, *Trichomanes reniforme,* bearing sporangia clusters around the margins of the fronds, sometimes grows on the bases of tree trunks. Its undivided fronds are unusual among ferns. New Zealand.

Left: A tree in a cloud forest with the trunk and branches enveloped by lichens, mosses, and small ferns. New Zealand.

Epiphytic orchids

Many people believe that orchids are rare, exotic, and expensive. Some of them are, but many more are quite common, and orchids can be found from tropical forests to Arctic tundra and even in deserts. Nevertheless, there are about 10 times as many orchid species in the tropics than in temperate and polar regions. Many additional species are being discovered in the tropics, and it seems likely that the orchid family (Orchidaceae), with 30,000 or more species, will displace the daisy family (Asteraceae) as the largest family of flowering plants.

The orchids with large, elaborate, and colorful flowers that people buy or cultivate are mostly tropical epiphytes and their horticulturally derived hybrids. Orchids of temperate regions are mostly terrestrial, and in some of them the flowers are small and inconspicuous though often still quite elaborate in form. The varied and elaborate forms of orchid flowers have evolved in relation to pollination by insects (Chapter 7).

Epiphytic orchids mostly have long, narrow leaves that are in tufts attached to very short stems, but in others the leaves are spread along elongated stems. The inflorescences, sometimes bearing many flowers, may arise at the ends of stems or in the angles between leaf and stem.

Epiphytic orchids generally attach directly to the bark of tree trunks or branches with their roots often spreading widely. Orchid roots are very distinctive. They have several to many layers of dead and empty cells on the outside that quickly absorb and store water when it rains. This dead, absorbing layer is known as the velamen, and the living tissues of the root draw water from it. Epiphytic orchids operate on the edge of viability so far as water avail-

A *Cymbidium* orchid. Hybrids of this genus are widely cultivated.

ability is concerned, but they are able to conserve it in several ways. Many, including the commonly cultivated cymbidiums, have leaf bases that are swollen into pseudobulbs, which store water. In some, the leaf blade, too, is thick or fleshy and water storing. Obtaining mineral nutrients is also a problem. Some nutrients leach out from the bark to which the orchid roots are attached, and some are provided by wind-borne dust.

Some small orchids, especially some bulbophyllums, branch freely and form dense mats. Others are very strange indeed in that the plant body is almost entirely made up of roots. The stem is hardly discernable and bears no leaves, but it does form clusters of small flowers. The living cells of the roots, as in many orchids, contain chlorophyll and so are able to manufacture sugars in the absence of leaves. Many of the orchids attached directly to bark have thick to fleshy leaves and utilize the water-conserving CAM type of photosynthesis.

Shrub and strangling tree epiphytes

There is a wide range of small epiphytic shrubs in tropical and subtropical forests. They belong to a number of families with the Ericaceae (*Vaccinium* and the vireya rhododendrons), Gesneriaceae (including *Aeschynanthus* and *Streptocarpus*), Melastomataceae (including *Medinilla* and *Miconia*), and Rubiaceae (including *Coprosma* and *Psychotria*) having the strongest representation. These shrubs mostly establish in the humus of nest epiphytes or on mossy branches and live out their lives in the treetops without root contact with the ground. Most do not appear to have any special modifications. The leaves may be somewhat fleshy and water storing, and the waxy cuticle on the leaf surfaces may be quite thick, reducing water loss. Some rubiaceous shrubs, however, are very unusual in that they are swollen at the base into relatively large and somewhat ugly tubers. The latter are fleshy and therefore water storing, but they also have a much more specialized purpose as we see under "Epiphytes and ants," page 53.

Strangling epiphytes, or hemi-epiphytes, start off in the same way as the smaller shrubby epiphytes but eventually send a root or roots to the ground and, in some cases, become freestanding after the death of the supporting tree. The most conspicuous and numerous examples of the latter are the strangling figs (*Ficus*) of tropical forests. The genus *Ficus* is quite remarkable. Apart from the one commercially grown species (*F. carica*) of the Mediterranean, there are about 800 others in the tropics and subtropics. Some of these are banyans, whose branches extend laterally, supported by column-like roots, sometimes for remarkable distances, and many others are epiphytes. The smooth, pale, descending roots of these epiphytes branch and fuse to form a cage-like network around the trunk of the supporting tree.

Among other genera with some epiphytic species that establish root contact with the ground are the widespread *Schefflera; Clusia* in the American tropics; *Fagraea* in the Asian tropics; *Metrosideros* in New Zealand, New Caledonia, and some smaller

A young strangling fig on a supporting tree. Southern Queensland, Australia.

A descending branch of a banyan fig propped up by column roots. Singapore.

Pacific islands; and *Griselinia* in New Zealand and Chile. At least some of these become established directly from seeds that land on rough bark and so would be water stressed from time to time. In some, parts of the young roots swell into fleshy, presumably water-storing tubers. Eventually, one or more slender roots begin to grow down to the ground, keeping closely pressed to the bark, where rainwater flows down from time to time. Once the soil is penetrated, water and nutrients are readily available, and the growth rate of the epiphyte increases greatly.

In some if not most genera of such hemi-epiphytes there is generally one main descending root that may have major branches near the ground. Arising from the main root, there may be a number of girdling roots that extend horizontally around the supporting trunk, sometimes many times. In *Ficus* and *Metrosideros* at least, the epiphytes become freestanding trees after the death of their supporting trees, supported by a pseudotrunk of their own coalesced roots. In most of these epiphytes, however, the main descending root does not become large enough to support its crown independently, and the epiphyte falls with its supporting tree.

Do these epiphytes actually strangle the supporting tree by compressing the living tissues of the trunk as it expands within the confines of the epiphyte's roots? Some

A descending main root of *Metrosideros robusta* with clasping girdling roots. New Zealand.

botanists think not. They point out that the light-demanding epiphytes will establish only in the well-lit crowns of mature trees, and that by the time the epiphyte itself is mature the support might then just die of old age. However, the presence of the epiphyte is certainly not helpful to the tree and probably shortens its life. There is competition for water and minerals by the roots, and the crown of the epiphyte usually overtops and shades the crown of the tree.

Fibrous tree fern trunks are also a favored site for some epiphytes. Some of these are mosses, small ferns, and allied plants, but others become small or even large flowering trees that are stranglers and stand independently when the tree fern dies. Some tree ferns retain their old fronds in thick skirts. It has been suggested that the skirts are advantageous for the tree ferns, preventing the establishment of vines and epiphytes. Twining vines can damage young uncoiling fronds, and woody epiphytes can weaken tree fern trunks and cause them to break (Page and Brownsey 1986).

The tree fern *Dicksonia fibrosa* with long-persistent skirts of dead fronds. New Zealand.

Left: A tree combination—the crown of an epiphytic *Metrosideros robusta* in flower is at the top, with the smaller, shiny crown of *Griselinia lucida* immediately below, and the remaining crown of the supporting *Dacrydium cupressinum* just above the tree fern. New Zealand.

At left is *Pseudopanax arboreus*, growing on a still living tree fern. At right is *Weinmannia silvicola* on a collapsed tree fern. New Zealand.

Epiphytes and ants

One of the most remarkable mutually beneficial associations between plants and animals is that between some epiphytes and ants (Huxley and Cutler 1991). Ants are the commonest insects in tropical tree crowns. They build nests with internal gallery systems out of a cardboard-like material they manufacture, which is known as carton and includes a combination of soil and plant fragments. Such nests are desirable sites for epiphytes because they are a good source of nutrients, which are provided by the soil and the plant fragments of the carton, leftover fragments from ant food brought from elsewhere, and the feces and decaying bodies of the ants themselves. To increase the chances of their seeds getting to ant nests, some epiphytes have structures such as fleshy arils, oil bodies, and the like attached to their seeds. The ants collect such seeds preferentially, take them into their nests where they eat the edible attachments, and leave the seeds intact to germinate. Some ant epiphytes also have nectaries on their stems or leaves (extrafloral nectaries) to encourage ants to establish nests in their vicinity. It is also advantageous for the ants to site their nests adjacent to nest epiphytes as they are able to use the debris they accumulate as a building material.

Even more remarkable are epiphytes that provide housing for ants, such as the rubiaceous shrubs with enlarged tuberous bases that belong to several genera, of which the two largest are *Hydnophytum* and *Myrmecodia*. As the tubers enlarge, cavities develop within them that link up into a gallery system with external openings, occupied by the ants. These tuberous shrubs are found from Southeast Asia through Melanesia. Less elaborate ant houses are formed in leaves and rhizomes of some ferns, orchids (hollow pseudobulbs), bromeliads, and *Dischidia*, a genus of the milkweed family (Apocynaceae, including Asclepiadaceae).

How ancient are epiphytes and where did they come from?

There are differing views on the age and origin of epiphytes. It is probably true to say that if, in a particular vegetation type, there are unoccupied habitats where it would be possible for suitable plants or animals to make a living, then species will evolve to occupy them. So some botanists suggest that the ancestors of light-demanding epiphytes are, or were, shade-tolerant plants beneath the canopy in the forest or on the forest floor. Variants of these shade tolerators, requiring more light, would have colonized progressively higher levels in the forest until the sunny tree crowns were attained. If this is the case, then epiphytes have probably existed as long as the rain forests dominated by flowering plants—approximately 100 million years.

Other botanists suggest that epiphytes are derived from plants of arid terrestrial habitats that would have had little difficulty in adapting to the dry conditions of tree crowns. Because extensive deserts are geologically more recent than rain forests, they further suggest that epiphytes may not be very ancient. That there is no clear fossil evidence of epiphytes in earlier times is considered to support this view. However, fossils of epiphytes would be mostly of leaves or other detached bits and pieces, which would provide no evidence of their epiphytic mode of life.

Students of fern epiphytes favor forest floor ferns as ancestors because ferns are rare in arid terrestrial habitats. Similarly, orchids are not conspicuous desert inhabitants. With the bromeliads, there are desert species but also thin-leaved forest floor species. The cacti may provide the best case for a desert derivation of epiphytes. Most species grow in the deserts of North and South America, but there is a significant minority of epiphytes and vines in tropical forests. Even there the drought-tolerant epiphytic cacti could be ancestral, colonizing and diversifying when the deserts expanded at the expense of the forests in more recent geological times.

It is appropriate to conclude with a quotation from David Benzing (1989), a notable student of epiphytes: "Future inquiry is likely to reveal that earthbound precursors of the modern epiphytic flora occupied various habitats, including deserts, wet savannas, and the lower reaches of dense forests."

Plant pirates—The parasites

Particularly in the tropics, many trees have to put up with curtains of vines and masses of epiphytes on their trunks and branches. These can slow the growth or shorten the life of trees by shading their foliage or competing with their roots for water and nutrients. But at least epiphytes do not steal food whereas truly parasitic plants do. Those parasites with green leaves (hemiparasites) manufacture most of their own carbohydrates and, for the most part, steal only water and inorganic nutrients the host has absorbed from the soil, but those that have entirely lost their chlorophyll (holoparasites) depend completely on their hosts for water, carbohydrates, and soil nutrients. Holoparasites behave more like animals and fungi in this respect, as indicated by the name of one of the earliest of them to be described, *Balanophora fungosa*. Parasitic plants belong to a number of families and only some are entirely parasitic, so this way of life has evolved a number of times (Kuijt 1969).

Holoparasites

We begin our review of the parasitic plants with the most spectacular of them all—*Rafflesia arnoldii*—described and named in 1821. The genus is named after Sir Stamford Raffles, founder of Singapore, and the species after the naturalist who observed and reported the plant, Joseph Arnold. When Arnold first saw the enormous flower on the floor of the jungle he must have wondered for a moment whether he was hallucinating before being overtaken by excitement. He was taken to the flower by a local guide when he was on an expedition, led by Raffles, in Sumatra. In a letter he said, "To tell you the truth, had I been alone, and had there been no witnesses, I should, I think, have been fearful of mentioning the dimensions of this flower, ..." It was almost 1 m (39 inches) in diameter! Arnold sent a description of the plant to London, but unfortunately he died soon afterward from malaria, so he had little time to savor the discovery.

The huge flowers of this species are heavy, fleshy, and colored a rich, meaty red with contrasting white polka dots. There are five large, rounded petals and a deep cavity at the center, partly roofed by a diaphragm with a central opening. Within the cavity is a stout column that expands into a flat disk at the top. In male flowers the pollen-producing stamens are attached around the rim of the disk, as are the pollen-receiving stigmas in female flowers.

The flowers emit a smell of rotting meat, suggesting they are pollinated by carrion flies or beetles. Observations confirm that carrion flies visit the flowers. Unfortunately for them, the enticing smell is a deception as there is no sustenance for the eggs they lay to develop into larvae. Within the flower the flies climb up the column and receive a blob of sticky pollen from the stamens. If they then visit a female flower and column-climb again, the stigmas pick up the pollen.

A huge flower of *Rafflesia arnoldii*, with John Whitehead. Malaysia.

The flower buds are described as being like brown cabbages with a covering of scales, which are all that could be interpreted as leaves. The flowers generally open at night and last only a week before turning black and breaking down into a slimy mass. If a female flower is fertilized, the ovary at the base of the flower enlarges into a fleshy spherical fruit containing thousands of small seeds. A plantain squirrel (a rodent) and a tree shrew (an insectivore) have been observed feeding on the fruit, so they and perhaps other animals disperse the seeds.

Rafflesia arnoldii and a few other species of the genus have the largest known flowers in the world, but what about *Amorphophallus* of the arum lily family? The apparent flower of this spectacular plant, also evil smelling, has a central column up to 2 m (6^1/2 feet) high. The flower, however, is actually an inflorescence with many small flowers crowded on the column.

Rafflesias are restricted to Southeast Asia (Nais 2001) and include some species with smaller flowers only about 15 cm (6 inches) across. The species parasitize the stems and roots of two genera of the Vitaceae, the family of the grape vine. The exact details of the establishment of the parasite are not known, but presumably small seeds on or near a host stem or root germinate and penetrate the living tissues of the host. The cells of the parasite do not form a discrete mass of tissue but give rise to one-cell-wide filaments of elongated cells that spread far and wide through the host's tissues, particularly in the sugar-transporting phloem, right up to the growing points of the stems and roots. These filaments are very reminiscent of the filaments of parasitic fungi. When a flower bud is initiated, a localized part of the filamentous network divides to form a nodule of parasite tissue. This gradually enlarges and eventually bursts through the bark of the host as a flower bud.

There are a number of other genera of Rafflesiaceae. These are also mostly tropical, though there are some species of *Cytinus* extending to the Mediterranean, South Africa, and Madagascar, and of *Mitrastemon* in Japan. The genus *Pilostyles*, which has the smallest flowers in the family, parasitizes leguminous shrubs in arid habitats of northern Africa, Western Australia, and from the southwestern United States to South America.

Balanophoraceae are also widespread in tropical forests, mostly at higher elevations, with a few outlying species in temperate regions. There are three regional groups of genera, in the Americas, Africa, and Eurasia–Australasia. The parasites of this family differ in a number of ways from the those of the Rafflesiaceae and related families. They attack only the roots of trees and form a tuberous growth, attached to the host, which in some cases becomes quite massive. The tubers are often difficult to find as they are at least partly covered by leaf litter. Their surfaces are often covered with warty protuberances, and the inflorescences originate deep in the tissues between them and eventually break through the surface. There are many overlapping scale leaves on the inflorescence stalk, and the very small and numerous flowers, either male or female, are crowded on a single expanded fleshy axis or on many slender axes. So, again what appears to be a flower is an inflorescence, in marked contrast to the Rafflesiaceae.

Inflorescences of Balanophoraceae range in color from leaf litter brown to yellow, red, and dark purple. Not much is known about the pollination of their flowers. Some do not require pollination at all as they are able to form embryos by a type of cloning. In some genera the inflorescences stand well above the scale leaves, as in *Hachettea* of New Caledonia, but in others the scales form a sort of cup around them. In the only species of the New Zealand genus *Dactylanthus* (*D. taylori*), this cup contains a considerable amount of nectar. A small native bat, which spends as much time scrabbling on the forest floor as in the air, has been observed feeding on the nectar.

Fruits of Balanophoraceae, each containing a single seed, are very small. In *Mystropetalon* the fruit is seated on a ring of fleshy, fatty tissue (an oil body) typical of ant-dispersed seeds. In *Sarcophyte* and *Chlamydophytum*, groups of fruits are fused into a fleshy mass, so they may be dispersed by fruit-eating animals. *Balanophora* may have the smallest of all known flowering plant fruits at about 0.2 mm ($1/128$ inch) in diameter. It has been suggested that these may be wind-dispersed.

The way in which water and nutrients are drawn from the host varies in the Balanophoraceae. The part of the parasite that enters the host is known as the haustorium. In *Balanophora* and other genera, the haustorium becomes a mixture of host and parasite cells. The invaded part of the host root is stimulated to enlarge, and its cambium forms strands of water-conducting xylem that extend deeply into the parasite. So the host has to provide the pipelines for the thief. In the haustoria there seem to be no connections to sugar-conducting phloem cells, but as organic nutrients are definitely transferred this must happen in some other way, perhaps through unspecialized thin-walled cells, or even through the xylem.

In *Dactylanthus* and some other genera the haustorium is more clearly defined and there is no incursion of host tissue. The inner part of the haustorium in the enlarged host root is in the form of radiating flanges that tap directly into conducting tissues. The wood of the host root is also distorted into radiating flanges that, when the parasite is removed, have a somewhat flower-like appearance. These flower-like structures are known as wooden roses.

Broomrapes and Indian paintbrushes are

Scaly inflorescence of *Hachettea austrocaledonica*. New Caledonia.

more familiar parasites to people of temperate regions, and they can even be found in polar and alpine habitats. There are very few species of these in the tropics. The broomrapes completely lack chlorophyll, but Indian paintbrushes have green leaves and are therefore hemiparasites. However, both are in the same family, Orobanchaceae, related to the plantain family (Plantaginaceae, including many genera formerly placed in Scrophulariaceae), which is widespread and includes many garden flowers, such as snapdragon (*Antirrhinum*) and *Penstemon*. The parasites attach to the roots of a wide range of hosts, mostly small annuals or perennials but also a few shrubs. The three best-known genera of Orobanchaceae are the broomrapes (*Orobanche*), of which some species can be garden weeds, the Indian paintbrushes (*Castilleja*) in western North America, whose brilliantly colored flowers suggest the name, and eyebright (*Euphrasia*), widespread throughout the world, with species in polar and alpine habitats.

The flowers of these parasites are mostly pollinated by insects, but some (*Castilleja*) are pollinated by birds, including hummingbirds. The seeds are released from dry capsules. In some cases they are extremely small and numerous and are probably wind-dispersed.

Inflorescences of a broomrape, *Orobanche,* parasitic on clover roots.

Indian paintbrush, *Castilleja angustifolia,* with scarlet flowers.

There is evidence that host roots, to their cost, exude chemicals that stimulate the parasites' seeds to germinate and also attract the roots of seedling parasites to grow in their direction. *Castilleja* and *Euphrasia* have branching root systems that attach to host roots with many haustoria. Broomrapes have very small seeds and equally small embryos; when the embryo germinates, the primary root penetrates a host root to form the usually one and only haustorium. Secondary roots are sometimes formed, but these do not form haustoria. Instead, they enlarge into irregularly shaped tubers that may serve for food storage.

Dodders (*Cuscuta*) are widespread throughout the world though they are poorly represented in Southeast Asia and Australasia. As surprising as it may seem, dodders belong to the morning glory family (Convolvulaceae). The botanically unrelated *Cassytha* has species concentrated in Australia with a few in Africa, and *C. filiformis* is widespread in the tropics. Even more surprisingly, *Cassytha* belongs to the laurel family (Lauraceae). We review these two genera together, not because they are share a common ancestry but because they share a distinctive lifestyle. As well as being parasites, the species of these genera are also very slender, twining vines. Their small scale leaves are barely visible, and when the plants smother herbs, shrubs, or trees, they look very much like tangles of string.

On germinating, the primary root of a dodder seedling grows into the ground, and the stem elongates and begins to spiral in a counterclockwise direction. Again, there seems to be a chemical attraction of the stem toward certain hosts. If after about 7 weeks a host is not encountered, the seedling dies. If support is found, the dodder stem twines around it and penetrates the host with haustoria, followed by another freely spiraling phase that may encounter additional support. At an early stage, the root and the lower part of the stem die. The small dodder flowers occur in lateral clusters and are probably pollinated by insects. Their capsules split open to release a few seeds.

A dodder, *Cuscuta*, growing on a glasswort, *Salicornia*, in a salt marsh in northern California.

Despite their absence of relationship, the germination and development of *Cassytha* are remarkably similar to *Cuscuta*. The small flowers are typical of the family Lauraceae, however, and the fruits are fleshy and probably dispersed by birds.

On New Caledonia there is a holoparasite that is especially notable as it is the only known parasitic conifer (Kopke et al. 1981). The genus is appropriately named *Parasitaxus*, and there is only one species, *P. ustus*. It belongs to the largely southern hemisphere family Podocarpaceae and has the single round seeds, each with a fleshy coat, typical of some members of that family. It grows on deeply shaded forest floors and is a spindly, red-purple shrub about 1 m (39 inches) high; its leaves are reduced to scales. *Parasitaxus* parasitizes another member of the Podocarpaceae, the tree *Falcatifolium taxoides*. There is no well-defined haustorium, and the parasite has no external roots, but within the host, *Parasitaxus* forms branching, finger-like processes, perhaps modified roots, that are in close contact with the host's conducting

Parasitaxus ustus with red-purple twigs and whitish seeds. New Caledonia.

tissues. The tissues of *Parasitaxus* can extend up into the trunk of the host for more than 1 m (39 inches), but its leafy shoots mostly grow out from the host roots. Nothing is known about the germination and establishment of the seeds.

Indirect parasites—The mycotrophs

The mode of life of mycotrophs—distinctive plants that parasitize hosts indirectly through the intermediary of a fungus—has not received much attention from botanists until relatively recent times. They have been classified as saprophytes—plants that feed on dead rather than living matter—and like many fungi they were thought to obtain their energy by breaking down organic compounds in nonliving plant material, such as leaf litter.

Mycotrophs are mostly small plants, sometimes very small, that lack chlorophyll or have very little of it and live in moist, shady forest habitats, often in the leaf litter. Some are pale or even pure white, so they have a ghostly appearance in the shadows, or they may be so slender, delicate, and hidden that they can easily be missed. *Monotropa uniflora*, a member of the heath family (Ericaceae), is widespread in North America, where it is mostly known as Indian pipe. It is entirely white, and the turned-down flower at the top of the stalk looks quite like the bowl of a pipe. Other names for this plant are ghost flower or, less kindly, corpse flower. Other species of *Monotropa* are more colorful, sometimes a rich orange-brown.

Species of *Thismia*, a genus belonging to the monocotyledonous family Burmanniaceae, can also be very colorful. *Thismia rodwayi* has small, bright red flowers that have been likened in their shape to small lanterns. Curiously, although most species of the genus are found in Australia and New Zealand, one (*T. americana*) was discovered near Chicago, Illinois, in the early 20th century.

A number of orchids belong to the group of mycotrophic parasites, and some can be quite tall. *Gastrodia cunninghamii,* for example, can be as much as 1 m (39 inches) high. The plants are anchored by roots, sometimes arising from short rhizomes enlarged into food-storing tubers.

Doubt that these plants are truly saprophytes was first raised when it was noticed that the roots and rhizomes of *Monotropa hypopitys* are invaded by fungal filaments connected to the roots of surrounding beech trees (Bjorkman 1960). After the beech trunks were injected with carbon-14, radioactive organic compounds were recovered from the *Monotropa* plants. The fungus takes sugars from the tree roots and in return supplies water and some mineral nutrients to the tree; the *Monotropa* takes some of

The flower of *Thismia rodwayi*. New Zealand.

Right: A close view of the flowers of a *Gastrodia* orchid, not yet named, related to *G. cunninghamii*. New Zealand.

the sugars and other organic compounds from the fungus and probably gives nothing in return.

Since the first investigation of mycotrophy in *Monotropa,* many plants have been shown to have fungal connections to tree roots, so they are probably all indirect parasites. Bjorkman (1960) used the term epiparasite for such plants, but they are currently known as mycotrophs. Because mycotrophs belong to a number of different families, including Ericaceae, Gentianaceae, Orchidaceae, and Burmanniaceae, it seems that this way of life, too, has evolved independently a number of times.

Hemiparasites—Mistletoes and their relatives

Mistletoes are the best known of the parasitic plants largely because the few species in Europe form conspicuous clumps in tree crowns, particularly in winter when many of the trees are leafless and the mistletoes retain their green leaves. They have also played a role in folklore from the times of the Druids. Nevertheless, most species of mistletoes are found in the tropics, though there is also a significant representation in the southern temperate lands.

Two families of mistletoes are recognized. These are partly based on anatomical and morphological details, but in general, the Loranthaceae have large, bisexual, often colorful, bird-pollinated flowers (see page 12), and the mistletoes of the Santalaceae (including Viscaceae) have small, mostly unisexual, modestly colored, insect-pollinated flowers. Included in Santalaceae are the dwarf mistletoes, with leaves reduced to scales and often with flattened stems. Most mistletoes grow on the trunks and branches of trees where their foliage can get sufficient light for photosynthesis and food production.

The fruits of mistletoes are berries, each containing a single relatively large seed. Most seeds have an enclosing layer of tissue that secretes an extremely sticky glue. The berries are mostly eaten by birds for the outer fleshy layers, and the still-sticky seeds are later excreted, often onto tree branches. In Australia, southern Asia, and Africa, there are remarkable associations between particular birds and mistletoes. In Australia and Asia, the birds are known as mistletoe birds and belong to the genus *Dicaeum.* The birds squeeze the fruits with their beaks, and the seeds, enclosing pulp, and sticky tissue pop out and are swallowed. The seeds can pass through the bird in only a few hours, and as the bird moves along a twig or branch, it plants, or rather pastes, the seeds. In Africa the specialized mistletoe-dispersing birds are tinkerbirds belonging to the genus *Pogoniulus.* They swallow fruits whole, and the sticky seeds are regurgitated onto branches, sometimes after only a few hours.

It has often been suggested that when birds feed on mistletoe fruits, some of the sticky seeds become attached to their beaks and feathers, later to be groomed off onto branches. Some botanists do not believe this is a significant mode of dispersal for mistletoes. Some mistletoe seeds, particularly those of dwarf mistletoes, are self-propelling. Pressure builds up within the berry, and the seeds are suddenly shot out as if from a cannon. In one species they travel on average for 5 m (16 feet) and for a maximum distance of 15 m (49 feet).

When a seed attaches to a tree trunk or branch, by whatever means, moisture enables it to germinate, and the embryo curves away from the light, its tip making contact with the bark of the host. There is no clearly defined primary root at the tip, and some botanists have claimed that mistletoes do not have roots, only variously modified stems (Kuijt 1969, 39). The embryo tip expands on contact with the bark to form an attachment disk, and from the center of this an outgrowth penetrates to the living tissues of the tree and forms a haustorium. In some cases, outgrowths from this primary haustorium extend longitudinally within the bark and form wedge-shaped secondary haustoria. In others, the haustoria have radiating flanges that lead to the formation of "wooden roses" in the wood of the host.

Some mistletoes have only a primary haustorium at the base of a shrub-like system of branches and green leaves. In others, axes grow out from the base of the parasite and spread over the bark of the host, forming secondary haustoria at intervals. Some consider these axes to be roots, others stems, and some refer to them, noncommittally, as runners. The runners may form a network over the trunk of the host and give rise,

A germinating seed of *Peraxilla tetrapetala* with glue and a white attaching disk. New Zealand.

Right: The right-hand partner in this embrace is the mistletoe *Peraxilla colensoi*, attached to a slender branch of the host, *Nothofagus menziesii*, by three secondary haustoria. New Zealand.

Cross section through part of the trunk of *Nothofagus menziesii* with the flattened stem of the mistletoe *Peraxilla colensoi* above. Haustoria extend into the tree from the primary attachment of the parasite.

here and there, to new clusters of stems, leaves, and ultimately, flowers and fruits.

Some of the mistletoes with larger, colorful flowers have a specialized mode of bird pollination. In the mistletoes involved, the four long, narrow petals cohere at their margins, and the buds are distinctly swollen at the tips where the petals are under tension. To open the flower and get to the nectar, a bird tweaks the swollen tip or, if the petals have partly separated below the bulge, inserts its beak and unzips the flower. The flower opens explosively and scatters pollen onto the head of the bird. In New Zealand the birds belong to the honeyeater family (Meliphagidae), in southern Asia to the mistletoe bird or flowerpecker family (Dicaeidae), in Africa to the sunbird family (Nectariniidae), and in the Amazon they are short-billed hummingbirds.

A few members of the Loranthaceae have unusual growth habits (Kuijt 1969, 15). In *Gaiadendron punctatum* of the Central American tropics, the host is not the tree on which the mistletoe grows but the epiphytes on the tree. In disturbed sites this species can become a small tree on the ground, where it parasitizes the roots of other plants. *Phrygilanthus acutifolius* of Brazil is even more unusual and not fully understood. There are stems, foliage, and haustorial attachments in the crowns of trees, and a woody axis, which may be a stem or a root, that extends down to the ground. Below the ground it connects to a far-extending and branching root system. In one, the roots were found to connect with and parasitize trees of five different species.

The largest mistletoe of all is *Nuytsia floribunda* of Western Australia, which is always terrestrial and becomes a tree up to 15 m (49 feet) high. It is known as the Christmas tree because it has masses of bright yellow flowers at Christmastime, that is, in midsummer. This, the only species of *Nuytsia*, has an extensive underground system of rhizomes, with small scale leaves and roots. Haustorial connections are made with a wide range of shrubs and smaller plants, including cultivated wheat. The underground system can also give rise to leafy shoots that can become trees. *Nuytsia* is also unusual among mistletoes in having dry, winged fruits that are presumably wind-dispersed.

The mistletoes mostly parasitize a wide range of hosts, including other mistletoes. It is also not uncommon to find one branch of a mistletoe forming haustoria on another of its own branches. Sometimes haustoria can be found attached to rocks. The most remarkable case of all, however, was recorded in Western Australia, where an underground cable that had failed was dug up and found to be encircled by several haustoria of *Nuytsia*, some of which had penetrated through the plastic covering to the wires.

Sandalwoods and some other members of the family Santalaceae form a relatively small group of somewhat different parasites. Among other things, they differ from mistletoes in not having a sticky layer enclosing the seeds, but instead a hard woody layer, which is in turn enclosed by an outer fleshy layer. The flowers are small and insect-pollinated. Most of the species are parasitic on roots, though there are some branch parasites. Once again, most are found in the tropics, though some can be found in cooler, even polar climates.

Santalum and related genera are mostly small trees. Sandalwood (*S. album*) has been notable since the earliest times, particularly in China and India. The wood is used for ornaments, and the aromatic oil is particularly prized for body anointing, soaps, and perfumes, and it is also believed to have many medicinal properties. Sandalwood is now widely cultivated, but fortunes were made in earlier times by exploiting natural populations of it and related species throughout the tropics. Olacaceae, related to Santalaceae, is notable for some of its species, which are vines as well as parasites, climbing by recurved hooks or tendrils.

The effect of parasites on their hosts

As they invade the living tissues of their hosts, parasites cause more damage to their hosts than vines and epiphytes do to their supporting plants. In woody hosts the presence of a parasite haustorium can induce abnormal trunk and branch growth and, where twigs are affected, excessive proliferation of shoots, forming what are known as witches'-brooms. Often, the portion of a tree branch beyond the attachment of a parasite does not produce flowers or cones and sometimes dies and drops away.

Sometimes, tree crowns support such an abundance of bushy mistletoes that there seems to be as much foliage of the parasites as of the host. In such a case, the parasites must be depriving the host of enormous amounts of water and nutrients. The growth and reproduction of the host trees are depressed, and this can be a major problem in some temperate forests, natural or planted, where only one or a few tree species form most of the vegetation.

Smaller herbaceous parasitic plants such as broomrapes and dodders have a similar deleterious effect on smaller hosts such as crop plants. Here, the holoparasites are the worst offenders as they depend on the hosts for all their water and nutrient needs. Unfortunately, there seems to be no easy way of combating the problem of plant parasites that attack cultivated plants.

CHAPTER TWO

Not Enough Water

◆ ◆ ◆

The Plants of Deserts and Seasonally Arid Places

The ideal conditions for plant growth are where year-round temperatures are warm and rainfall is abundant. This is why the tropical rain forests are so luxuriant and rich in species. Where even one of these important conditions is deficient, most plants are unable to cope. In the deserts, only those plants that have evolved special modifications to make the most of the meager water supply are able to grow, even if only slowly and sporadically, and reproduce (Evenari et al. 1985, 1986).

Why there are deserts

With so much water in the world, covering about 70% of the globe's surface, we might expect that there would be enough evaporation to provide sufficient rain to keep the land areas constantly moist. This is true of many parts of the world, but there are deserts and seasonally arid habitats on every continent. To appreciate why this is so, we need to understand how air and ocean currents are generated by heat from the sun.

Because the world's axis of rotation is not far from a right angle to the plane of its revolution around the sun, the sun's rays are vertical or almost so at midday in the equatorial region. As the Earth's surface curves away to the north and south, the sun's rays

A heavily armed cholla cactus of the North American deserts, *Cylindropuntia bigelovii*, with fruits.

are more and more slanted. Vertical sunshine causes maximum heating of water or land, but as it becomes increasingly oblique with latitude (or when the sun is lower in the sky during the day), the heating effect steadily diminishes. Why is this so?

A simple analogy helps explain why. If you point a flashlight reasonably close and at right angles to a wall, its light will appear as a bright disk. If you then angle the flashlight so it is oblique to the wall, the disk of light enlarges to a pale ellipse. In other words, the disk of bright light is now spread thinly over a larger area and has lost intensity.

In the equatorial belt, surface heating from the sun is at a maximum and the heated ground or sea radiates excess heat to the air above. As a result the air expands, becomes less dense and lighter, and rises away from the surface. With the high temperatures, evaporation is also great, so the rising air is heavily charged with moisture. Heated air holds water as invisible vapor. As the air rises farther it begins to cool, partly because expanding gases lose heat but mostly because the intensity of the radiant heat from the earth's surface steadily declines with increasing altitude. With cooling, the capacity of the rising air to hold water vapor lessens, and water condenses in droplets that build up into impressive thunderhead clouds. Further condensation produces rain. The now dry and cooler rising air contracts, and gravity begins to assert itself again. The air masses diverge into two currents, one moving south and the other north. For a while these currents run more or less parallel to the ground but eventually descend to the earth along subtropical zones centered on 30° north and south. With the downward pressure against the earth, the descending currents are compressed and as a consequence heat up. If the equatorial zone can be described as hot, wet, and very favorable for plant growth, the northern and southern subtropical zones can be described as generally hot, dry, and very unfavorable, or even in some places impossible, for plant growth.

At the earth's surface, the trade winds, as they are called, move from the high air pressure of each subtropical zone to the low pressure at the equator. One would expect them to move due north to south in the northern hemisphere and due south to north in the southern hemisphere. However, in the north they blow from the northeast, and in the south from the southeast. This relates to the different speeds of the Earth's rotation at different latitudes. At the equator we find the maximum speed of rotation. A point there travels around the widest circle of latitude in a day. At 30° from the equator the speed of rotation is slower because a point there still takes a day to get around a smaller circle. The trade winds originating at 30° latitude start off with the slower rotational speed, lag behind the increasing rotational speed of the Earth, and so reach the equator at an oblique angle. On reaching the equator, the trade winds complete two circulating cells of air currents, forming somewhat flattened, doughnut-shaped, invisible tubes situated on each side of the equator to 30° north and south.

To complete the global picture there are two other pairs of atmospheric cells at higher latitudes. As well as winds blowing toward the equator from the high-air-pressure tropical zones, there are also winds blowing toward low-pressure belts centered on 60° north and south. In this case the winds veer to become southwesterlies in the northern hemisphere and northwesterlies in the south. These midlatitude south- and northwesterlies meet north- and southeasterlies coming from regions of high atmospheric pressure over the poles induced by intense cold. For part of the year in the polar regions there is no sun at all, and when it returns it is at such a low angle that it contributes very little heat. The only way the opposing winds can go is up, and cooling at higher altitudes results in cloud formation and rain. As before, the now dry ascending air diverges into two currents, one going toward and down to a tropical belt to complete the second circuit and the other toward and down to the poles to complete the third. So the low-pressure temperate belt could be described as cool and wet, and the polar zones, cold and dry.

In the two subtropical belts, one would expect that all land areas would be desert. The descending air is dry and hot, and because of the high pressure resulting from compression, the winds are outward, tending to take with them what little moisture there may be. However, the actual pattern in these latitudes is that deserts extend to the sea on the west of continents but generally not on the east. This results from the influ-

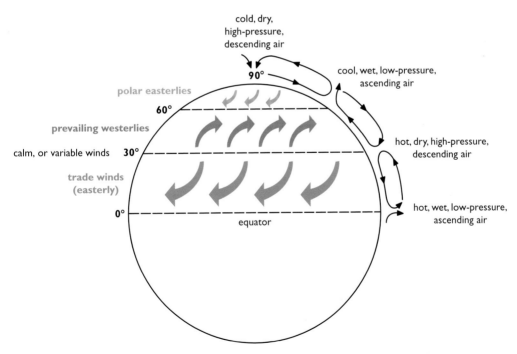

Diagram of the Earth, showing air circulation patterns in the northern hemisphere.

ence of circulating currents in the oceans, which are largely generated by the tropical easterly and the temperate westerly winds. These currents are most fully developed in the wide Pacific Ocean. The northeast and southeast trade winds of the northern and southern hemispheres, respectively, converge on the equator, generating a warm ocean current moving from east to west. When this current reaches the Asian and Australian tropical coasts it diverges into two that follow the coasts to the north and south. These currents remain warm into the subtropical zones, and because of this, the air above them is moist despite the dry, descending air above. On the western sides of oceans, the easterly trades are onshore winds, carrying the moist air over the warm ocean currents onto the land where the moisture condenses as rain when lifted and cooled by hills or mountains. This rain is sufficient to support forests, so on the eastern sides of the continents, forests are, or were, continuous from the equator to the temperate regions, ranging in the northern hemisphere from tropical to cool temperate coniferous. By the time such winds in the subtropical zones move toward the western sides of continents, they have lost their moisture, and the desert, with its sparse vegetation, prevails.

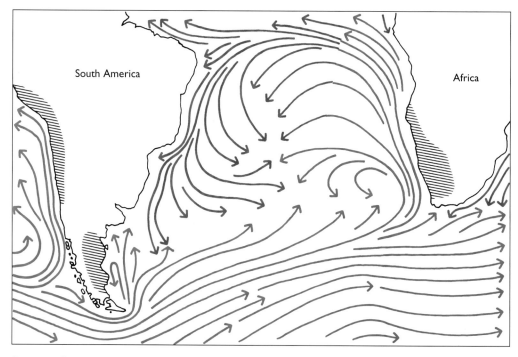

Diagram of ocean currents in the South Atlantic. Cold currents are shown in blue, and warm currents in red. Hatched areas are deserts. The hot deserts of west-central South America and southwestern South Africa lie in the generally dry southern subtropical zone, and their aridity is intensified by the easterly trade winds, which lose their moisture on mountains to the east, and the minimal evaporation of moisture from cold currents to the west. The cold Patagonian desert of southeastern South America lies in the generally moist southern temperate zone and owes its aridity to the prevailing westerlies, which lose their moisture on the Andes to the west, as well as to the influence of a localized cold current to the east.

The warm ocean currents now continue into temperate latitudes where the westerlies now steer them from west to east through colder higher latitudes. In the South Pacific the now westerly current forms part of the very cold seas circling Antarctica. When the Humboldt Current diverges from the Circum-Antarctic Current to run up the South American coast, it is cold though it provides sufficient moisture to the temperate onshore westerlies to support forest growth. Most of these forests are dominated by species of southern beech (*Nothofagus*), some evergreen and others deciduous. When the Humboldt Current reaches the subtropical region of hot, dry, descending air, its tendency to swing away from the coast, partly under the influence of the offshore trade winds, allows the upwelling of extremely cold water from the depths. These extracold waters are slow to evaporate, providing little rain for the land though coastal fog is common, and with the easterly trade winds having lost their moisture to the Andes, desert conditions prevail on South America's western coast in the subtropical zone. There is a similar strongly developed cold current in the South Atlantic along the southwestern African coast. The Circum-Antarctic Current runs well to the south of Australia, so there is no cold current along its western coast. In the northern hemisphere, the cold currents along the southwestern coast of North America and the northwestern coast of Africa significantly affect the coastal climates.

The hot deserts—Landforms and habitats

Hot deserts and semideserts are generally defined as receiving less than 400 mm (15 3/4 inches) of rain per year. For true deserts it is less than 120 mm (4 3/4 inches) and extreme deserts less than 70 mm (2 3/4 inches), but the boundaries are not sharply defined. These deserts are largely found between 20° and 40° north and south, though in eastern Africa the Sahara extends close to the equator.

At the western coastal edges of most of the hot deserts there are narrow zones with relatively cool temperatures that result from offshore cold currents and cold upwelling water. These coastal fringes are often swathed in fog that forms over the cold currents. The cold currents themselves evaporate little moisture, but the sea beyond them is somewhat warmer and the moisture in the air above it condenses into fog or drizzle as it passes over the cold current on its way to the land. These landward winds are mostly what are known as sea breezes, which result during the day from the movement of higher-pressure, contracted air over the cold current toward the lower-pressure, expanded air over the warmer land. The sea fog drifts onto the land but rarely generates any rain. But the fog condenses on plants and rocks, and runs down to or drips onto the ground. As an example, the tallest tree in the world, the coast redwood (*Sequoia sempervirens*), is largely restricted to a narrow, foggy coastal strip in northern California and southwestern Oregon where it obtains much of its moisture during the dry season from fog drip.

The Sahara is by far the largest of the hot deserts, occupying most of northern Africa, and it is virtually contiguous with the deserts of Arabia, the Middle East, Afghanistan, Pakistan, and northwestern India. Most of these are true deserts, including extreme desert, with more limited peripheral belts of semidesert. Plants are absent from large areas of these deserts and are mostly low in stature with relatively few species even in the more favorable sites. They include a number of grasses, such as the spiny *Aristida pungens*, and species of *Euphorbia* (Euphorbiaceae) and *Acacia* (Fabaceae).

The other hot desert in the northern hemisphere is smaller and occupies the southwestern United States and much of Mexico. There has been much crustal movement and faulting in this region with raised blocks forming the mountain ranges, and sunken blocks the basins. The rain-shadow effect of the mountains at some localities increases the aridity induced by dry, descending air masses. Most of the North American deserts are semideserts with relatively rich and diverse floras. There is true desert in Death Valley, California, and at the head of the Gulf of California in Mexico, both dipping below sea level.

In South America the high and very long mountain range of the Andes plays a major role in desert development. Moisture in the trade winds precipitates on the eastern side of these mountains, so this rain shadow in combination with dry, descending air currents and cold ocean currents result in desert and extreme desert in the narrow lowland strip west of the mountains from about 30° south to near the equator. Under these conditions there are only a few specialized plants. East of the Andes, from about 28° to 33° south, is the Monte Desert. This is largely semidesert and results partly from the rain shadows of surrounding mountain ranges, which deprive the trade winds of their moisture before they reach the Andes. The less extreme conditions here allow a greater diversity of plants, including tall cacti.

In southern Africa there are mountains near the eastern coast, less imposing than the Andes but still sufficiently high to remove most of the moisture from the trade winds. The Namib Desert, a narrow coastal strip in the west bordered by a cold current, is mostly extreme desert with vast extents of sand dunes but few plants, of which *Welwitschia mirabilis*, shown on page 97, is without doubt the most remarkable. The next belt inland, Namaqualand and the Karoo, is desert to semidesert with small shrubs and tufted, spiny-leaved grasses predominating.

In Australia there is an even lower mountain range paralleling the east coast, but it still manages to remove most of the moisture from the trade winds. Also, as Australia is much wider than South Africa, the winds are quite dry before they reach the center of the continent. The deserts extend to the western coast and occupy more than half of Australia. They are mostly semideserts with some central locations just qualifying as true desert. There is no extreme desert; as in Namaqualand and the North Karoo, tufted grasses with spiny leaves are conspicuous.

Looking down into Death Valley, California, with its extensive salt flats.

The central parts of some deserts, particularly the Sahara, may never receive any rain at all, but most hot deserts have some rain even if only sporadically. The paucity of rain might suggest that water would not play a significant role in erosion and that surface abrasion by sand storms would be the major factor. However, everywhere in the deserts there is evidence of extensive water erosion: ravines often narrowing to slot canyons in the mountains; extensive fans of debris radiating from the mouths of these canyons; deep deposits of sand, silt, and rocks in the basins; dry river beds (dry washes or wadis); and sand dunes, shaped by wind, certainly, but the sand itself mostly formed by water action. So how can this be explained?

Energetic storms from the sea or from low-latitude rain forests sometimes penetrate into hot deserts. There, the moist air rises to cooler altitudes where clouds form, and the rain is often accompanied by thunder and lightning. In some cases this rain completely evaporates because the temperature increases closer toward the ground. More often,

A dry wash in San Diego County, California, with a variety of
small trees and shrubs. The shrub in flower is *Justicia californica*.

though, there is a cloudburst followed by a deluge. Anyone who has been out in such
a storm will see the washes fill from bank to bank, with the narrow canyons churning
with raging torrents and sheets of water spreading over the fans and plains, ending up
as temporary lakes in the lowest parts. Unfortunately, some observers do not live to tell
the tale, especially if they are caught in a canyon. Those who do are convinced that such
deluges, infrequent though they are, fully explain the present landforms and habitats in
the deserts. However, there is more to it than that.

During the Ice Age there was a series of glacial periods when ice sheets spread from
the polar regions into middle latitudes in the northern hemisphere, alternating with
warmer interglacials. We may be in such an interglacial now, with the period of maximum warmth some thousands of years ago, according to fossil evidence. There are
shorter periods of ups and downs in temperature superimposed on the broader trends.
From historical evidence, there was a warm period of about 500 years during the Mid-

dle Ages, followed by what has been called the Little Ice Age of about 500 years, and now there is another warming trend. Some attribute this last period to an accumulation of "greenhouse gases" generated by humans; others see it as a natural event. Perhaps it is both.

During the glacials, with less evaporation from the seas, the deserts would have been cooler and drier than they are now, and it has been estimated that during the coldest phase of the last glacial—about 20,000 to 12,000 years ago—they would have occupied five times their present area. The interglacials are warmer and moister, and the deserts shrink. There is evidence from the last period of maximum warmth and moisture—about 10,000 to 7,000 years ago—that at least some of the present dry washes had permanently flowing water. Salty lakes at the lowest points in basins or plains—such as the Great Salt Lake in Utah, the Dead Sea in the Middle East, and Lake Chad in the Sahara—were much larger, and at other places there were permanent rather than temporary lakes. The deserts were smaller than now and better vegetated, even in the central Sahara.

Some of the water that fell in the deserts in pluvial times still exists at depth and is sometimes referred to as fossil water. This is the source of oases, either where wind has blown sand away down to the water table or, in hilly terrain, where faulting has opened deep fissures, allowing water, under pressure at depth, to push to the surface. Such oases, often shaded by palms and with a garden of Eden atmosphere, are a stark contrast to the barren surrounding desert.

Apart from rain, another source of moisture in hot deserts is dew. In these deserts it is said that there is summer during the day and winter at night. During the day, temperatures can reach 40°C (104°F) or more and drop to single figures or even below freezing overnight.

Although secondary to water in its various forms, wind also plays a significant role in erosion. Hot, dry winds can generate dust storms, carrying dust to high altitudes. Sometimes the dust eventually settles in moist regions beyond the deserts, even as far from the Sahara as the rooftops of Paris. Larger sand particles are lifted only 1–2 m (3–6 feet) above the ground and cause great discomfort to travelers. The sand and wind sandblast rock surfaces, and where they funnel through ravines and narrow openings in thin-layered sandstones, striking wave-like formations result.

Fragmentation of rock in deserts is brought about in several ways. In the heat of the day the rock expands, and it contracts with the nighttime cold. This results in the development of fissures in the rock surface and eventual separation of slabs and fragments, which accumulate as an apron of debris at the base of the outcrop or cliff. This process is accelerated if there is frost at night. Moisture in crevices expands when it turns to ice, as do any salt deposits when they are moistened.

In younger desert landscapes, erosion creates dramatic rock formations, particu-

A wave-rock canyon at Coyote Buttes near the Arizona–Utah border.
Note the loose gravel left behind on ledges by a flash flood.

larly so where plateaus with horizontal strata have been lifted by earth movements. The temporary rivers, and permanent rivers flowing through from wet mountains, now cut down into the plateau, forming steeply cliffed sides. The cliffs slowly erode back from their faces, and the plateau is cut into segments. Further erosion, by gravity assisted by occasional cloudbursts, slowly but steadily reduces these to narrow, flat-topped columns or buttes, as in Monument Valley in northeastern Arizona and adjacent Utah. In time, these buttes, too, are reduced to stumps and disappear, leaving a new plain at a lower elevation.

In older deserts, such as the Sahara, featureless plains are widespread, sometimes extending from horizon to horizon. The plains are covered with the products of erosion: sand, silt, and small rocks. The latter lie on the surface, close together, forming what is known as desert pavement. It is believed that the rocks are concentrated at the surface

At Goosenecks State Park, Utah, the San Juan River has cut down into its bed following uplift of a former plain.

Monument Valley on the Utah–Arizona border. The buttes
are mantled with fallen debris around their bases.

A view in the Negev, Israel, with desert pavement in the foreground.

when winds blow away the lighter particles of sand and silt, but it is also suggested that they work their way to the surface as a result of expansion and contraction of the fine-grained matrix in response to wetting and drying. The rocks are usually dark as a result of dew or rain dissolving iron and manganese compounds and leaving reddish iron oxides and blackish manganese oxides as surface deposits when the water evaporates. Calcareous rocks form calcite crusts in a similar way. These surface crusts, known as desert varnish, also form on bedrock surfaces. The sand, and some of the dust, removed by wind from the plains, and especially from the beds of former lakes, is deposited elsewhere in the desert, often in depressions, where it builds up into dunes.

Water dissolves minerals from rocks, particularly salts of various kinds. In wetter regions of the world, rivers flow permanently and carry dissolved salts and other compounds right to the sea, adding to its saltiness. In deserts the temporary rivers never reach the sea, disappearing at the lowest parts of the plains or forming temporary lakes, which evaporate and leave the salts behind. The latter form thick crusts at the surface, which are added to when moisture persisting at depth percolates up to the dry surface and adds more salt when it evaporates. This is a hopeless situation for the establishment of plants. Especially thick salt beds may be found in Death Valley in California, at

On the sand plain leading to the Kelso Dunes in the Mojave Desert, California, the dark green shrubs are creosote bush (*Larrea tridentata*), and the yellow flower heads belong to desert marigold (*Baileya pauciradiata*).

Bonneville Salt Flats in Utah, and at Lake Gairdner in South Australia, the latter two notable as locations for attempts on the world land speed record. Other desert soils are salty, too, but less so.

Plant strategies for desert survival—The hot deserts of North America

In hot deserts the sun's potential to evaporate moisture far exceeds the amount of water available from rain or dew. It has been estimated that the heat of the sun in deserts has the potential to evaporate 2,000–4,000 mm (80–160 inches) of moisture per year, sometimes more. Even after a deluge, water on sunlit rocky surfaces quickly evaporates. The only water that persists long enough to sustain plants sinks into the substrate, where it is protected from evaporation. On rocky outcrops, water can persist in deep fissures or under large boulders; on debris fans it sinks into the beds of stones, sand, and silt; and on sand dunes it readily penetrates to deeper levels. Even small accumulations of sand on rocky terrain can shelter sufficient moisture for small plants to grow. The

A small desert shrub at Coyote Buttes, near the Arizona–Utah border, with roots extending into a rock fissure to reach moisture.

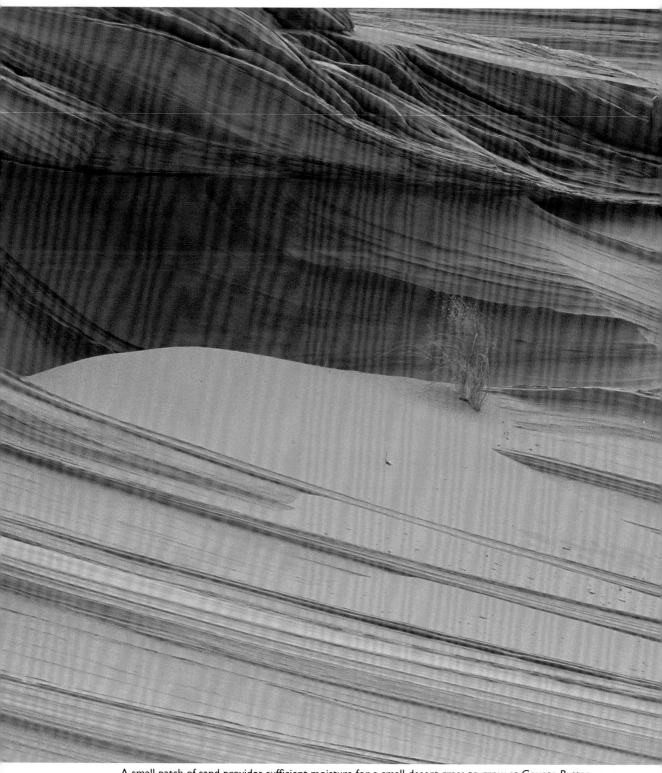
A small patch of sand provides sufficient moisture for a small desert grass to grow at Coyote Buttes.

best hidden water supply is in the dry washes or wadis. There, water from occasional floods sinks into the deep beds of sand and stones to some depth. On desert plains with some depth of sand and silt it is a different story. Wetting and drying of the surface results in the development of a crust, preventing easy penetration of water except when it is broken up by a flash flood. Most of the rain runs off with some penetrating only a few centimeters or an inch or more, and that does not last very long once the sun comes out.

So there are habitats in deserts where water is available permanently, or more often sporadically, for plants. The plants have evolved a variety of adaptations to enable them to grow and reproduce in each of these habitats. The North American hot deserts are diverse in their climates and landforms and are relatively well known. We begin with these deserts and their plants, then make comparisons with deserts elsewhere.

Three hot deserts are recognized in North America. The Mojave Desert lies mostly in southeastern California with extensions east into Nevada, Utah, and Arizona, between 33° and 37° north and 600 to 1,600 m (1,900–5,200 feet) in elevation. Any rain comes from the temperate westerlies in winter. Succulent plants are not conspicuous in this desert though there are some smaller cactus species. The characteristic plant is the Joshua tree (*Yucca brevifolia*).

Yucca brevifolia is very distinctive in the Mojave Desert, with a thick, corky trunk and diverging branches raised like arms to the sky. Below the Joshua trees are a number of shrubs and grasses, including annuals in spring.

The Chihuahuan Desert lies mostly in Mexico with extensions east into Texas and north into New Mexico and Arizona, between 24° and 34° north. Rains come in summer from the subtropical Gulf of Mexico. Yuccas and agaves are conspicuous in this desert along with smaller cacti and, particularly at higher elevations, grasses.

The Sonoran Desert has the lowest elevational range and extends from 34° north in southernmost California and southern Arizona to the Tropic of Cancer (23.5° north) in Mexico. The striking and visually dominating plants of this desert are columnar cacti, including the saguaros and organ pipes. Lying partly between the two other deserts, the Sonoran Desert can receive some rain from the Gulf of Mexico in summer and some from the Pacific westerlies in winter. The Sonoran Desert reaches the Pacific coast on the narrow peninsula of Baja California. The cold current offshore generates fog from time to time, and condensation from this provides additional moisture but not to the same extent as in the western coastal deserts of Chile and South Africa.

Desert plants with a more or less permanent water supply

Where permanent rivers, arising in mountains that receive enough rain, flow through the North American deserts, small trees, shrubs, and marsh plants grow along their banks, where they are able to avoid the periodic water stress suffered by most desert plants. Plants in this community include cottonwoods (*Populus*), willows (*Salix*), mesquites (*Prosopis*), and paloverdes (*Cercidium*). Introduced species of tamarisk (*Tamarix*) from Eurasia are also well established in this habitat.

Similarly well watered conditions can be found in the vicinity of springs, where groundwater comes to the surface along faults in southern California and western Arizona. The notable plant favoring such sites is the California fan palm (*Washingtonia filifera*) with its conspicuous skirt of persistent dead fronds. Associated trees, also found along river edges, are an alder (*Alnus rhombifolia*) and a sycamore or aliso (*Platanus racemosa*) in addition to cottonwoods, mesquites, and willows.

The third habitat with a good but not quite so reliable water supply is in the dry washes, which are much more common in deserts than permanent rivers and springs. Water from occasional floods sinks into the stones, sand, and silt, and in the deeper and moderately sloping washes, persists at some depth, where it moves slowly downslope. Small trees and shrubs that develop deep roots, sometimes as long as 50 m (160 feet), are able to tap this water supply. Drought-resistant shrubs and herbaceous plants from surrounding slopes may also establish for a time but are often swept away by floods.

Cottonwoods, willows, and other broad-leaved trees do not form part of the dry-wash community as they are basically moist-climate plants with no special modifications to reduce water loss from leaves. Young plants would not survive long enough to extend roots to the water table. Two genera of the pea family (Fabaceae), mesquite (*Prosopis*) and paloverde (*Cercidium*), cope well with these problems by dropping their leaves during dry spells to reduce water loss at the young stage. Other small, dry-wash trees are desert willow (*Chilopsis linearis*)—not really a willow but a member of the *Bignonia* family with attractive, tubular, pale purple flowers—and catclaw (*Acacia greggii*), of the Fabaceae.

Most of the seeds of these dry-wash inhabitants germinate after a flood, which provides moist conditions for young plants, allowing them to get established before drought sets in again. Seeds of mesquite and catclaw in particular will not germinate until their coats are broken, and this is achieved by the tumbling rocks during floods.

Most plants spread over the desert landscape are subjected to long periods of drought. Two broad categories, in terms of drought-surviving strategies, can be recognized: drought evaders and drought tolerators.

Drought evaders

Drought-evading plants, along with some organisms formerly classified as plants—lichens and blue-green bacteria—enter a state of dormancy during periods of drought. They maintain life but do not grow or do so at a much-reduced rate. This is achieved in several quite different ways.

Deciduous shrubs lose their leaves, from which most water is lost, for long periods when there is a well-marked dry season: winter in the Chihuahuan Desert, summer in the Mojave Desert, or for shorter periods where dry spells are scattered through the year as in the Sonoran Desert. They mostly grow on rocky slopes, outcrops, and in canyons, where water persisting in fissures and under boulders can be tapped, as well as in dry washes. In washes, the roots mostly do not extend down to the water table but take advantage of the fact that after heavy rain, water persists longer in the recently flooded upper wash layers than in the surrounding desert.

Some of the deciduous species of moister sites such as washes and canyons have relatively large and thin leaves, for example, a bur-sage (*Ambrosia ambrosioides*) and species of *Acacia*. Their leaves take in carbon dioxide for photosynthesis speedily and lose water just as rapidly, but they build up food reserves quickly and grow vigorously while the water lasts. Deciduous shrubs of more open sites have smaller leaves, and their rate of growth is slower. An example is the distinctive ocotillo (*Fouquieria splendens*) with its clumps of tall, slender, arching stems tipped with clusters of bright red flowers. When there is rain, its stems produce many small round leaves, which drop off when drought sets in again.

The deciduous shrubs use the C_3 method of photosynthesis, which they share with the many plants of moist habitats where there is little or no drought. A number of them have green stems, including the ocotillo and the paloverdes, so they do not stop functioning completely during drought but grow at a slower pace.

A view in the Sonoran Desert, with bright, lemon yellow flowers of paloverde, *Cercidium floridum,* at center right. The more golden yellow flowers below are those of creosote bush, *Larrea tridentata,* and the purple flowers belong to desert willow, *Chilopsis linearis.*

In contrast, resurrection plants do shut down during drought and appear to be quite dead until the rains come. This adaptation is not common in the North American deserts. Examples include species of spike mosses (*Selaginella*), a fern (*Cheilanthes parryi,* also known as *Notholaena parryi*), mosses, and lichens as well as the photosynthetic blue-green bacteria. During drought, they dry up and shrivel but remain alive if only just. They are in this state most of the time, but when it rains they quickly rehydrate and resume their typically slow rate of growth. Most resurrection plants grow in shady places in canyons or under large rocks, where moisture is more persistent. The blue-green bacteria grow under smaller rocks. Crustose lichens are an exception in that they often grow on sunny rocks, where they are virtually incorporated in the rock surface. In some cases, the edges of the slowly advancing lichen wedge themselves under thin, translucent layers of the rock surface. Growth of these almost indestructible organisms is so slow that patches no more than 10 cm (4 inches) across may be hundreds of years old.

A much larger group of drought evaders do die during drought but survive in the form of seeds, either in the soil or in the capsules of dead parent plants. The capsules only open to release the seeds when they are moistened by heavy rain. In years when there is little or no rain, the seeds in the ground do not germinate and one could be quite unaware of the existence of the many species involved. Germination does not take place after only a light shower as the young plants would die as the soil rapidly dried out. A heavy shower or a succession of showers is required to leach germination inhibitors from the seed coats, and the desert becomes a spectacular flower garden. The flowers are often large and are mostly brightly colored to attract pollinating insects. These plants fall into the category of annual plants, which germinate, reproduce, and die in a single growing season. Desert annuals, however, are very short-lived; they have to fit their life cycles into spells when moisture is abundant or at least adequate, ranging from a few months down to a few weeks. In the latter case, some of the species are minute with flowers only a few millimeters or small fractions of an inch in diameter. Because of their short life spans, desert annuals are often termed ephemerals.

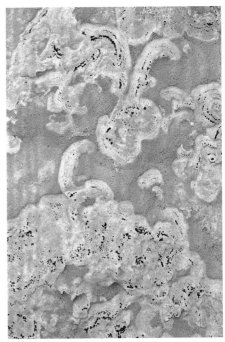

A desert crustose lichen etched into the surface of a rock.

Many ephemerals grow in spring, following winter rains. They are mostly similar to herbaceous plants of moist climates in their morphology and growth processes, including the C3 mode of photosynthesis. Other ephemerals, appearing after summer rain, are unrelated to those that appear in spring. Their seeds will only germinate when temperatures are high, unlike the spring ephemerals, which require cooler temperatures. The summer ephemerals generally utilize the C4 mode of photosynthesis, which unlike the C3 and CAM modes is not inhibited by high temperatures.

Ephemerals are mostly a spring phenomenon in the Mojave Desert (for example, the evening primrose *Oenothera californica* subsp. *avita*) with its winter rains, though others appear with occasional summer rains. There is a more equal balance in the Sonoran Desert (for example, the ephemeral *Calycoseris wrightii*, tackstem), and mostly summer ephemerals in the Chihuahuan Desert (for example, sand penstemon, *Penstemon ambiguus*) with its summer rain.

There are also some herbaceous perennials in this temporary flora. When drought sets in, they die down to bulbs, corms, or rhizomes. Following rain, they quickly produce leaves, flowers, and seeds. Plants that die down to food-storing organs during an unfavorable dry or cold season are known as geophytes. Examples include desert lily (*Hesperocallis undulata*) in the Mojave, the mariposa lily *Calochortus kennedyi* in the Sonoran, and desert hyacinth (*Dichelostemma capitatum*) in the Chihuahuan.

A Mojave Desert scene with spring flowers, including
California poppy (*Eschscholzia californica*, orange).

Drought tolerators

Plants that tolerate drought are widespread through the hot deserts of the world. They maintain a moderate state of activity throughout the year with an increase following rain and a decrease during drought. Several strategies are involved.

Evergreen shrubs retain their leaves throughout the year, though they sometimes produce a new crop to add to the old when it rains. The leaves are generally small and have a number of modifications to reduce water loss not generally found in the drought evaders. They may be densely covered with hairs, a varnish-like film, or a thick waxy cuticle. The pores (stomata) for gas exchange in the leaves are often sunken so breezes are less able to hasten the evaporation of water.

Evergreen shrubs are most frequent on older soils of the lower slopes of fans and on plains. There, with evaporation, calcium carbonate precipitates from saturated solution to form a hard, impervious layer (also called hardpan, calcrete, or caliche) at no great depth. Such layers are particularly well developed in regions of calcareous rocks, widespread in American deserts, where there is an abundance of calcium. Lakebeds that dried after the last rainy period some thousands of years ago also contain significant amounts of calcium, and dust storms have spread it over most desert landscapes of all rock types.

So far as the plants are concerned, the impervious layer is a fact of life that limits their source of moisture to quite a shallow zone. As a result they have shallow, widely spreading roots that take up water quickly after rain. The most widespread shrub in this habitat is the creosote bush (*Larrea tridentata*). It is found in all three North American deserts and sometimes forms almost pure associations. The common name reflects the creosote smell of rain-wet or crushed leaves, though it is perhaps more reminiscent of the gunpowder smell of childhood cap guns. The small leaves are covered with a shiny, varnish-like film. Creosote bushes can be 2–3 m (6 1/2–10 feet) high, and they are found with a number of smaller shrubs such as white bur-sage (*Ambrosia dumosa*) with gray-white foliage, and cheese bush (*Hymenoclea salsola*) with long, narrow, bright green leaves. A number of the smaller shrubs have very small leaves and are almost ball-like in form with densely interlaced twigs, some with needle tips, others not. There is also a widespread species of Mormon tea (*Ephedra*) that forms small shrubs with upright twigs. Most of the photosynthesis is carried out by the twigs as the leaves are reduced to small scales. *Ephedra* belongs to the unusual Gnetales, included in the same phylum as conifers.

Rather different shrubs and small trees are the yuccas and related plants with their densely tufted, tough, long, narrow leaves. Some species lack trunks, others have short, mostly unbranched trunks, and the Joshua tree (*Yucca brevifolia*) has tall, stout trunks with much-branched crowns. Yuccas tend to favor somewhat higher elevations and extend into the zone dominated by junipers and piñon pines.

Several saguaros, *Carnegiea gigantea*, rise above a thicket of paloverde, *Cercidium floridum*, in the Sonoran Desert. Creosote bush, *Larrea tridentata*, is at the lower left.

Water-storing plants are a special group of drought-tolerating plants. They grow in sites similar to those of the evergreen shrubs and also have shallow, widely spreading root systems that take up water quickly even after the lightest rain. The cacti, of which there are a wide array, have no leaves, so photosynthesis is carried out by the green stems, which are enlarged and also store water. In agaves, the water is stored in long, fleshy leaves that are arranged in often massive rosettes at ground level.

The most spectacular and best known of the cacti are the columnar types of small tree dimensions: the saguaro (*Carnegiea gigantea*) and the organ pipes (*Stenocereus* and *Lophocereus*). Saguaros can be as tall as 15 m (49 feet) and are unbranched when young but eventually form clusters of branches high above the ground. Organ-pipe cacti are much-branched from the ground upward.

Large cacti can store considerable quantities of water, as much as several tons in a saguaro. Such a watery mass of tissue would collapse if it were not for a cylindrical network

An organ-pipe cactus, *Stenocereus thurberi*, in the Sonoran Desert.

The creeping devil, *Stenocereus eruca*, of the Chihuahuan Desert can spread to cover quite large areas.

of woody tissue in the interior of the stem that functions rather like reinforcing steel in concrete. The stems of these tall cacti have a pleated appearance with alternating longitudinal grooves and ridges. These are most pronounced during droughts when the stems shrink as their water content becomes depleted. When the water supply increases, the pleats allow for considerable expansion before there is any danger of splitting. There are many other species of smaller, sometimes prostrate cacti, including the chollas (*Cylindropuntia,* page 66, and related genera) and prickly pears (*Opuntia*). All the desert species are notable for their daunting armor of spines, to dissuade thirsty animals, as well as their large, multipetaled, often brightly colorful flowers.

Cacti conserve water by storing it; by restricting photosynthesis to the stems, which have fewer stomata than would leaves; by secreting a thick waxy cuticle over the stem surface; and by utilizing the water-conserving CAM mode of photosynthesis. Thus the cacti are well suited to life in the desert. They do not tolerate cold well, however, so they are most diverse and conspicuous in the Sonoran Desert, the warmest of the three North American deserts. Even there the tall, columnar species are often found near small trees, such as paloverde, providing shade and protection from occasional frosts when the plants are young.

The fleshy-leaved, water-storing agaves are most diverse and conspicuous in the Chihuahuan Desert. Like the cacti they are heavily armed against browsing animals, with steely spines along the leaf margins and at their tips, as shown on page 211. It is many years before some agaves produce flowering stalks though "century plant" is an exaggeration. The massive, tall stalks bear clusters of yellow or purple flowers. As the fruits are forming, the leaf rosette dies but is soon replaced by a ring of new rosettes that develop from offsets. In this way agaves can form quite large colonies.

Evergreen plants of saline habitats, or halophytes, have to cope with lack of water as do other desert plants but also with an excessive concentration of salts in the soil (Chapter 4). These conditions prevail in the lowest parts of desert basins or plains, where floodwater ends up and evaporates, leaving behind the salts it has dissolved from the rocks and debris of the landscape in the form of salt pans. No plants can grow under such conditions. Plants first appear at the periphery of the salt pans, where there is exposed rock, gravel, or sand, albeit still very salty. A number of these plants are fleshy and water storing. Farther from the salt pan, salt-tolerant shrubs predominate, and this vegetation is known as saltbush scrub.

Plants of sand dunes

When people think of deserts they generally picture sand dunes, like those illustrated on page 80, but although dunes are to be found in all deserts, they only occupy a quarter to a third of the total desert area of the world. In North America, as elsewhere, desert dunes have been built up largely from dry sediments blown out from former lakes, some of them quite large, of wetter times. The material of the grains varies but is mostly silica. In Death Valley, California, the dunes are calcium carbonate, and in New Mexico the dazzling White Sands are calcium sulfate, or gypsum.

Sand dunes look arid and sterile but in fact support quite a variety of plants. Rainwater penetrates readily, and when it reaches a sufficient depth it is protected from evaporation. Some small trees and shrubs from other desert habitats can grow quite happily here—cottonwoods from the edges of desert rivers, mesquite from dry washes, and creosote bushes from even drier habitats.

Particularly in sometimes-shaded hollows, smaller perennial plants grow, including evening primroses (*Oenothera*), sand verbena (*Abronia villosa*), and desert lily (*Hesperocallis undulata*). Coarse grasses send widely spreading stems through the sand and form deeply penetrating roots.

Many desert dunes are largely fixed in position. This may be because they were formed by wind regimes in former times that no longer prevail, or because there are strong winds from opposing directions. The dunes of the White Sands in New Mexico move steadily across the landscape. Between the dunes are sand plains where the water table is not far below the surface and the often-moist sand is not so easily moved by the wind. The plains are quite favorable, if temporary, sites for plants as there is a good water supply at no great depth, and the plants improve the soil by adding some organic material. As well as small trees and larger shrubs, there are small shrubs, including the widespread *Ephedra*, and a number of perennial herbs, including grasses, evening primroses, and sand verbena. In the wetter winter season, if the rains come, colorful ephemerals make an appearance. The fate of most of these plants, however, is to be buried under a sand dune. The exceptions are some of the small trees and larger shrubs, such as soap-tree yucca (*Yucca elata*), which is able to cope by growing vigorously, staying above the sand as it tries to bury the plants. The buried stems form roots to fully tap the water supply. From the advancing edge of one sand dune to the retreating edge of the next at the other side of a sand plain, the plants grade from oldest and tallest, just before they are inundated, to youngest and smallest, where new sand plain is being exposed.

Hot deserts outside North America

South America

The Monte Desert in northwestern Argentina lies just east of the Andes between 27° and 35° south. This is largely a semidesert caused by rain shadows of the surrounding mountains and dry, descending air currents. It has many similarities to the Sonoran Desert of North America. There are tall, columnar cacti of which some genera are shared as well as relatives of the creosote bush, mesquite, and paloverde. Unlike the North American deserts, there are no ephemerals in the Monte Desert.

The Atacama Desert on the western side of the Andes is long and narrow, extending from approximately 20° to 27° south on the inland side of a coastal range. The high Andes block any moisture from the east. Winds from the cold ocean to the west, which bring winter fog and drizzle to the coast, heat up as a result of compression as they descend the inland slopes of the coastal ranges, so any moisture they still contain is in the invisible vapor form. It is probably the driest desert in the world with some localities recording no rain at all for as long as 45 years. As a result, the Atacama Desert is virtually rainless and plantless.

In summer, when higher land temperatures prevent condensation of fog and drizzle, even on the coast, winds from the west produce rain only when cooled at elevations of 1,000–3,000 m (3,300–9,800 feet) on the western slopes of the Andes. The amount of rain is sufficient to support a semidesert dominated by tall cacti.

The narrow coastal fog desert, which extends much farther north and south than the Atacama, has a number of specialized plants and animals that depend on condensation from fog for their water needs. Because of the cool temperatures induced by the cool current, evaporation is also much less along the coast than even a few kilometers or miles inland.

When the fogs begin in fall, many small annual plants appear in sandy sites, and sprawling cacti and tillandsias resume growth. The tillandsias, relatives of the epiphytes discussed in Chapter 1, form strands or loose mats that can be lifted away from the sand. Water absorption is entirely through leaf scales, and there are few roots. In rocky sites, including erosion debris, many of the cacti are erect, but there are also strange forms known as soil cacti. In these, most of the plant body is below ground in the form of fleshy tubers that give rise to profusely branched roots near the surface of the soil. The aboveground shoots are small, brownish, and close to the surface, so they are generally only noticed when they are in flower.

In some places, small blue-green bacteria predominate in the fog season. The microscopic filaments of *Nostoc*, in their matrix of jelly, can turn the ground surface black. Lichens can form large cushions on sandy sites.

At about 500 m (1,600 feet) in the coastal ranges, cooler temperatures intensify precipitation from the fog, which may be in the form of drizzle. This results in places in a low, dense, mostly evergreen forest of *Acacia macracantha*, *Caesalpinia tinctoria*, and *Tournefortia undulata*, supporting masses of bryophytes and lichens. There are slender lianes and a ground cover of shade-loving plants, including some ferns. The rainfall in these sites is only about 150 mm (6 inches) a year, but it is estimated that fog condensation provides another 1,500 mm (59 inches) a year.

Southern Africa

In southern Africa, deserts and semideserts extend inland from the western coast (Werger 1978). In latitude they range from about 15° south to near the southern coast at 34° south, a distance of about 2,400 km (1,500 miles). The northern part is quite narrow at 100 km (62 miles) wide, but there is a gradual widening southward to about 800 km (500 miles), which brings semidesert toward the center of the land mass.

The Namib Desert is a narrow coastal strip from about 15° to 30° south. It extends inland from the coast to an elevation of 1,000 m (3,300 feet) at the foot of the escarpment of the great interior plateau of southern Africa. This is the driest of the southern African deserts, where in some localities there is no rain in half the years and less than 10 mm (3/8 inch) in each of the remaining years. Near the coast, fog generated by the cold current is present for an average of 120 days per year, and condensation from it ranges from 30 to 130 mm (1 1/4–5 1/8 inches) per year.

Extensive areas of the Namib Desert are covered by moving sand dunes, some of them as high as 240 m (790 feet). These dunes are practically plantless, though there are a few grasses, which gain a significant proportion of their moisture from fog condensation. In other places there are plains of desert pavement with surface stones of mostly light-colored quartz. This habitat, too, is virtually devoid of plants.

Rocky outcrops and ridges with moisture hidden in deep crevices and under debris support a range of small succulent plants mostly belonging the ice plant family (Aizoaceae), and on rare occasions when there is a period of heavy rain, similar succulents may also appear on the dunes and pavement, only to disappear when drought returns.

Welwitschia mirabilis, the only species of its genus, is the best-known and most remarkable plant of the Namib Desert. It looks like something conjured up for a movie set on an alien planet. The stem is like a woody bowl set close to the ground. There are only two leaves, very broad and leathery, attached on opposite sides at the top of the woody stem. The leaves grow continuously from the base like fingernails and die back from the tips. As they age, they split into narrow longitudinal segments that tumble untidily along the ground for 1 m (39 inches) or more. In season, pollen cones or seed cones, on different plants, arise within the rim of the stem. With *Ephedra* (Mormon tea) and *Gnetum,* which grow elsewhere, *Welwitschia* forms the small group of cone-bearing plants, the Gnetales, very different in appearance from cycads and coniferous trees. *Welwitschia* is a plant of dry washes, gravel fans, and other habitats where its roots can extend down to moister levels. It does best in washes where the occasional floods are not too turbulent.

Namaqualand and the Karoo extend inland from the Namib Desert on a plateau that is mostly semidesert with 100–300 mm (4–12 inches) of rainfall per year. Any rain mostly comes in summer, from the east. The most common type of vegetation in this desert comprises dwarf evergreen shrubs with small leaves and deep roots. Many or

Two plants of *Welwitschia mirabilis* in the foreground with others scattered over sandy slopes and hollows.

them are of a rounded, cushion form and include a number of euphorbias. There are also almost shrubby grasses with stiff, spiny leaves. Quite common here and in other arid areas of southern Africa are ferns, flowering perennial herbs, and shrubs that fall into the category of resurrection plants. During drought they can remain shriveled for as long as several years, but when there is a good rain, their leaves quickly absorb water, spread out, and become green. When there have been particularly good rains, large areas of the desert become covered with quickly growing annuals bearing masses of large, brightly colored flowers.

Namaqualand also extends to the south of the Namib Desert in a coastal strip that includes the escarpment mountains. The rainfall is similar to that of the Karoo, but in this case any rainfall comes in winter when with the cooler temperatures it is more effective, rather than summer. With the generally lower elevations and proximity to the sea, frosts are uncommon and light, and as in the Sonoran Desert, water-storing succulent plants, belonging to many families, are conspicuous. Some of the taller succulents with water-storing, spiny, strongly ridged stems look very like the organ-pipe cacti of the Sonoran Desert. In fact, there are no members of the cactus family (Cactaceae) native to southern Africa. The look-alikes belong to the spurge family (Euphorbiaceae), which is evident when they produce their distinctive flower-like inflorescences, which contrast so strongly with the much larger, more flamboyantly colored cactus flowers. This is an example of parallel evolution, where a similar adaptation has evolved independently from unrelated ancestors in response to similar habitat conditions.

Succulent plants generally in southern Africa vary in form from perennial and annual herbs through small, cushion-like shrubs to small, branched and unbranched trees. In some species only the stems are succulent, and leaves are often absent; in others, only the leaves, or both leaves and stems, are succulent. A few species have greatly enlarged water-storing roots. Bulbs of some of the species of the lily (Liliaceae), daffodil (Amaryllidaceae), and *Iris* (Iridaceae) families, which die down during periods of drought, are also unusually large and water storing.

Euphorbia ingens in South Africa.

Among the most curious of the southern African succulents are the euphorbias; the stapelias of the Apocynaceae (including Asclepiadaceae), in which the attractiveness of the broad, flat flowers is rather outweighed by their fly-attracting odor; the small stone plants, *Lithops*, of the Aizoaceae, whose pairs of rotund leaves are well camouflaged among the pebbles where they grow; shrub to small tree species of *Aloe*

A close view of *Euphorbia* inflorescences, each with a female flower surrounded by male flowers.

A *Stapelia,* with fleshy, leafless stems, a striped, hairy flower, an empty seed capsule to the right, and many seeds, each with a plume of hairs.

Cultivated "stone plants" (*Lithops*), one of them with two flowers.

Pachypodium namaquanum, with swollen, heavily spined stems, each topped by a tuft of leaves and flowers.

The grotesquely enlarged lower stem of *Adenia spinosa* with climbing stems arising from the near end. The stem is said to weigh 4 tons.

(Asphodelaceae); species of *Pachypodium* (Apocynaceae), whose stems are strongly swollen and are each topped by a tuft of leaves that seem too small for the bulky stems; the climber *Adenia spinosa* (Passifloraceae), which seems more like a figment of the imagination than a real plant; and *Dioscorea elephantipes* of the yam family (Dioscoreaceae), also a climber but with a more elegant, hemispherical, swollen, basal stem. The succulent plants mostly have very shallow root systems so that they can quickly absorb and store moisture when it rains.

Madagascar

With a length of 1,601 km (995 miles), Madagascar is a large and also mountainous island. Although only 400 km (250 miles) east of southern Africa, its rich flora and fauna differ dramatically from that of the continent. In the southwestern part of the island there is a narrow coastal strip of semidesert about 50 km (30 miles) wide, extending from the southernmost cape along the western coast for about 200 km (120 miles). Average rainfall is about 350 mm (13¾ inches), mostly coming in thunderstorms for a month or two in summer. In some places there may be no rain at all for 1–1½ years. The aridity largely arises from the trade winds' losing their moisture on the mountains and descending on the west as dry winds. Opposing sea breezes moving over the relatively cool sea to the heated daytime land can also be strong, but they bring only fog to the coasts. So this Madagascan desert is also a fog desert, apparently resulting as elsewhere from the presence of a cold offshore current. This is unexpected as currents on the western sides of oceans come from equatorial regions and are warm. In the case of Madagascar the southward-moving warm current splits into two around the island. The eastern branch divides again at the southern end with one branch continuing southward and the other curving up around the southern cape to meet the western branch moving southward. Perhaps the turbulence resulting from dividing and conflicting currents in this region results in the upwelling of cold waters from the depths.

The substrates for plants range from sand dunes and saline sands to soils derived from sandstone or limestone. The vegetation is very distinctive: "A most remarkable abundance of endemics and strange life- and growth-forms is concentrated in the relatively small area of this region and creates a unique vegetation, which has no counterpart anywhere else in the world" (Rauh 1986). Many of the plants are succulent and spiny, and are either leafless or lose their leaves during the long droughts. The vegetation is generally a low, open woodland with an overstory, sometimes sparse, of trees 10–15 m (33–49 feet) high above an often dense lower story of shrubs to 3 m (10 feet) in height.

Among the small trees, euphorbias, usually much-branched, and species of the family Portulacaceae (including Didiereaceae) predominate. *Didierea* and related genera are unusual and found only on Madagascar. They belong to the same botanical order as the cactus and ice plant families. The species are extremely spiny and fleshy, and produce small leaves when it rains. A number of species of *Didierea* and *Alluaudia* have short trunks with clusters of very long, slender, wand-like, outward-curving branches. They are quite similar in appearance to the ocotillo (*Fouquieria*) of North America. Others have untidily branching, often entangled, horizontal branches. There may also be scattered, taller "bottle trees" with swollen, water-storing trunks. Some of these are baobabs, of the genus *Adansonia*, and others are species of *Pachypodium*.

The shrubs belong to many different families, and many of them are densely twiggy and spiny, with small leaves that are shed during the dry spells. In the aloes and kalanchoes the somewhat larger, fleshy leaves are persistent. The stems of the shrubs are often fleshy, as are the roots of some species. After a good rain, leaves and large, colorful flowers quickly develop.

Although pushing through the spiny, intertangled shrubs to investigate the many species must be a painful experience, most botanists would consider this a small price to pay for the opportunity to see such a strange and remarkable type of vegetation.

Australia

The Australian desert is second in size only to the much larger Sahara-to-India desert complex. It occupies 55% of its continent, reaching the sea along the central western coast and the western part of the southern coast where the porous limestones of the Nullarbor Plain retain little moisture. There is no extreme desert in Australia. Rain in the north comes mostly in summer, and in the south in winter. The Simpson Desert near Alice Springs is the driest region and is marginally true desert with about 125 mm (4 7/8 inches) of rainfall; most of the rest is semidesert.

Most of the desert region is of low relief, with some mountain ranges of modest height in the northwest and near the center. Dry washes are abundant and carry water after heavy rain. They end in flat depressions that are sometimes shallow lakes but mostly salt flats. Some of these are large, for example, Lake Eyre (9,300 km^2, 3,600 square miles), but most are small and numerous.

Extensive sandy deserts occupy most of the central region and reach the coast in the northwest. The sand is derived from the erosion of rocks by permanent rivers, ancestral to the present dry washes, in much wetter times. Also, in these wet, tropical times the continental shield in the west was subjected to deep weathering, resulting in an iron-rich, rock-like, lateritic crust (duricrust) that can be as much as 20 m (66 feet) thick.

The desert vegetation of Australia differs from that of other hot deserts in the world in several respects: all species are evergreen; there are few ground plants that die down to underground storage organs; there are few spiny plants; and perhaps most notably, there is no array of distinctive water-storing plants, though there are some small succulent plants in saline habitats.

In the peripheral desert zone there is a tall shrubland dominated by mulga (*Acacia aneura*) up to 8 m (26 feet) high on infertile, sandy soils. The acacias are usually quite widely spaced, providing only 10–30% cover. Other small trees are much less common and include small species of *Eucalyptus, Grevillea,* and *Pittosporum.* There may be quite a dense ground cover of small shrubs of many species, or the ground may be largely open and support herbaceous plants among which the daisy, pea, and grass families are strongly represented.

The drier central region, mostly comprising sandy plains and dune fields, is quite well vegetated. There may be scattered small trees and shrubs, but the general cover is called a *Triodia* hummock grassland. Species of the grasses *Triodia* and *Plectrachne* are almost cushion-like in form with stiff, erect leaves with needle-like tips. During periods of drought the leaves roll up into slender tubes to reduce water loss from the pores on the inner surface. When it rains, the leaves unfold and function actively once more (Jim Tyler, personal communication). The hummocks gradually extend at their mar-

An Australian *Triodia* grass of spreading, cushion-like form with many central flower spikes.

gins but die at their centers so they end up ring-like in form. The hummock grasses provide a less than 30% cover. Between the hummocks, ephemerals provide a colorful display after rain.

Northern Africa to southwestern Asia

In northern Africa to southwestern Asia the largest desert is the vast Sahara of Africa, but desert continues, barely interrupted by the Red Sea, through to northwestern India. The total area of this hot desert zone is about four times that of Australia.

In the Sahara, true desert with rainfall of 70–120 mm (2 3/4–4 3/4 inches) occupies the largest area, more than 10 times that of the fringing semidesert with rainfall of 120–400 mm (4 3/4–15 3/4 inches). Some central parts are extreme deserts with rainfall from 70 mm (2 3/4 inches) down to none at all. In the north, any rain comes in winter, and in the south, during summer, often in the form of thunderstorms.

In the central Sahara there are some mountain clusters attaining elevations up to 3,000 m (9,800 feet). Apart from that the landscape is rather monotonous with reg, desert pavement covered with small stones, occupying 70% of the area; hammada, plateaus of solid rock covered with large boulders, 10%; and erg, "sand seas" of dunes, 20%. The extensive desert pavement is essentially plantless. Dry washes or wadis support shrubs and tufted grasses, as do occasional depressions where sand has accumulated. Plants are also rare on the rocky plateaus. Sand dunes support scattered shrubs, including water-storing euphorbias and leafless ephedras, but robust grasses, mostly species of the genus *Stipa*, predominate.

Succulent vegetation on nonsaline sites is mostly found in the far west, near the Atlantic coasts of southern Morocco to Mauritania and also on dry, low-elevation sites in the Canary Islands. There are fleshy euphorbias that look like cactuses, and kalanchoes and members of the ice plant family, reminiscent of plant communities near the sea in Namaqualand in South Africa.

The semidesert is best developed on the southern side of the true desert. The vegetation includes scattered small trees, many of which are species of *Acacia*, and particularly in rocky sites there is also a variety of small shrubs. Both the trees and shrubs are often spiny. Perennial grasses are also conspicuous even if widely spaced. Like the grasses of the Australian and some southern African deserts, they have narrow, rolled leaves, often with sharp points. Following rains, the perennial grasses produce new growth and other ephemeral grasses quickly appear, as well as a wide range of more showy ephemeral flowering plants. When drought settles in again, the ephemerals die, so for a time the ground seems to be littered with straw.

In northern Africa true desert reaches the Atlantic coast on a broad front where there is a cold offshore current, as is usual on the western coasts of continents at these latitudes. In the east the desert reaches the Red Sea with an extension southward along the Somalian coast, reaching almost to the equator. This southern extension of the desert is puzzling because ocean currents on the eastern sides of continents come from the equator and are warm, with warm, moist air above them. However, on the landward side of the warm currents along the Somalian coast, as also along the southern Arabian coast, there is cold upwelling water, which provides only relatively cool, dry air for the land. Perhaps this results from restriction of the circulation of the warm currents imposed by the limited extent of the Indian Ocean north of the equator and the blocking effect of the Indian peninsula.

The temperate deserts

Temperate deserts are beyond the range of the dry, descending air masses of the tropics, and they are arid mostly because mountain ranges precipitate the moisture from prevailing winds so that little or no moisture reaches the land on the lee side. In winter these temperate deserts can be extremely cold, but in summer temperatures can sometimes be very high (West 1983).

In North America the desert of the Great Basin lies between the ranges of the Sierra Nevada and the Cascades to the west and the Rocky Mountains to the east, which dry out winds from both west and east. The largest area of temperate desert in the world is in central Asia, where the distance to the sea in almost all directions is so great that most incoming winds are dry. In particular, moist monsoon winds from the Indian Ocean in summer are stripped of their moisture by the Himalaya. In the southern hemisphere the Patagonian desert in southern South America, where the prevailing winds are westerlies, lies in the rain shadow of the high Andes. The short, cold Falkland Current, coming from circum-Antarctic waters, runs along the Patagonian coast on the east and contributes little moisture to the land.

The Great Basin

With rainfall between 100 and 400 mm (4–15¾ inches) the Great Basin is mostly semidesert. It occupies much of Nevada except in the far south, extending north through eastern Oregon and Washington and east through southern Idaho to western Wyoming. Much of Utah is also included, and there are limited extensions into California, Arizona, Colorado, and New Mexico. The landscape mostly comprises extensive plains, or flat mesa tops in the southeast. The elevational range is mostly between 1,000 and 2,000 m (3,300–6,600 feet). Temperatures can be very high in summer and bitterly cold in winter. There can be occasional rain in some parts in spring and summer, and snow in winter, particularly in the north.

There are two main types of vegetation. On plateaus, the extensive coalesced debris fans, hills, and plains, where the soils are not saline or only moderately so, there is a far-extending association of shrubs, bunchgrasses, and other herbaceous flowering plants. The shrubland has fewer species than similar vegetation in the hot deserts. In fact, just about everywhere the grayish-leaved sagebrush (*Artemisia tridentata*) is the overwhelming dominant. Other species of *Artemisia* dominate locally, and shrubby species of other genera are scattered throughout. In the spaces between the shrubs, the short, tufted bunchgrasses can be common, together with a range of smaller flowering plants. Bunchgrasses are particularly abundant in northern parts of the Great Basin, where the plains are underlain by volcanic basalt rock or where the soil is alluvial.

Central Asian deserts

The central Asian deserts extend from the vicinity of the Caspian and Aral Seas in the west to the Gobi, not far from the ocean in northern China. Many plant genera are shared with the North American temperate deserts, including *Artemisia* and milk vetches (*Astragalus*), and in salty sites, genera of the goosefoot family (Chenopodiaceae).

The temperature swing from winter to summer in the central Asian deserts is extreme, often from −40 to 40°C (−40 to 104°F). The landforms of the temperate Asian deserts are very similar to those of the hot deserts. As in the Sahara, there are extensive desert pavements with plants largely restricted to dry washes and sandy hollows, sand dunes that sometimes support tall shrubs to small trees as well as smaller plants, and salt flats with fringing, salt-tolerant plants.

Gray-green sagebrush (*Artemisia tridentata*) shrubs in the Great Basin at Arches National Park, Utah.

The Patagonian desert

The Patagonian desert is a region of semidesert in southern Argentina, extending from approximately 40° to 52° south. Much of the landscape consists of plains and plateaus that support a low vegetation cover of tufted grasses, including many species of *Stipa*, rounded shrubs, and dense cushion plants, some of which are spiny, and a few dwarf cactus species. Apart from the small amount of rain, the frequent westerly gales that sweep across the plains add to the aridity by increasing evaporation. These relentless winds also prevent the establishment of taller plants. Wide, braided rivers extend from the mountains across the plains and transport heavy loads of gravel, sand, and silt. The sand is blown into dunes in the vicinity of the rivers.

Seasonal drought in Mediterranean climates

There are two climate regimes characterized by seasonal drought: Mediterranean with a summer drought, and savanna with a winter drought. If the Earth's axis of rotation were exactly at right angles to the plane of its revolution around the sun, then the air pressure belts would be constant in position year-round. The Earth's axis is in fact inclined at an angle of 23.5° from the vertical.

This means that in the northern summer, the northern hemisphere is tilted toward the sun and the angle of the sun's rays steepen toward the North Pole and impart more heat. The effect of this is that the pressure belts move northward, and the northern part of the desert climate over the Sahara, for example, comes to lie over the lands bordering the Mediterranean and they experience a summer drought. At the same time, the savanna zone on the other side of the desert is experiencing a wet equatorial climate. The opposite takes place during the northern winter: the pressure belts move south and the southern part of the wet temperate zone now lies over the Mediterranean, giving a wet winter. The savanna, in contrast, is now subjected to desert drought. Both climate types have greater rainfalls than the desert, but life is still not easy for the plants—they have to survive through a season of desert climate.

The Mediterranean Basin

The North African, Middle Eastern, and southern European lands bordering the Mediterranean Sea constitute the largest area of winter-wet, summer-dry vegetation at 60% of the world total. Smaller Mediterranean climate areas occur in California (10%), central Chile (5%), the southern extremity of South Africa (3%), and in Western Australia and South Australia (22%) (Dallman 1998).

Mediterranean-type vegetation is found in Portugal, much of Spain, near the sea in southern France, in Italy, the Balkans, through much of western and southern Turkey, and near the sea in the Middle East. In northern Africa it is found in Morocco, Algeria, and Tunisia but is largely absent from the lower-latitude coasts of Libya and Egypt, where the desert comes to the sea. In southern parts of the region the dry season accounts for about half the year but reduces to a few months in the north.

The lands surrounding the Mediterranean Basin have been occupied by humans for thousands of years and have seen the rise and fall of several civilizations. With the human presence, the vegetation has been much modified by the clearance of land for crops and the felling of trees for firewood and construction. For example, Lebanon was originally covered by dense forest dominated by the cedar of Lebanon (*Cedrus libani*), which is now restricted to a few stands in the mountains. Also, although there would have been natural fires following lightning strikes in pre-human times, human-caused fires are much more frequent and have had a devastating effect on the vegetation.

Where natural vegetation still occurs it is mostly dominated by shrubs and is generally known as maquis. The shrubs are about 1–3 m (3–10 feet) high and include species of rosemary (*Rosmarinus*), heaths and heathers (*Erica*), often brightly colored rock roses (*Cistus*), brooms (*Cytisus* and *Genista*), and sometimes somewhat taller evergreen oaks (*Quercus*) and pines (*Pinus*). In gullies along streams, oleanders (*Nerium*) are a colorful sight when in flower. Often, there are open spaces between the shrubs, and in spring, after the winter rains, these fill up with colorful ephemerals and geophytes. Of the regions with a Mediterranean climate, the Mediterranean Basin has the greatest abundance of ephemerals and is second to South Africa for geophytes. Among these herbaceous Mediterranean plants are many genera familiar in gardens, such as tulips (*Tulipa*), daffodils (*Narcissus*), species of *Iris*, *Cyclamen*, and *Anemone*, and poppies (*Papaver*) and snapdragons (*Antirrhinum*).

Most of the shrubs are evergreen and have small to very small, hard leaves called sclerophylls, which have modifications to reduce water loss, so they are drought tolerators, while the geophytes and ephemerals are drought evaders.

A second type of shrubby vegetation, known as garrigue, is found on the driest and sunniest sites, especially on porous limestone rocks. The shrubs are low, mostly less than 50 cm (19 inches) high, rounded, and often have densely interlaced twigs. Many of the shrubs are very spiny, deterring browsing animals. A number of the genera are shared with the maquis, with the addition of euphorbias, lavender (*Lavandula*), sage (*Salvia*), and thyme (*Thymus*). Once again in open spaces between the shrubs, a wide range of ephemerals and geophytes makes an appearance in spring.

The shrubs of the garrigue have shallow roots that can quickly absorb moisture from a shower but are not sufficient to sustain active growth during the dry season. For this reason some of the shrubs, such as *Euphorbia dendroides* and the spiny broom *Calycotome villosa*, lose their leaves during summer. Other species, particularly those belonging to the mint family (Lamiaceae), have relatively large, soft leaves during the wet winter, but these drop off in spring and are replaced on new growth by generally smaller, hard leaves that are more drought resistant. Many of the leaves contain aromatic oils or resins, for example those of lavender, thyme, and rosemary, which in the heat of summer days fill the air with a pleasant aroma.

The other major type of Mediterranean vegetation is a low, evergreen, sclerophyll forest dominated by evergreen oaks bearing small leaves that are smooth-margined or lined with spiny teeth. There are also a few species of deciduous oaks, mostly in northern parts of the region where winters are cooler. Sometimes mixed with the oaks, or more often forming their own forests in the driest and hottest sites, are small, round- or umbrella-crowned species of pine. The trees are up to 15 m (49 feet) high and form a closed, dark green canopy. Below are smaller trees, such as *Arbutus*, *Viburnum*, and in places, *Clematis*, honeysuckle (*Lonicera*), and other vines. The true laurel or bay laurel (*Laurus nobilis*), with its aromatic leaves, demands more moisture than the species of the oak and pine forests and is mostly restricted to shady ravines and gorges.

A number of plant ecologists believe that before human occupation around the Mediterranean Sea, low sclerophyll forests would have been much more widespread than they are now, and maquis and garrigue much more limited. They further suggest that if fire could be kept out of the maquis and garrigue, much of the region would eventually convert to various types of closed-canopy forest.

California

The Mediterranean-type vegetation of California is similar in many ways to that of the Mediterranean Basin itself—the chaparral can be compared to the maquis, the coastal sage scrub or soft chaparral to the garrigue, and the evergreen sclerophyll forests of both regions share the oak (*Quercus*), pine (*Pinus*), and cypress (*Cupressus*) genera. Physically, California is mostly hilly to mountainous with the only extensive area of flat land being the long and wide Central Valley, lying between the Coast Ranges of moderate height and the much higher Sierra Nevada. North of the Central Valley, hills and mountains extend across the state, and in the south, deserts and mountains lie inland from the Coast Ranges.

Chaparral is commonly encountered in the Coast Ranges, the western foothills of the Sierra Nevada, and also in the rain shadows of mountains in the north of the state and southern Oregon, where rainfall is otherwise very abundant. The sclerophyllous shrubs of the chaparral are up to 3 m (10 feet) high or more, and most have a deep taproot but also branch roots near the ground surface to collect water from showers that wet only the upper layers. Much of the chaparral has a great mixture of species, including chamise (*Adenostoma fasciculatum*) with its small narrow leaves, and species of manzanita (*Arctostaphylos*) with their handsome, polished, red-brown stems, California lilacs (*Ceanothus*) with their masses of small blue flowers, and scrub oaks. A number of annual and perennial herbaceous plants appear after fires, but they eventually disappear

Chaparral, dominated by chamise, *Adenostoma fasciculatum,* is in the foreground and also in the distance, where it is the smooth-textured vegetation on the hills. Also on the hills are coarser-textured patches of oak woodland, which tend to be on moister, north-facing slopes. Mount Diablo, east of San Francisco Bay, California.

after the chaparral canopy is reestablished. There are not as many geophytes as in the Mediterranean maquis.

Coastal sage scrub is found mostly near the shore from just north of San Francisco to northern Baja California. The shrubs are usually no more than 1.5 m (5 feet) high, and like the Mediterranean garrigue, a number of species of the aromatic-leaved mint family are conspicuous, including salvias. As in the garrigue, some of the shallowly rooted shrubs lose their leaves during the summer drought, and others have different wet- and dry-season leaves (for example, *Salvia leucophylla*).

Oak woodlands are common in the Coast Ranges, the Sierra foothills, and set back from the sea in the north. Their preferred climate is warm and dry in summer, with relatively mild winters; they generally grow upslope from the grasslands of the hot, dry valleys and plains. Quite a number of oak species are involved, but only two or three dominate in any locality. They range in height from 5 to 20 m (16–66 feet); some are

Open oak woodland in the Coast Ranges of northern California with a mixture of coast live oak (*Quercus agrifolia*), blue oak (*Q. douglasii*), and California black oak (*Q. kelloggii*). The dead annual grasses between the trees have been introduced from the Mediterranean.

deciduous, others evergreen. In many places the oaks do not form a closed canopy but are quite widely spaced. Sometimes, chaparral species occupy the spaces between, but more often grasses cover the ground. These are now introduced grasses, which replaced the original native bunchgrasses. Species of pine and cypress may also be present.

Northern California has more rainfall and a shorter dry season, and the forests there could be regarded as a transition between the temperate coniferous forests of the Pacific Northwest and the oak forests of central and southern California. Also in the north, in a belt close to the coast, is one of the world's most awe-inspiring forests. It is dominated by the world's tallest tree, the coast redwood (*Sequoia sempervirens*). This forest is sometimes considered to be part of California's Mediterranean-type vegetation, but this is questionable as the climate is moist year-round. The rainfall can be as much as 2,500 mm (98 inches), and fog drip during the relatively short summer drought, together with low evaporation in the cool cloudy conditions, keeps the soil moist.

Chile

The narrow zone of typical Mediterranean-type vegetation extends in Chile from about 30° to 37° south, to the west of the high Andes. In the north it grades into extreme desert, and in the south into moist temperate forests dominated by species of southern beech (*Nothofagus*), now accorded its own family, Nothofagaceae, allied to the Fagaceae of the oaks (*Quercus*) and true beeches (*Fagus*). To the east are the ramparts of the Andes, attaining heights of about 6,500 m (21,000 feet), and to the west the cold Humboldt Current that is even colder than the California Current.

Topographically, central Chile is similar to California. There is a coastal range up to about 2,200 m (7,200 feet) in height, a central valley, then the high Andes. However, the Valle Central in Chile is only about 40 km (25 miles) wide whereas the Central Valley in California is about 100 km (62 miles) wide, and the Andes are about 50% higher than the Sierra Nevada.

The Chilean equivalent to the Californian chaparral is the matorral. It is widespread in the coastal ranges and along the foothills of the Andes and once also occurred in the central valley. The matorral comprises often quite widely spaced small shrubs and small trees. Mostly in the shelter of the shrubs there are many perennials, and geophytes and some annuals. About half the herbaceous genera are shared with California, a contrast with the woody plants where very few genera are shared. Among the herbaceous plants, the best-known and most prolific genus is *Calceolaria* with 86 Chilean species, and among the geophytes the genus *Alstroemeria* is well known to gardeners.

The northern coastal strip of central Chile supports coastal matorral, which includes a range of small shrubs with soft foliage that is lost during the dry season. Evergreen sclerophyll forest is now very restricted in distribution, having been heavily exploited after European settlement. Patches can be found in the cooler, moister southern half of central Chile, both in the coastal ranges and the Andean foothills. There is a closed canopy mostly 5–10 m (16–33 feet) above the ground, though some species can reach 20 m (66 feet) where conditions are favorable.

Cryptocarya alba is a common tree that is related to the California laurel (*Umbellularia californica*) and the bay laurel (*Laurus nobilis*) of the Mediterranean. It is also found in a stunted form in the matorral. *Lithraea caustica* is related to the poison oak (*Toxicodendron diversilobum*) of California and causes similar rashes on contact. Unlike poison oak, *Lithraea* can become a tree up to about 7 m (23 feet) tall, but it is also common as a shrub in the matorral. The soapbark tree (*Quillaja saponaria*) is found in a wide range of sites, including sclerophyll forest. It is tolerant of both drought and cold. The common name derives from the fact that the inner bark foams like soap in water and has been used for washing clothes and as a shampoo. These are some of the trees. There are also some subcanopy shrubs, including species of *Escallonia*, and species of the myrtle family (Myrtaceae) and a few vines. Unlike California and the Mediterranean, conifers are not represented in the sclerophyll forest of Chile.

South Africa

The area of Mediterranean climate in the southwestern corner of South Africa is the smallest at 3% of the world total. In many ways, however, it is the most spectacular with several times the concentration of species of the other regions (Werger 1978). The total flora numbers about 8,500 species, and the narrow Cape Peninsula alone, which is only 50 km (30 miles) long, supports about 2,600 species. This is perhaps the greatest species density in the world. The Cape flora has also contributed more than its fair share of colorful garden plants to the world.

The Mediterranean climate forms an arc bordering the sea from about 150 km (93 miles) north of Cape Town on the Atlantic coast to Mossel Bay, about 370 km (230 miles) east of Cape Town on the Indian Ocean. In the western part, the summer drought is mostly unrelieved by any showers, though fog from the cold Benguela Current provides some condensation, but in the east there is some summer rain. There is a series of mountain ranges paralleling the coast, similar in height to the coastal ranges of Chile and California. The coarse sandstones, shales, and granites of these mountains provide an infertile soil. North of Cape Town are sandy coastal plains where in places the soils are reasonably fertile.

The main type of vegetation is known as fynbos, which is similar in form to the shrubby vegetation in other Mediterranean climate regions. The species involved, however, are mostly unrelated to those of the northern hemisphere and have only weak links with Chilean plants. There are stronger connections with the plants of this type of vegetation in Australia. Fynbos is also often easy to walk through as the shrubs are well spaced, unlike those of the other regions except Australia. In the spaces between are dwarf shrubs and herbaceous plants, including geophytes. This pattern may be one reason why the concentration of species is so high.

There are three main growth forms in the fynbos. There are shrubs to small trees of the southern hemisphere family Proteaceae, with relatively large, thick leaves held erect to avoid overheating by the midday sun. Species of this family often have large and distinctive, compact inflorescences with brightly colored flowers, so proteas, leucadendrons, and leucospermums among other genera from South Africa are well known as ornamentals. The family is also strongly represented in Australia but less so in Chile.

The second plant form involves mostly small, twiggy, rounded shrubs with small, often rolled leaves. The family Ericaceae is strongly represented, the Cape heaths (*Erica*) alone having more than 600 species. In addition, there are genera from a number of other families that have species of similar form.

Protea flower head, South Africa.

Tubular flowers of a Cape heath, *Erica cerinthoides.*

The third form is grass-like with the southern hemisphere family Restionaceae predominant, but true grasses (Poaceae) and sedges (Cyperaceae) are also represented.

Fynbos on the lower mountain slopes is generally three-layered with an upper discontinuous layer of proteaceous shrubs up to about 2.5 m (8 feet) tall and, in places, the only conifer, *Widdringtonia cupressoides.* Below that are small, dense shrubs mixed with large, tufted plants mostly belonging to the Restionaceae. On the ground in more open places are herbaceous perennials, including *Pelargonium.* Annuals are uncommon, but geophytes are abundant and many are eye-catching when in flower during the moist time of year. Some of the larger geophyte genera, such as *Freesia, Gladiolus,* and *Watsonia,* are well known in horticulture.

Coastal fynbos is found on sand north of Cape Town and mostly limestone elsewhere. On sand, the shrubs are mostly of the rounded, small-leaved type; on limestone, proteaceous shrubs are also present. Particularly on sand there is an abundance of perennial and annual herbaceous plants, and geophytes are spectacular when in flower in spring. The daisy family and ice plants (*Mesembryanthemum*) are conspicuous among the former, and among the latter, as well as genera already mentioned, there are large, tufted species of such genera as *Kniphofia* and *Agapanthus,* of which only some die down during summer.

Quite a number of the fynbos plants have plentiful nectar and are pollinated by birds. This is the case in Australia, too, but it is uncommon in the other regions. Some of the Proteaceae can become small trees in the absence of fire, but there does not seem to be any equivalent to the sclerophyll woodland of the other regions.

Australia

There are two regions of Mediterranean climate in Australia: in the southwestern corner of Western Australia and, on the other side of the Great Australian Bight, southern South Australia with some extensions into Victoria and New South Wales.

The pattern in southwestern Australia is similar to that of the Western Cape in South Africa. The Mediterranean climate begins north of Perth at Shark Bay on the Indian Ocean, extends and widens southward, then curves around toward Esperance on the south coast. Beyond Esperance this climate regime dwindles and stops where the semidesert of the Nullarbor Plain reaches the sea. This area has the distinction of having the most infertile soils of the Mediterranean climate type in the world. This is partly because there are no young, actively eroding mountains providing nutrient-rich sediments and partly because Western Australia is essentially a plateau that has been above the sea for hundreds of millions of years, with the consequence that the soils are very old and leached of much of their mineral nutrients. The region in South Australia comes next to that of Western Australia in soil infertility for similar reasons.

As in South Africa, the areas of Mediterranean vegetation in Australia are rich in species and diverse. There are also strong links at the family level between the plants of the two regions, but the genera are mostly different. Important shared families are Proteaceae, Ericaceae—if the Epacridaceae is included in that family as more recent study suggests—Restionaceae, and Fabaceae. One family, though, which plays only a minor role in South Africa, has an overwhelming presence in the woody vegetation in Australia. This is the Myrtaceae with the predominant genus *Eucalyptus*, comprising over 500 species, providing a backdrop to almost every scene. There are many other genera in the family, though, including the bottlebrushes (*Callistemon*, *Melaleuca*, and other genera), *Leptospermum*, and many more, some of which are restricted to Western Australia.

As in South Africa, the flowers of many species are spectacular. Flowering is concentrated in spring, and the display is such that it attracts human visitors from all over Australia and beyond every year. Many flowers are pollinated by birds, and as a result, the flowers or their compact inflorescences are relatively large, brightly colored, and produce an abundance of nectar. There are many species of trees, shrubs, and perennial herbs. Annuals are less common, though particularly in sandy sites, everlasting daisies (*Helipterum* and *Helichrysum*) provide a colorful display after good rains. Geophytes, too, are not so prominent as elsewhere though ground orchids are frequent.

Mostly near the coasts is a shrubby type of vegetation without trees, growing on deep, infertile sands derived on the sand plains north of Perth from calcareous rocks but elsewhere from the weathering of laterites. Broad-leaved banksias and other Proteaceae are prominent. This shrubland is known as kwongan and it is comparable to chaparral, maquis, matorral, and fynbos. As well as banksias there are many other genera of Proteaceae present. Shrubby species of most of the other larger families are also represented. In the ground cover there is a wide range of monocotyledons. Most notable is the genus *Anigozanthos*, species of which are commonly known as kangaroo paws and cat's-paws. The flowers are furry, strongly curved, and brightly colored. A most striking species is *A. manglesii*, with two-tone flowers, bright red and bright green.

Farther inland where there is a pronounced summer drought we come to a vast extent of a sclerophyll woodland dominated by eucalypts known as mallees. The numerous species of mallee eucalypts are tall shrubs to small trees with many stems arising from the base. The stems are attached to swollen woody structures in the ground known as lignotubers. After a fire these distinctive eucalypts resprout from the lignotubers (Chapter 3).

Shrubs in the mallee vegetation are sparse to abundant and include *Melaleuca* and other Myrtaceae; *Casuarina; Grevillea, Hakea,* and other Proteaceae; species of the conifer *Callitris; Boronia* of the citrus fruit family (Rutaceae); and some species of *Acacia.* Where the soils are salty, particularly near the many salt pans, gray shrubs of the family Chenopodiaceae and other salt-tolerant plants become conspicuous.

Caladenia flava, a Western Australian ground orchid.

Flower heads of the Western Australian *Banksia coccinea.*

Hakea victoriae of Western Australia, a mostly unbranched small shrub with multicolored leaves.

The tall Western Australian *Grevillea excelsior*, with orange inflorescences.

Seasonal drought in savannas

The word savanna conjures up images of tall elephant grass, safaris, and perhaps giraffes, reaching up to the tops of small trees to browse on the foliage. This, however, is only one of many variations on a theme. Savanna is the other type of vegetation subjected to seasonal drought. It is found in low latitudes, much warmer on average than those of the Mediterranean type, and lying between tropical rain forest and the hot deserts (Cole 1986). The climate pattern is the reverse of the Mediterranean type. In summer these regions come under the influence of moist equatorial air masses, so the summers are wet. In winter, dry subtropical air moves in, so the winters are dry. The winters, of course, though cooler than the summers, would not be regarded as wintry by people from temperate regions. The vegetation resulting from this climate pattern is characterized by a ground cover of grasses that range from short, tufted species to very tall elephant grass (*Pennisetum purpureum*, in Africa). Small trees and shrubs, clumped or scattered, are generally also present.

Much of the savanna vegetation in the world grows on extensive plateaus that were formed by erosion, perhaps beginning as far back as the time when their now separate, mostly southern hemisphere land masses were united in the continent of Gondwana. Later, these lands enjoyed moist tropical climates, their soils became heavily leached, and under the influence of the high temperatures their silica compounds were largely lost, and iron and aluminum oxides accumulated near the soil surface. The latter form hard, rock-like laterites that can be meters or yards in thickness. The plateaus slowly erode back from their peripheral scarps, providing colluvium and alluvium for plains and shallow valleys at lower elevations.

It has been suggested that much of the savanna may not be original vegetation but has been brought about by fires following human settlement, destroying former forest of a drought-resistant type. A current view is that much of it is largely natural, and that long before human presence, fire as an accompaniment of drought was an important influence in its development.

In Africa, savanna occupies more than half the continent and extends across the north from west to east, south of the Sahara, then links southward to another extensive area to the south of the tropical rain forest. Savanna is also well developed in western Madagascar in the rain shadow of the north–south mountain range. In South America, savanna is also extensive though it occupies less than half the continent. It is found south of the Amazon rain forest, mostly in Brazil and to the north mostly in Venezuela. In Australia there are areas of savanna in the north, but these occupy a relatively small part of the continent. On the other side of the equator there are limited areas of savanna in Southeast Asia and southern India.

A baobab, *Adansonia grandidieri,* in the savanna of Madagascar.

Africa

The African savanna can be divided into zones related to decreasing rainfall. The zone nearest the rain forest is known as savanna woodland and extends from the sea on the West African coast about 5,000 km (3,100 miles) eastward, then turns around the eastern end of the Congo rain forest and expands into a very wide belt in the south from the Indian to the Atlantic Oceans. The general rainfall range for this type of vegetation is 700–1,000 mm (28–39 inches) with 4–5 months of drought. The preferred terrains are the ancient plateaus where a sandy, very infertile soil overlies a lateritic hardpan. The scattered or sometimes clumped trees are mostly species of *Brachystegia, Isoberlinia,* and *Julbernadia,* all belonging to the Fabaceae. These trees can be 15–20 m (49–66 feet) high, and they have small leaves with pinnately arranged leaflets. Their trunks arise from large lignotubers, which store food and water. Their roots go very deep and can make their way through the lateritic layer to considerable depths. As usual in the pea family, the roots bear nodules containing bacteria that, as part of an energy-gaining process, convert nitrogen into nitrates that the trees are able to use. So these trees are adapted in a number of ways to cope with drought and the infertility of the soil. Some of the shrubs present also have deep roots; others have shallow roots and only grow actively after rain.

Depending on rainfall, the tufted grasses covering the ground range from about 1 to 3 m (3–10 feet) high. Their aboveground parts dry and shrivel during the dry season and are replaced when the rains come from underground rhizomes.

Except for the Proteaceae, the trees lose their leaves during the dry season, though generally several months after the rains stop. Those trees and deep-rooting shrubs with a water supply at depth produce new foliage and showy flowers in abundance several weeks before the wet season begins. This is probably triggered by rising temperatures, extending the period for reproduction. Species with shallow roots generally do not resume growth and produce flowers until there have been several good rains.

As rainfall decreases toward the deserts, the savanna woodland changes to savanna parkland. Rainfall ranges down from 700 mm (28 inches) to about 500 mm (19 inches) with 5–7 months of drought. With a further decrease in rainfall there is a transition to semidesert. Savanna parkland mostly grows on the more arid parts of plains and broad river valleys at a lower elevation than the ancient plateaus. Lateritic hardpans are not present, and soils range from loams to sand.

In the savanna parklands there is a closed cover of grasses mostly less than 1 m (39 inches) high, and scattered trees up to 8 m (26 feet) high, among which species of *Acacia* predominate. An infrequent but conspicuous taller tree is the water-storing baobab or bottle tree (*Adansonia digitata*). The acacias have spreading, flat-topped, spiny crowns with small leaves whose leaflets angle away from the sun, and very long roots, sometimes penetrating to a depth of 50 m (160 feet). They also have roots nearer the ground surface to take advantage of water from showers. Species of *Terminalia* and *Combretum* also have both deep roots and shallow roots. Most of the acacias and the other trees, as well as shrubs, are leafless in the dry season.

South America

In South America the greatest extent of savanna is found south of the Amazon rain forest in southern Brazil on an ancient plateau where infertile soils overlie laterite or sandstone. The vegetation cover, as in Africa, is mostly savanna woodland. There is a ground cover of tall grasses and an overstory of small trees whose crowns often touch. These trees differ from those of the savanna woodland in Africa and Australia in being shorter, 4–8 m (13–26 feet), and having contorted trunks and branches with thick, often deeply fissured, corky bark. A further contrast is provided by the large, leathery leaves of many of the trees (for example, *Eugenia dysenterica, Jacaranda brasiliana,* and *Terminalia argentea*). As in the other regions, the leaves are retained well into the dry season, and new foliage is produced when temperatures rise before the first rains. Again, this is made possible by lignotubers, and roots that extend down to the water table.

Going east in Brazil, rainfall decreases, and on the plains at lower elevations, resulting from the erosional retreat of the ancient plateaus, there is a very different type of vegetation whose plants are quite unrelated to those of savanna woodland. This is known as caatinga and, though it is considered to be a type of savanna, grasses are not a conspicuous element. In the driest sites where the soils are thin and stony, small spiny mimosas mingle with succulent plants—the creeping cactus (*Pilocereus gounellei*), a semiprostrate, branching, columnar type that spreads widely over the ground, several opuntias and other small cacti, thorny euphorbias, and bromeliads.

Australia

In Australia, savanna is found in the north of the Northern Territory and adjacent northern Western Australia, and in inland eastern Queensland from Cape York to about the Queensland–New South Wales border in the south. Across the Torres Strait from Cape York there is also savanna on the southern plains of New Guinea. In Queensland the savanna borders coastal tropical to subtropical rain forest in many places, but elsewhere, in northern parts, it is separated by the sea from the tropical forests of Malesia.

Savanna woodland is particularly extensive, being found in Arnhem Land of the Northern Territory and the adjacent Kimberley Plateau in Western Australia, and, on suitable sites, throughout the savanna zone of eastern Queensland. As in Africa and South America, it is mostly found on old tablelands with infertile lateritic soils. Rainfall ranges from 500 to 1,500 mm (19–59 inches) with, in the northern areas, a particularly pronounced winter drought following the monsoon summer rains. The dominant trees are mostly single-trunked species of *Eucalyptus*, standing above a ground cover of tall grasses belonging to several genera. Shrubs may be absent, but where they occur they include small species of *Eucalyptus, Acacia,* and *Grevillea.*

Savanna parkland is of very limited extent in Australia, occurring on alkaline soils derived from basalt and limestone. The otherwise ubiquitous *Eucalyptus* is not represented but is replaced by genera also present in the savanna parkland of Africa: *Acacia, Bauhinia,* and the occasional baobab (*Adansonia*).

Savanna grassland with few trees or shrubs is more widespread, particularly in northern Queensland. It is found on plains at a lower elevation than the lateritic plateaus. Decreasing rainfall from north to south and from east to west is the basic determinant in the sequence of savanna vegetation types, but local factors, particularly different types of soil, can result in complicated patterns.

CHAPTER THREE

Rising from the Ashes

♦ ♦ ♦

Plants and Fire

Much of the world's population lives in regions where there is year-round rainfall with only occasional and short periods of drought. People living in the humid tropics and the forest climates of the humid temperate regions do not associate fire with forests as a natural phenomenon. Nevertheless, devastating forest fires often make the international news in places where high temperatures and drought coincide during summer, such as California and eastern Australia. These fires often result in loss of life and extensive destruction of property and are a constant background concern to many who live in these places.

Before human intervention, fire in moist tropical and temperate forests would have been a rare occurrence; the litter on the forest floor is too moist, and the water content in living foliage too great to burn readily following lightning strikes. So for moist forest plants, fire has not been an important evolutionary factor. Desert plants, too, at the other extreme, have not had to cope with fire, even though the high temperatures and aridity are conducive to it. In deserts the vegetation is mostly sparse so that even if one plant were set on fire by lightning, the fire would probably not spread. Too, desert plants produce little litter as fuel for fire. The larger plants grow slowly, and many have dispensed with leaves to reduce water loss.

Banksia praemorsa, with a seed head so densely covered by dead flower parts that any follicles are completely concealed. Western Australia.

Between these extremes, fire has been a frequent occurrence, particularly in vegetation subjected to seasonal drought: savanna with winter drought, and Mediterranean-type vegetation with summer drought. Temperate grasslands, including the prairies of North America and the steppes of Russia, were also very fire prone (Bond and van Wilgen 1996).

Some might wonder how effective lightning is as an initiator of fires in susceptible vegetation. It is often followed by heavy rain, but not always, and in regions where summer thunderstorms are frequent, there may be many lightning strikes. For example, in Yosemite National Park, California, hundreds of such strikes in a year have been observed, spread throughout the park, and some of these have resulted in fires. In northern Australia, the first lightning strikes at the end of the dry season are not accompanied by rain, and they readily ignite the tinder-dry savanna grasses (Jim Tyler, personal communication).

Nevertheless, little attention was initially given to fire as a factor in the natural evolution of plants and plant communities. It was assumed that fire is largely a result of human activities and that in pre-human times it was infrequent. This attitude has changed in more recent decades, most notably in Australia, where adaptations to fire are strikingly obvious in many plant communities and have been the subject of much research (Gill et al. 1981).

Why do some plants burn so well? Some have small to very small, hard-textured leaves, known as sclerophylls, that have thick waxy cuticles, thick-walled cells, and that are low in moisture content. Such leaves may live for several seasons and, being relatively dry, catch fire quite easily. If these leaves and other plant parts also contain what could be called natural fire accelerants, such as resins in pines and other conifers, and oils in glands of a number of flowering plants, fierce and rapidly spreading fires can result.

Grasses also are very fire prone with their long, narrow, and usually quite thin leaves. As they also often grow quite close together as tussocks or in continuous swards, fire can quickly spread over considerable areas. In temperate grasses, the outer persistent, dead leaves catch fire first and gradually ignite the living leaves; the savanna grasses, whose entire aboveground parts die and dry out during dry summers, are even more susceptible.

In vegetation dominated by woody plants, fire generally starts in the litter on the ground. This litter is made up of fallen leaves, twigs, empty seed capsules or cones, and bark flakes. Their tough texture and dryness prevent rapid decay, so the litter increases in quantity year by year. With a moderate amount of litter a fire will kill annuals and the aboveground parts of shrubs and geophytes, but apart from being blackened on the lower parts of their trunks, trees are largely unaffected. If it has been some years since the last fire and there is a deep bed of accumulated litter, the fire is much more fierce and flames can reach up the trunks of the trees, sometimes aided by bark strips acting as wicks, to set fire to the crown. If the trees are conifers with resin or eucalypts with oil glands, the fire can quickly spread from tree crown to tree crown into a general conflagration that may become an all-consuming firestorm.

How do plants survive these fires? Trunks of trees of fire-prone regions are protected by thick bark. Bark is largely made up of dead corky cells that are heat resistant and protect the living inner tissues, particularly the tissue-renewing cambium, from the heat of all except the fiercest fires. The thickness of the bark is critical; a doubling of thickness does not just double the heat resistance, it increases it several times. Trees with thick, fire-resistant bark include many eucalypt species in Australia and the redwoods (*Sequoia* and *Sequoiadendron*), pines, and other conifers of North America as well as evergreen oaks there and in the Mediterranean Basin, of which the most notable is the cork oak (*Quercus suber*). Trees of moister habitats with thin bark are generally killed by fire. This is the case with some eucalypts in Australia, including the tallest of all, *Eucalyptus regnans*.

A remarkable phenomenon that illustrates the great resistance of some tree trunks to fire has been observed in eucalypts in Australia and redwoods in California. Fire can burn away bark and living tissues, down to the wood, in a patch on one side of a tree trunk. Observations suggest that this patch is on the lee side of the trunk relevant to the fire direction, where flames curving around the trunk on each side concentrate their heat on what should be the more protected side. The trees can continue living as there are plenty of conducting tissues elsewhere around the trunk to provide for the leafy crown.

Even more remarkable is the fact that subsequent fires can burn farther into the wood and, probably as a result of slow smoldering, completely hollow out the trunk so that it is like a black cave. Sometimes the fire even breaks through on the other side, and one can walk right through the tree. It is difficult to understand how the living outer tissues of these trees are protected from the heat of fires burning inside their trunks.

Some tree monocots, including agaves and cordylines, have corky bark, giving some protection against fire, and all have conducting tissues scattered throughout their stems. This means that the centrally located conducting tissues, at least, of monocot trunks are well protected from fire, unlike the conducting tissues of dicotyledons, which form a narrow zone just inside the bark. Some of these tall monocots retain their old leaves as a thick skirt around the trunk. In *Aloe ferox* of South Africa it was found that few of these single-stemmed tall shrubs were killed by fire if the skirts were intact, whereas mortality was 90–100% when the skirts had been removed. Some palms, including the California fan palm (*Washingtonia filifera*), and some yuccas and cordylines, also retain skirts of dead leaves, but these look as if they would burn so fiercely that the trees would be killed rather than protected. On the other hand, the distinctive grass trees

Pinus ponderosa with thick, patterned bark. California.

The living *Sequoiadendron giganteum* to the right has had the base of its trunk burned out by fire. Giant redwoods now are restricted to about 75 groves, some quite small, in the Sierra Nevada of California.

A trunk of *Kingia australis* (right) in Western Australia and an adjacent eucalypt, blackened by a recent fire. The flower heads of the *Kingia* were stimulated to develop by the fire.

(*Xanthorrhoea* and *Kingia*) of Australia are protected from fire by the persistent bases of their dead leaves. These are densely packed, partly glued together by resin, and occupy most of the diameter of the stout trunks, from the ground to the crowns of narrow leaves. Virtually all trunks of living grass trees are charred and blackened from frequent fires, attesting to the insulating capability of the leaf bases.

The sprouters

Some of the plants known as sprouters, whose aboveground parts are killed by fire, resume growth by activating dormant epicormic buds on the still-living stem bases at or below ground level. Epicormic buds are formed in the angles between leaves and the stem of young plants and become dormant. In woody plants, as the stems increase in thickness, these buds extend to keep pace with the enlarging cylinder of wood but become enclosed by the outside layers of cork. The corky blanket insulates them from fire, aided by soil in the lowermost parts, and when the dormancy is broken by the heat of the fire they break through the cork and form leafy stems.

Trees of a small species of Western Australian *Eucalyptus* regrowing from the base following fire.

A number of trees with single trunks form basal shoots in this way after their upper parts have been killed by fire or felled by windstorms or humans. The shoots can eventually become trees themselves, which because of the way they originated are in closely crowded groups. Examples of trees that survive in this way are species of oak, some conifers, including the coast redwood (*Sequoia sempervirens*) of California, and several eucalypts.

A special case of trees regenerating from epicormic buds can be found in some Australian eucalypts and melaleucas. Epicormic buds are present along the full length of the trunk and along the major and minor branches. After a ground and crown fire the trees appear completely blackened and dead, but sometimes after only a few weeks, tufts of leafy shoots push out through the blackened bark, from the trunk to the tips of the branches. Trees do not normally come to mind as examples of resurrection plants, but these would certainly qualify.

Some small trees and shrubs have many stems arising from an irregularly shaped, burl-like, woody structure at ground level known as a lignotuber. When these first came to attention they were thought to be uncommon, but they are now known in species from a number of families, including Ericaceae, Fabaceae, Myrtaceae, Proteaceae, and Rosaceae in Australia, Africa, and North and South America. Lignotubers are particularly common and well studied in *Eucalyptus* in Australia. Almost all the

Southern Californian redshank (*Adenostoma sparsifolium*), a chaparral shrub, resprouting after fire.

many species known as mallee gums have them. Initially, some botanists thought that these structures are not genetically determined but result from the enlargement and deforming of the rootstock as a result of repeated fires. However, later research revealed that in the seedlings of these species, swellings develop early in the angles of the first leaves, including the cotyledons or seed leaves. These modified branchlets continue to enlarge and presumably fuse if there is more than one, forming a large, woody, plate-like structure, sometimes several meters or yards in diameter, partly or completely buried in the soil. Lignotubers contain food reserves, some water, and many dormant epicormic buds. After the stems and branches of these small trees and shrubs are killed by fire, they are often quickly replaced from the lignotubers.

An apparently less common phenomenon related to lignotubers has been observed in several species of *Eucalyptus* and some of *Melaleuca, Syzygium, Tristaniopsis,* and *Xanthostemon,* all genera of the Myrtaceae, in the savanna of northern Australia and also in several tree species in the African savanna, including a species of the myrtaceous genus *Eugenia.* Slender, scaly rhizomes arise from the bases of the trees or their seedlings and spread out and branch to form a far-extending network as much as 20 cm (8 inches) below the surface of the ground. In seedlings these arise from small lignotubers, and in mature trees from large basal lignotubers. Shoots from the rhizomes grow up above the ground to form thickets of foliage. If these are killed by fire, they can be quickly re-

An eastern Australian *Eucalyptus* with three trunks rising from a lignotuber between the trunks.

placed, but if there is a sufficient period without fire, then some of these shoots can develop into trees up to 10 m (33 feet) high. Plants spreading by rhizomes are quite common among perennial herbs, but it is unusual for trees to behave this way. In an African study of this phenomenon, the thickets of leafy shoots were termed underground trees, an exaggeration as the underground stem system must be quite shallow.

In most plants, leafy shoots only arise from stems in their various forms, but in some they can arise directly from roots. This is another very effective method of recovery after fire.

We have considered resprouting of conifers and dicotyledonous flowering plants. The resprouting after fire of monocotyledons is different. In dicots the growing points of branchlets are killed by fire and are replaced by shoots from dormant buds. In monocots the growing points are well insulated by the closely packed bases of the long leaves, including those of the often persistent, outer dead leaves. The leaves themselves may be burned by fire, but the growing point usually survives and is able to resume growth. In grasses and some other monocots, leaves grow more or less continuously from the base, so often, when the outer parts of leaves are killed by fire, they are able to quickly regrow from the base.

Most geophytes are monocots. If their aboveground foliage is killed by fire it can be replaced from the food-storing bulbs, corms, or rhizomes below the ground. These structures are often pulled deeper into the soil by contractile roots, where they are well insulated from the heat of fires.

The seeders

Some of the plants of fire-prone areas are killed by fire and depend on seeds for their replacement. These include trees with thin bark, many shrubs, and perennial and annual herbs. Seeds are scattered on the ground every year and build up as a seed bank in the soil. Most are dormant and can remain viable 1–30 years. Seeds of some species, mostly legumes (Fabaceae), are potentially able to remain viable for centuries, but their dormancy is generally broken long before that. The seeds are unable to germinate because their coats are hard and thick, have a waxy cuticle, and are impervious to water. The seed coats are breached when fire passes through the vegetation and sufficient heat penetrates into the soil to melt the waxy cuticles and either split the seed coat or break down groups of weaker cells where the seed stalk was originally attached. Water can now be absorbed, and the seeds germinate. Examples of seeds with hard, impervious coats are many of the legumes, particularly the species of *Acacia* found in dry habitats in many parts of the world; species of a number of genera of the Proteaceae in Australia and South Africa; *Ceanothus* in California; and the rock rose (*Cistus*), around the Mediterranean.

An unexpected way for fire to break seed dormancy, which does not involve rupture of the seed coat, has been discovered but is not yet completely understood. It was found in California that seeds of a number of fire-following annuals, subshrubs, and shrubs are stimulated to germinate in the presence of charred wood. The same result was obtained by subjecting the seeds to extracts or leachates from charred wood, and similar results were obtained in South Africa and Australia. More recently, it has been discovered that smoke alone can break the dormancy of seeds of many heathland species in South Africa and Australia.

In chaparral in California it is notable that after some years have elapsed since a fire, herbaceous ephemerals, annuals, and perennials become very scarce, and the ground is often quite bare under the shrubs and even in open places. It is believed that some of the shrubs manufacture toxins that leach into the soil with rain and inhibit the germination of seeds. Fire destroys these toxins, and the seeds then germinate abundantly. In following years, the herbs steadily diminish as shading increases and toxins from the shrubs build up in the soil.

The breaking of dormancy by fire ensures that the seeds germinate at the best time for their establishment and survival. More light gets to the ground, the soil is temporarily enriched by ash from the fire, and more moisture is retained in the soil as many of the plants are either dead or leafless and extract little or no water with their roots.

Another type of seed bank is more unusual. Seeds are retained in dry fruits or cones—not in the soil—until there is a canopy fire in the shrubland or forest. This type of storage is known as a canopy seed bank. The fruits or cones are bulky structures and are mostly hard and woody. Often, the space for the seeds within them is very restricted, and the seeds are few and quite large. Plants with canopy seed banks are not always killed by fire, but the release of their seeds after a fire ensures that the seedlings have the best conditions for survival, which includes a temporary drop in the number of seed predators such as insects.

In the northern hemisphere, canopy seed storers are all conifers. In North America there are pines, a spruce (*Picea mariana*), cypresses (*Cupressus*), and the mountain redwood (*Sequoiadendron*). Some grow where there is a summer drought; others, including the redwood, the spruce, and some of the pines, grow at cooler, moister elevations or latitudes. The latter are fire prone because they often dominate in their forests, form a deep litter, and catch fire readily because of their resinous secretions. In the Mediterranean region, Aleppo pine (*Pinus halepensis*) is a canopy seed storer.

In the southern hemisphere, conifers that store seeds in the canopy are few and all belong to the mainly northern hemisphere cypress family (Cupressaceae): *Widdringtonia* in summer-drought vegetation in South Africa, and *Actinostrobus* and *Callitris* in Australia. However, there is a good representation of flowering trees and shrubs with this adaptation, belonging to a range of families and genera. In South Africa there are such species in several genera of the Asteraceae and Bruniaceae; *Leucadendron, Protea,* and other genera of the Proteaceae; but only one of the hundreds of species of Cape heaths, *Erica sessiliflora.* In Australia there are species of *Callistemon, Eucalyptus, Lepto-spermum,* and other Myrtaceae; the genera of the Casuarinaceae; and *Banksia, Dryandra,* and *Hakea* of the Proteaceae.

Thick-walled hard fruits protect the seeds from the heat of the sun and the stronger heat of fire, and also keep them safe from all but the most determined seed-eating animals. In the absence of fire, the number of seeds stored in the canopy increases season after season. How does fire cause the cones and fruits to open? In some pines, the tips of the woody scales of the cones are glued together with resin. Fire melts the resin, and the scales are able to separate. In most other plants, the heat of the fire dries and shrinks the outer woody tissues more than the inner, and opening follows. The banksias are interesting. Their cone-like seed heads are a result of the aggregation of many narrow flowers. Only a minority of the flowers form woody fruits known as follicles; the others form a dry, tangled mass of petals and other parts that, when it catches fire, provides the level of heat necessary for the follicles to open.

Only some of the canopy storers have an absolute requirement for fire to release their seeds. In others, most seed release results from fire, but some also can take place on particularly hot summer days, or after a plant has died and dried up for a reason other than fire.

Presumably, the first seeds released by fire are likely to be incinerated, but others that sift out in following days will find cooler conditions on the ground. The best time for seed release is at the end of the dry season when rainfall is likely to follow soon afterward. Fires are most likely to happen at this time as after many months of drought, everything is at its driest. Fires do occur at other times, however, and if there are still some months of drought to come, many of the released seeds will be killed by the heat of the sun before they can germinate. At least some of the species have an adaptation to at least partly solve this problem. In some banksias the two rows of seeds in open follicles are largely kept in place by a two-winged, diaphragm-like structure when conditions are dry. In the rainy season when the follicles are alternately wet and dry, the wings undergo movements that result in the gradual release of the seeds.

In addition to storing seeds in the soil or canopy, there is a third pattern for coping with fire, involving plants whose flowering is stimulated by fire. Most of these plants are not killed by the fire, but there are often no seeds ready to germinate, to take advantage of the favorable postfire conditions. Instead, flowering is initiated, followed by seed formation and release in a relatively short period of time. The grass trees (Xanthorrhoe-aceae) are excellent examples of this with about 80% of their flowering initiated by fire. With each fire, their trunks are blackened again, and the spreading crowns of long,

A *Banksia* grove in Western Australia recently killed by fire.

Charred seed heads of *Banksia* from the recently killed grove, with the follicles wide open and three recently germinated young plants nearby.

narrow leaves, attractively moving in the lightest breeze, are often burned down to their bases. The trees look completely dead, but it is not long before a new crop of leaves emerges along with inflorescences. In *Xanthorrhoea* the upright, remarkably long and narrow inflorescences arise singly from the crown of leaves. Their upper portions bear closely packed small flowers that form seed capsules, and the seeds are released while postfire conditions are still favorable for germination and establishment. In *Kingia* there are circular clusters of short inflorescences that resemble drumsticks as the terminal groups of flowers are spherically arranged. Some undershrubs and vines, too, flower abundantly after fire.

A number of monocotyledonous geophytes also flower abundantly after fire, often producing striking colorful displays, particularly in South Africa. Some flowers are also produced in years when there have been no preceding dry-season fires, but in these circumstances most plants only form leaves. Families represented include the Amaryllidaceae, Iridaceae, Liliaceae (broadly defined), and Orchidaceae. Fire also stimulates flowering in a number of grasses and sedges, and some dicot shrubs such as species of *Leucadendron, Telopea,* and other genera of the Proteaceae in South Africa and Australia. There is evidence that smoke is the trigger for flower initiation in *Xanthorrhoea* and some geophytes.

Fire and vegetation in human times

Since humans have spread throughout the world, more frequent fires have greatly affected much of the world's vegetation. In regions with seasonal drought, shrubby sclerophyll vegetation has expanded at the expense of evergreen forest. Temperate grasslands, such as the prairies in North America and the steppes of Russia, were probably partly maintained by natural fires in pre-human times. These grasslands do not have abundant rainfall, but in many places it seems sufficient to have supported some sort of forest. However, repeated fires would have maintained a cover of grasses, which can quickly recover from fire by resprouting, flowering, and seeding. Human fires probably increased the extent of these grasslands. Nowadays, of course, most of them have been replaced by fields of cultivated crops.

The human influence has probably been most marked in moist forests of the temperate zones and the tropics. In the temperate zones, trees were removed, mostly by felling, for timber and to clear the land for pastures and crops. In the tropics, however, human ingenuity, aimed at clearing the forest for crops, was able to overcome the reluctance of the forests to burn. This is known as slash-and-burn agriculture and has been practiced for a very long time. The trees and shrubs in an area of forest are felled, and the litter is allowed to dry out. When there is a dry spell, the litter is set afire; the ash added to the forest soil provides sufficient fertility for crops to be grown for several years. Eventually though, the lack of decomposing litter, increased leaching in the

The silver-leaved form of *Kingia australis*, with flower heads on the taller tree. Western Australia.

The pea *Kennedia coccinea*, flowering abundantly after fire. Western Australia.

absence of a forest cover, and loss of nutrients to the crops lead to the soil's becoming so infertile that the plots are abandoned, and a new clearing is made. Forest regenerates in the abandoned plots, and the gap in the canopy is closed. Traditional slash-and-burn methods do not greatly threaten the integrity of the forests, but the modern equivalents, particularly in Brazil and Malaysia, certainly do. There, trees are felled for timber, and in Brazil, particularly, the litter is ignited to clear the land for agriculture. This is not a matter of relatively small plots but of extensive areas where the fires can spread and race out of control. Inevitably, the soils deteriorate, and even when attempts at cultivation are abandoned, the forests take a long time to recover.

CHAPTER FOUR

Serpentine and Salt

♦ ♦ ♦

Coping with Toxic Soils

Serpentine soils

As far as plants are concerned, soils in general range from fertile and encouraging to infertile and challenging, but it is a surprise to find that some are actually toxic to most plants. Some of these soils are derived from rocks that are commonly known as serpentine, though strictly speaking this is only one type of a group of rocks termed ultramafics. Ultramafics originate from a layer of the Earth's crust, below the oceans, that underlies the uppermost layer of basalt. Both these layers are derived from molten magma from the Earth's interior that hardens into rock. Over time, crustal pressures at certain places forced these rock types above the sea and over the land. Basalts weather to form quite fertile, nontoxic soils for plants, but the serpentines are quite a different story (Brooks 1987).

The special nature of the soils formed on serpentine derives from their very low concentrations of minerals useful to plants, such as phosphates, potash, nitrates, and calcium, and often high concentrations of toxic metals, such as nickel, chrome, magnesium, and cobalt. Iron is also abundant, and it is required by plants in small amounts. Localized areas of serpentine are scattered throughout the world from the tropics to the

An ice plant, *Disphyma australe,* growing
in a rock crevice near the sea.

polar regions. Often, their vegetation strongly contrasts with that on surrounding nonserpentine soils. In otherwise densely forested regions in temperate latitudes, the serpentine has a sparse cover of stunted small trees, shrubs, and herbaceous plants belonging to relatively few species. Some of these are serpentine-tolerant varieties of widespread species; others are restricted to serpentine and are known as serpentine endemics. It is not clear yet how these plants cope with the toxic soils. Some are able to exclude the toxic metals from their roots, but others take them in freely and accumulate them in their tissues to high concentrations. For example, a nickel accumulator on New Caledonia, the tree *Sebertia acuminata,* has such a high concentration of nickel that the milky latex it exudes when cut is bright blue-green. Perhaps the tree essentially quarantines the nickel compounds in the latex-containing tubes. Rather fewer species are accumulators of chrome, cobalt, or magnesium.

Blue-green latex weeping from a cut in the bark of *Sebertia acuminata.*

Olivine Range, New Zealand. The sparsely vegetated strip, extending through
the forest, is an outcrop of ultramafic rock, as is the crest of the range.

New Caledonia has the highest number of hyperaccumulators of nickel—more than 0.1% nickel in dried leaves—with 47 species. Next come Anatolia and Cyprus (28), the Balkan Peninsula and Aegean Islands (25), and central Europe and Italy (17). In other parts of the world, including North America, there are 5 species or fewer. On New Caledonia, 9 of the species have greater than 1% concentration of nickel.

Serpentine endemics do not require serpentine soils. Rather, they are able to tolerate them and often grow better on normal soils.

The unusual appearance of serpentine rock and the "blasted heath" appearance of its vegetation has long been noted, but Andrea Cesalpino, in his *De Plantis Libri XVI* (1583), may have been the first to give an account of this phenomenon based on observations near Florence. Sometimes the weathered rock is red-brown, and there a number of "Red Mountains" named as a consequence throughout the world. The redness results from the high iron content and it is essentially rust.

In earlier times the serpentine terrains were not of much use to local inhabitants. The stunted growth of the plants indicated that the soil was unsuitable for crops, and this would have been confirmed if cultivation were attempted. Even weeds abundant on surrounding areas rarely establish themselves on serpentine soils. It has been found, however, that if lime is added liberally, their toxicity is greatly reduced, and if fertilizers are also added, some crops can be grown.

In more recent times the various types of ultramafic rock have been mined for nickel, chrome, copper, asbestos, and talc. These rocks are smooth and sometimes dangerously slippery, and often greenish in hue. Serpentinite is bright green, and when subjected to heat and pressure at depth it forms a hard, green stone—jade—widely used for ornaments. New Zealand jade is known as greenstone, and it was much prized by the Maori for making weapons, ornaments, and tools until iron was introduced.

In general, in temperate and polar serpentine localities, there is a sharp change between the serpentine vegetation and that on normal soils. There are also fewer species and varieties, and fewer serpentine endemics, than in the tropics. California may have the richest serpentine flora of temperate regions with an estimated 215 species and varieties of which about 90 are serpentine endemics. In contrast, although it is difficult to find an estimate of the total number of serpentine plants in Europe, the serpentine endemics are far fewer. At the coldest end in the Shetland Islands there is just one (a mouse-ear chickweed, *Cerastium*), in central Europe as many as 5, and at the warmest end in Albania perhaps as many as 30.

Serpentine outcrops in California are scattered through the Coast Ranges and along the Sierra Nevada foothills. The most extensive area is found in the Siskiyou Mountains, which straddle the California–Oregon border. There, the forests on serpentine have a rather open upper layer of tall conifers: Douglas fir (*Pseudotsuga menziesii*) and Port Orford cedar (*Chamaecyparis lawsoniana*). Below that is a layer dominated by two pines, western white pine (*Pinus monticola*) and Jeffrey pine (*P. jeffreyi*), with scattered incense cedars (*Calocedrus decurrens*). The relatively well lit forest floor has a dense cover of sclerophyllous shrubs, of which some are shared with the chaparral. On nearby nonserpentine soils there is an overstory of the same two tall conifers, but the dense lower story is dominated by flowering trees, with a complete absence of conifers. The forest floor is shaded and supports an open layer of mostly soft-leaved shrubs. So, on serpentine, conifers play a more prominent role than flowering trees, and this is a pattern found elsewhere in the world.

Farther south in the drier parts of California, where woodland or forest prevails, serpentine outcrops stand out with their extent of exposed rock, patches of chaparral shrubs, and scattered and rather stunted pines.

An outcrop of ultramafic rock with scattered, stunted pines, and chaparral shrubs and small trees in the Coast Ranges of California.

In the tropics, the richest and most diverse serpentine vegetation is probably that of New Caledonia, a narrow island 399 km (248 miles) long, lying about halfway between New Zealand and New Guinea. New Caledonia is a continental fragment that, along with New Zealand, separated from the ancient southern continent Gondwana 80–85 million years ago, so its original flora would have been derived from Gondwana. The Gondwanan element includes a number of southern hemisphere families, including the Araucariaceae and Podocarpaceae among conifers, and Casuarinaceae, Cunoniaceae, Ericaceae (including the Epacridaceae), Myrtaceae, Nothofagaceae, and Proteaceae among flowering plants.

A third of New Caledonia is occupied by ultramafic rocks that were pushed over the island as a result of crustal movements about 30 million years ago. About 1,500 species, almost half the total flora, grow on serpentine soils. Of these, 900 are serpentine endemics, a remarkably large number. The Gondwanan families are strongly represented, as are unusual growth forms. Outstanding among the latter is the only known parasitic conifer in the world, *Parasitaxus ustus,* shown on page 60, and a permanently and often deeply submerged fern, *Blechnum francii.* A number of the Casuarinaceae and some of the conifers have a distinctive candelabra form, and one dwarf podocarp, *Retrophyllum minor,* is semiaquatic and has a swollen trunk base.

A dwarf, semiaquatic conifer, *Retrophyllum minor,* with a swollen trunk. Plain of Lakes, New Caledonia.

A grove of *Gymnostoma deplancheanum* (Casuarinaceae) with a candelabra form of branching.
The yellowish shrubs are *Tristaniopsis guillainii* (Myrtaceae). Plain of Lakes, New Caledonia.

In a book on the serpentine vegetation of the world, R. R. Brooks (1987) says of New Caledonia, "Perhaps it is not too much to say that this island carries the richest, most interesting, and most diverse serpentine vegetation anywhere on earth and it will long continue to excite the interest of botanists throughout the world." Why is the New Caledonian serpentine flora so rich and diverse? Well, there have been tens of millions of years available for the plants on nonserpentine soils of the island to evolve forms able to tolerate the serpentine soils and for these forms to diversify into the many initially unoccupied habitats. The warm, moist climate has also helped as the plants have mostly not had to cope with cold winters and drought.

The southern part of the large, southern, serpentine massif has a mountain-and-basin topography with small lakes at the lowest parts of the basins. Much of the more level terrain has a thick, hard, dark layer at the surface that looks like volcanic rock but is in fact an iron-rich lateritic crust (carapace in French) that was formed by extreme leaching of the soils in ancient times. Even though rainfall is abundant in this Plain of Lakes region, the carapace and erosional material from it can support only small trees and shrubs, and a variety of sedges. There are few endemic grasses on New Caledonia. This shrubby vegetation is generally termed maquis as it is similar in appearance to that vegetation of the Mediterranean area. On swampy sites, sedges predominate along with scattered shrubs; some plants, including some conifers, are largely restricted to streambeds and margins.

On the slopes and ridges of the hills and of mountains farther north, where the bedrock is exposed at the surface in places, there are closed-canopy forests. Sometimes these are quite low and dominated by one or a few species of *Agathis* (Araucariaceae), *Arillastrum* (a *Eucalyptus* relative), *Gymnostoma* (Casuarinaceae), and *Nothofagus*. In other places, particularly where jumbled boulders of an ultramafic type of rock known as peridotite are present, it is surprising to find tall, species-rich rain forests that include large specimens of *Agathis, Araucaria,* and a number of flowering trees. The soil these plants grow on is largely derived from the breakdown of their own litter, and it is suggested that as a result the toxic influence of the parent rock is greatly diluted. At higher elevations where there is less accumulation of litter, the peridotite supports only small trees and shrubs.

Rain forests on nonserpentine rock on New Caledonia are similar in general appearance to those on serpentine, though there are more palms, of which New Caledonia has a number of endemic genera, more strangling figs, and a stronger representation of tropical Asian genera and a lesser representation of Gondwanan genera. Conifers, too, are less prominent, but there can be impressive groves of *Agathis* and araucarias, particularly at higher elevations.

Halophytes—Plants that grow on salty soils

Soils with a high concentrations of dissolved salts are widespread throughout the world, particularly along the many thousands of kilometers or miles of ocean coastlines. Nearest the sea, in estuaries, the soils become salty by inundation by seawater at high tide. A little farther inland, less salty soils derive their salt from windblown spray.

If one tries to grow a plant from sites far inland, where soils are not salty, it will usually die in salty sites near the sea. This is partly because of the toxicity of salt at high concentrations, but mostly due to the fact that instead of the plant's roots taking in water, they lose it to the soil. As a result the plant wilts and dies. Why does this happen? Without going into all the details we can say that water alone is able to move freely in and out of root cells—its direction is determined by the relative concentrations of substances dissolved in the cell sap and in the soil solution. Normally, cell sap has a higher concentration of dissolved substances, and water moves from the soil into the plant cells. In effect, the water is moving from where it is in higher concentration in the soil solution to where it is in lower concentration in the cell sap. When the soil water contains more dissolved substances than the cell sap, however, then the pattern is reversed—water flows from the plant into the soil, and death quickly follows.

In coastal areas, the soil solution often contains relatively high levels of dissolved salt. To avoid the problem of water moving out rather than in, halophytic seaside plants have evolved a strategy. Their roots absorb enough salt to give their cell sap a higher salt concentration than that of the soil solution. This enables normal water relations to be maintained (Reimold and Queen 1974). However, this adaptation can lead to a further problem—above a certain concentration, salt is toxic to plant tissues. Some of the salt taken in is transported in water up to the leaves. The water mostly evaporates through the pores known as stomata on the leaf surfaces, but the salt accumulates and gradually impairs the functioning of the leaf tissues. To overcome this, additional water is moved into the leaf cells to keep the salt concentration below dangerous levels. As a result, the leaves of many coastal plants are thick and succulent, from the water-filled tissues. Notable examples of this are the glassworts (*Sarcocornia* and related genera) and the ice plants (*Mesembryanthemum* and related genera), which are prominent in the saltiest places (see page 142).

Some species that grow inland on nonsalty soils can also be found on the coasts. In these, the coastal plants have smaller, thicker, and somewhat fleshy leaves.

Some halophytes actually excrete excess salt. Some mangroves, for instance, have glands on their leaf surfaces for this purpose, and plants of the goosefoot family (Chenopodiaceae), so strongly represented in salty habitats, develop them at the tips of leaf

A glasswort, *Sarcocornia australis,* growing where waves can reach it at high tide.

teeth. The fluid excreted is a saturated solution of salts that washes away with rain or blows away when dry. Many species of Chenopodiaceae also excrete salt into leaf surface cells, which increase in volume many times and assume balloon-like shapes.

Seacoasts are not the only places where there are salty soils and halophytes. In the deserts of the world, water flowing from occasional downpours rarely reaches the sea but evaporates in the heat, leaving behind the salts that it dissolved from the rocks. In some cases this water ends up in landscape depressions, forming mostly temporary ponds or lakes, which after repeated episodes of filling and drying out become at least as salty as the sea if not more so. Once again, as a parallel to the serpentine-tolerant plants, halophytes do not require high levels of salt in their soils—they can grow quite happily on normal soils.

The sea rush, *Juncus maritimus,*
flooded by the sea at high tide.

CHAPTER FIVE

Too Much Water

◆ ◆ ◆

Plants of Rivers, Lakes, Swamps,
and Margins of the Sea

Life is thought to have originated in the sea, probably at a time when it was much less salty than now. Many plant and animal groups evolved into a great diversity of forms in the sea and have never left it, but others eventually made the transition onto the land, where they had to adapt to a water supply that was both limited and readily lost by evaporation (Chapter 2).

Plants in the sea are mostly algae. Some biologists put the aquatics known as algae in a separate kingdom, Protista, along with Protozoa, nonphotosynthetic unicellular organisms that have long been regarded as animals. For the purposes of our wide-ranging look at vegetable life, however, algae are considered plants. Algae range in size from the often large and abundant seaweeds of rocky shores to the even more abundant, but microscopic, plant plankton of the upper layers of the vast oceans. Plankton are of great importance as they are the base of the food chain in the sea that leads up to the largest marine animals. In freshwater there are algae, too, but they are all small: unicells, or masses of slimy filaments, or small, pinhead-sized colonies.

There are three main groups of seaweeds: brown, red, and green. All have chlorophyll, but in the brown and red groups this is masked by other pigments. Among other functions, these additional pigments enable the brown and red seaweeds to obtain

The massive fronds of bull kelp, *Durvillea antarctica,* which narrow to whiplashes at their tips. New Zealand.

energy from a wider range of light wavelengths, allowing them to survive in the lower light intensities of deeper water.

Because they are battered by waves, seaweeds need to be firmly anchored. The anchoring device at the base of a seaweed is known as a holdfast. It may be disk-shaped, rather like a rubber suction cup, or it may be more like a root system, much-branched and wedging into cracks and crevices. Although holdfasts function well most of the time, severe storms can dislodge them, and an array of dying seaweeds then piles up on nearby beaches.

Some seaweeds grow between low and high tide and are exposed to the air for varying lengths of time each day, unless they grow in pools where seawater is retained between tides. Seaweeds have a variety of ways to prevent drying out and dying when they are exposed to the air. Many secrete mucilage over their surfaces; others are formed as clusters or strings of vesicles that retain seawater or contain mucilage. More delicate-looking forms, where the plant body is a thin sheet of cells, appear to dry up completely—the red alga *Porphyra,* for example. At low tide, this seaweed looks like yellowish handkerchiefs dried out against the rocks, but with high tide, their mucilaginous cells quickly revive. This is a marine example of a resurrection plant.

The holdfast of bull kelp, *Durvillea antarctica.*

Green seaweeds tend to grow at higher levels on the shore. They are mostly small plants, ranging from bright green sheets of cells, as in the sea lettuce *Ulva,* to delicate filaments, fern-like fronds, and variously arranged vesicles. There are also unicellular green algae that live in coral polyps, not unlike the association found between algae and fungi in lichens (Chapter 8).

Red seaweeds, too, are mostly smaller plants and range from the highest levels to the greatest depths. Some of them are attractively fern-like in appearance, made all the more striking by their red or purple coloration.

Toward the level of low tide and below is the realm of the larger brown seaweeds. These include the kelps with their large, divided, leathery fronds (page 154), buoyed up by air-filled internal cavities. Other large

Porphyra (foreground) dried out on rocks at low tide, with kelp in the background. New Zealand.

Filamentous green seaweeds in a rock pool. New Zealand.

browns, such as the bladder kelp (*Macrocystis*), have specialized air-filled bladders. Colonies of bladder kelp could be described as seaweed forests as the plants can be up to 30 m (100 feet) long, with the fronds at their tips lifted up to the well-lit sea surface by the bladders.

Some terrestrial plant and animal groups include species that have adapted to a watery existence. Among animals there are the marine mammals, including the largest animals of all, the whales. A wide range of plant groups, too, have made the return journey (Sculthorpe 1967), mostly to freshwater where water lilies (*Nymphaea* and related genera), sedges (Cyperaceae), and rushes (Juncaceae) are best known. Some of the freshwater plants belong to families or even genera that are otherwise terrestrial, some belong to families that are largely or entirely aquatic, and others are so modified by their habitat that it is difficult to determine what they are related to. In shallow coastal waters where there is a muddy or sandy bottom, there are also plants with terrestrial ancestors. In temperate regions these include the sea grasses (*Zostera*), and in the tropics, a number of herbaceous species as well as shrubs and trees from a range of flowering plant families that are collectively known as mangroves.

Many aquatic plants grow in some depth of water, which may be either mostly still, in ponds and lakes, or moving, by gravity in streams or rivers, or, as a result of waves and tides, at the fringes of the sea. For these plants water is in abundant supply, but the essential gas oxygen is often very limited. Oxygen dissolves in water at its interface with the air. Turbulent water of streams and the sea is much better oxygenated than still water—with the complex mixing of air and water, there is a much greater contact area for gas exchange. Another essential gas, carbon dioxide, is generally in better supply. It dissolves more readily than oxygen, but it is also added from the breakdown of bicarbonates in solution, particularly in limestone regions.

Fully submerged plants have to cope with the oxygen-supply problem all the time. Plants that have leaves floating at the surface or raised above gain access to the more abundant oxygen of the air, so they face the problem only when young or if they die down during winter. The submerged parts of these plants have little or no cuticle over their surfaces, and thin cell walls, so they are able to directly absorb water and mineral nutrients. However, most species also have well-developed root systems, embedded in the substrate or free in the water, that are often abundantly provided with root hairs. Roots, then, also play a significant role in the absorption of water, even in aquatic plants.

The intensity of light decreases with greater water depth. Where water is very clear, there may be sufficient light for plants to grow at depths of 10–15 m (33–49 feet). Where there is suspended silt or staining from decaying vegetation, the limit may be only 1–2 m (3–6 1/2 feet).

The most specialized aquatic plants—those that are completely submerged, or have leaves floating on the surface, or are completely floating—often reproduce abundantly by vegetative means, resulting in populations of identical individuals, or clones. Many form stolons, or runners, that end in new plants that become independent when the stolon decays (for example, water hyacinth, *Eichhornia crassipes*). In other species the plants break apart with water movement, and each segment can become a new plant (for example, duckweed, *Lemna*). In many of these specialized aquatics, cloning is the main means of reproduction, and sexual reproduction may be infrequent. When conditions are favorable, cloning can enable a water plant to spread rapidly over extensive areas.

Many species form tubers and other food-storing structures to survive in climates with cold winters or seasonal drought. Short rhizomes and tuberous roots allow individual plants to survive and regrow when favorable conditions return. Similar structures ensure both survival and increase in numbers of individuals. The tips of stolons enlarge into tubers, which break away and settle in the mud (for example, the arrowhead *Sagittaria sagittifolia*), or the tips of leafy shoots form enlarged buds of densely overlapping leaves, which also drop off (for example, *Elodea canadensis*). Each plant can form many of these tubers or buds, so an expanded population results when they form new plants on the return of favorable conditions.

Submerged plants

The algae, particularly seaweeds, have already been considered. In still freshwater, some submerged plants have short stems with roots extending into the mud, and rosettes of leaves. Others have free-floating extended stems with tufts of roots arising where the leaves are attached. The latter can spread extensively, and when the stems are densely crowded, some of the foliage can emerge above the water.

The rosette species mostly have long, thin, undivided leaves, sometimes 1 m (39 inches) or more in length, that are thread- or ribbon-like, providing a large surface area for the absorption of oxygen and carbon dioxide. Included here are species of quillworts (*Isoetes*) and eelgrasses (*Vallisneria*, actually a genus of the tape grass family, Hydrocharitaceae). *Isoetes* is of particular interest. It belongs to the group of spore-producing vascular plants that also includes *Lycopodium* and *Selaginella* and is considered to be a diminutive descendant of long-extinct tree ancestors that lived in swamp forests of the Carboniferous period.

Among the plants with extended stems are species of *Elodea* and *Lagarosiphon* (both Hydrocharitaceae). These are notable for clogging waterways where there is fertilizer-enriched runoff from surrounding land. They have relatively short but thin and narrow leaves. Other species have the leaves much divided into thread-like segments, which is another way of increasing surface area for gas and water absorption. Included here are some water milfoils (*Myriophyllum*), bladderworts (*Utricularia*), and buttercups (*Ranunculus*). Bladderworts are notable for trapping and digesting small aquatic animals in bladder-like structures (Chapter 7). It is also suggested that thin, narrow, sometimes deeply dissected leaves, also found in the submerged leaves of some partly emergent species, offer little resistance to water movement and so avoid damage.

Along with water plants in general, most plants of this submerged group have interconnecting systems of air chambers in their roots, stems, and leaves. The air chambers are elongate but interrupted at intervals by thin diaphragms of cells that allow passage of gas through the many small pores. The diaphragms prevent pressure from the surrounding water from collapsing the chambers when the air pressure is low. When the pressure is high, the plant parts are firm and flexible, able to avoid damage from water movement. The air chambers also provide buoyancy to stems and leaves, raising them nearer to the better-lit surface of the water.

Always-submerged water plants have no access to the air, so the gases in their air chambers are the by-products of metabolic processes, particularly photosynthesis and respiration. Photosynthesis produces oxygen, which mostly accumulates in the air chambers though some is released into the surrounding water. Respiration produces carbon dioxide, which is also stored in the air chambers, though because it is more soluble than oxygen, much of it diffuses from the roots and dissolves in the surrounding water. During the day when sunlight allows sugar-forming photosynthesis, oxygen builds up in the air chambers, inflating them considerably, and some of this is drawn off by respiration, which uses oxygen to break up sugars to release energy. Some, too, escapes as bubbles, rising to the surface. During the night when photosynthesis ceases, oxygen is steadily depleted as the plant continues to respire.

In the sea, species of *Zostera* (sea grass or eelgrass but a genus of Zosteraceae, not the grass family) are the most widespread of the submerged aquatic plants, often forming dense, grass-like meadows on the sea floor. The long, narrow leaves are in rosettes with spreading stems or stolons that form additional rosettes at their tips. The leaves are flexible but toughened with strands of fibers to resist the turbulence of the waves. Despite this, a good storm often results in the leaves being torn off, and some plants uprooted, and the debris is then washed onshore to pile up like hay, sometimes to a depth of 1 m (39 inches) or more.

The most remarkable of the submerged water plants belong to the Podostemaceae. They mostly grow in the fast-flowing, sometimes turbulent water of smooth, rocky streambeds or waterfalls. The plant body may be branched and ribbon-like or in the form of flat, irregularly shaped sheets of tissue glued to the rock by hairs or small, discoid outgrowths. When these strange plants were first observed it was not realized that they were flowering plants. Lichens or liverworts seemed more likely, and some seaweeds are quite like them in form. The plant body turned out to be highly modified roots that contain chlorophyll and so can function without leaves. Podostemaceae can cover extensive areas of rock, and some are brightly colored and conspicuous—bright green or crimson red—from secondary pigments. Stems bearing small leaves arise from the roots and range from very short with few leaves to long, branched, and trailing downstream with the current. The plant parts do not have air chambers; the churning water is well aerated and is constantly recharged with oxygen and carbon dioxide. Podostemaceae is a family whose relationships are obscure. It is largely restricted to the tropics, has about 45 genera and 120 species, and differs greatly from other families of submerged aquatics in the nature of its preferred habitat and in its morphology.

When they reproduce sexually, submerged aquatics have curious ways of bringing about the pollination of their flowers, as flowers generally usually function in an air rather than an aqueous medium. In the eelgrass *Vallisneria* there are separate male and female plants. The delicate, elongating stalks of the female flowers carry them up to the water surface where their slight weight results in each of them floating in a small depression. The male flower buds are formed deep in the water. Each encloses a bubble of air, and when a bud separates from its attachment it floats to the surface and unfolds. Two of the tepals act as rudders and the third as a small sail, enabling breezes to spread the male flowers far and wide over the water. If a male flower comes into the vicinity of a female flower, it slides down into the hollow, tips over, and its sticky pollen attaches to the stigma of the ovary of the female flower. This leads to fertilization and the formation of seeds.

In *Elodea* the stalks of both the male and female flowers extend to the water surface. The male flowers open in the air and the stamens dehisce explosively, spreading pollen onto the water where some of the floating grains encounter stigmas of female flowers, bringing about fertilization and seed formation.

In *Ceratophyllum* there is a curious sequence. Female flowers remain deeply submerged, and in the male flowers only the anthers float up to the surface where they release their pollen. The pollen floats only briefly, then sinks—some grains encounter the stigmas of female flowers.

Ceratophyllum tends toward the pattern in the marine eelgrass *Zostera*. In *Zostera*, probably because of wave turbulence at the sea surface, aerial pollination has been abandoned. Both male and female flowers remain submerged, and the stamens of the male flowers release thread-like pollen that drifts in tangles, sometimes wrapping around the stigmas of female flowers.

The seeds of the preceding examples mostly sink soon after they are released, and some can remain dormant for some time. The distinctive Podostemaceae apparently only flower when uncovered by receding water during the dry season. The flowers are small, sometimes brightly colored, and hermaphroditic. Some are insect-pollinated and others wind-pollinated. Abundant small seeds are produced, but only a few come to rest in a suitable place to germinate. Detached bits of these plants can grow into new plants.

Plants with leaves that float on the surface

Species with floating leaves include the pondweeds *Aponogeton* and *Potamogeton*. These also have submerged leaves that are narrower than the floating leaves.

The outstanding plants in this category, however, are the well-known and greatly admired water lilies and lotuses. About eight water lily genera are recognized with a total of about 60 species, and there are a couple of species of lotus (*Nelumbo*). Sometimes water lilies are included in one family, the Nymphaeaceae; sometimes they are split into several. Unlike plants with floating leaves that have extended stems with leaves arising to the surface at intervals, the water lilies have short, stout rhizomes filled with food reserves. In temperate regions the leaves die down during winter, and new clusters arise from the ends of the rhizomes in spring. The leaf blades are mostly circular in outline and from a few centimeters or an inch or so to 1 m (39 inches) or more in diameter. The leaf stalk or petiole is attached more or less centrally to the underside of a blade that, on the side nearest the rhizome, is often narrowly split as far as the attachment of the petiole. The blades are quite leathery and not easily damaged by wind, and they have a shiny, waxy cuticle over the upper surface that is water repellent. Any

Floating leaves and raised flower heads of the pondweed *Aponogeton distachyus*.

water drops tend to roll off the leaf. There are many stomatal pores in the upper surface, so once a leaf emerges at the water surface, a good supply of air becomes available for the air chamber system, which extends through the leaf stalks to the rhizomes and roots.

The first-formed leaves each season have very long, oblique petioles that extend quite a long way from the rhizome. This leaves plenty of space within the outer circle for later leaves to arrange themselves without overlapping. Even so, when growing conditions are conducive to vigorous growth and there are many plants, the leaf blades can be crowded and overlapping over large areas, with some of them lifting above the water surface.

In *Nelumbo nucifera*, the sacred lotus of Asia, in which the petioles extend upward more or less vertically, the leaves, as large as dinner plates, are at first floating but then lifted above the water surface. As this species is similar to the water lilies it is included here rather than with the group with leaves that rise above the surface.

The large flowers of the water lilies are among the most attractive to be found. Their abundant, spreading, pointed, petal-like tepals come in practically every color: white, red, yellow, purple, and blue. The watery setting enhances their appeal, the flowers seeming to float among rafts of perfectly circular leaves.

The most remarkable water lily is undoubtedly *Victoria amazonica* of tropical South America. The floating leaves are relatively enormous, sometimes attaining 2 m (6 1/2

A water lily (*Nymphaea*) cultivar with floating leaves, and large flowers with many tepals and stamens.

The lotus *Nelumbo nucifera* with several plate-like leaves,
a large flower, and the strangely shaped seed capsule.

Large leaves of *Victoria amazonica* with a white flower at left. A purple-flowered *Nymphaea* is on the right.

feet) in diameter. They are very leathery in texture and, unlike most water lilies, have turned-up edges several centimeters or an inch or more in height, making it difficult for water to flood over them. Rainwater is able to drain out through opposite pairs of notches in the raised rim. In *V. amazonica*, as in *Nelumbo*, there is no incision from the margin of the leaf blade to the leaf stalk. The leaf blades are perfectly circular with the massive petiole attached centrally on the underside. The network of veins projects very strongly on the leaf undersides, and the pressure in the air chambers of the ribs provides buoyancy and strength to the considerable area of the leaf surface. The leaves can support objects of some weight, as photographs of small children seated on them attests. The undersides of the leaves and the outsides of the buds of the large flowers are covered with prominent spines as a deterrent to herbivorous fish.

Water lily flowers are mostly pollinated by beetles and small flies. The flowers are often strongly scented but have no nectar, and the insects feed on pollen and other nutritious flower parts. The stalks supporting mature fruits often bend downward, submerging them, and when the surrounding tissue rots away, the seeds float on the surface for a while, then sink to the bottom. In *Nelumbo* and a few other genera the flowers are raised well above the water surface, and the fruits break away and drop into the water.

Seeds of temperate water lilies have a period of dormancy lasting from a few months to years. The record for seed longevity goes to the sacred lotus, *Nelumbo nuci-*

fera. As one example, a seed on an herbarium specimen at the Natural History Museum in London was found to have germinated after the herbarium was flooded following bomb damage in 1940. The specimen was 237 years old! Seeds of some tropical water lilies germinate as soon as they are mature, so the dormancy in temperate species probably ensures that germination is at least delayed until the warmth of spring. Prolonged dormancy might also enable a local population to survive a calamity such as a pond freezing solid during an unusually severe winter, or drying out following a severe drought.

Plants that float

Plants that float are freshwater plants, mostly of sheltered waters. The leaves are usually in rosettes or clusters and vary in size from minute—less than 1 mm (1/32 inch) long in *Wolffia microscopica*—to about 15 cm (6 inches) long in the water hyacinth, *Eichhornia crassipes* (see page 168). Two genera of water ferns, *Azolla* and *Salvinia*, differ in having extended stems with leaves in opposite pairs.

Most floating plants produce abundant roots, often well provided with root hairs, that hang down in the water but do not reach the mud. So all mineral nutrients have to be obtained from the water, and growth is most vigorous in water that is naturally rich in nutrients or enriched by runoff from fertilized farmland. Vegetative reproduction, by simple breakup of plants or through stolons, each forming a new rosette at its tip, is the predominant mode of reproduction for these plants. With favorable temperatures, enriched waters can quickly become completely covered with floating plants, which may block slow-moving streams and interfere with the recreational use of ponds and lakes.

There are three genera of ferns among the floating water plants. Two, *Azolla* and *Salvinia*, belong to a small, specialized group that stands well apart from the majority of ferns. To begin with they are not at all fern-like in appearance, and their mode of sexual reproduction is different from that of other ferns and more complex.

The species of *Azolla* are quite small. Their stems are much-branched and bear very small,

A close view of a cluster of small *Azolla* plants with their closely overlapping leaves.

overlapping leaves. Each leaf has two lobes, an upper one exposed to the air that is kept dry and buoyant by a covering of air-trapping hairs, and a submerged lower one that absorbs most of the water. There is only a sparse production of roots. The stems are brittle, readily breaking to form new plants that can spread to form a continuous layer over the surface of a pond. Often, azollas have a red pigment masking the chlorophyll, and a completely covered pond can be a remarkable and attractive sight.

Salvinias have larger leaves, up to 2 cm (3/4 inch) long, and the stems are more widely spreading and less branched. Again, there are two lobes to each leaf, the upper one exposed to the air and the lower one much and finely branched. The submerged leaf looks like and functions as a root; there are no true roots. *Salvinia* reproduces vegetatively in the same way as *Azolla*. Both genera can reproduce sexually below water to produce spores, resulting in new plants.

The fronds of the water fern *Ceratopteris* do occur in rosettes. Some species reproduce vegetatively by plantlets that arise on the upper surfaces of the fronds. On some raised fronds, sporangia are formed on the undersides. The spores are dispersed by wind.

Among flowering plants, the water hyacinth (*Eichhornia crassipes*) has much larger floating rosettes. The clustered leaves are angled upward, and the robust stalks are inflated into air-filled floats. Extensive, branching roots form a large proportion of the

Leaves and inflorescences of water hyacinth, *Eichhornia crassipes*.

total mass of the plants. The purple flowers, raised above the water surface, are very attractive, but unfortunately, in warmer parts of the world, the vigorous spreading of this species by stolons often results in the blocking of waterways. The water chestnut (*Trapa natans*) also has leaf petioles modified into floats, but its leaves lie flat on the water surface.

The duckweed family (Araceae, including Lemnaceae) includes not only the smallest water plants but also the smallest of the flowering plants. They are a remarkable contrast to larger members of the family, such as the arum lily (*Zantedeschia*). The plant body is made up of small groups of round to oval segments that are so reduced it is difficult to determine whether they are leaves or stems. Each segment can form a few new segments laterally, and the clusters break up quite easily, providing a very effective mode of vegetative reproduction. The segments have many air-filled compartments. Their exposed tops are flat to a little convex, and the submerged lower parts in the duckweeds (*Lemna*) are shallowly to deeply convex, and in watermeal (*Wolffia*), convex to narrowly conical. In *Lemna* there is one unbranched root per segment, and in *Wolffia*, none.

The flowers of the duckweeds are very small and only rarely seen, so reproduction is largely vegetative. As with the water fern *Azolla*, duckweeds are able to spread over large bodies of water and, attached to the swimming birds that frequent ponds and lakes, are easily transported to new localities.

Plants with stems, leaves, and flowers that rise above the water

Herbaceous species

In addition to submerged and floating herbaceous plants, there are aquatics that grow in shallow water or waterlogged soil near the margins of lakes, streams, and estuaries. In many, the roots, lower parts of the stems, and in some cases some of the leaves are submerged. The aerial parts conform to those of land plants except for having an extensive aeration system to provide oxygen to the roots. Examples of such plants are the wind-pollinated cattails (*Typha*), bur reeds (*Sparganium*), and a number of sedges and rushes, and the insect-pollinated water irises, arrowheads (*Sagittaria*), flowering rushes (*Butomus*), and water plantains (*Alisma*). Unlike fully submerged or floating aquatic plants, in which vegetative reproduction often predominates, these plants mostly reproduce by seeds spread by wind, water, or in mud adhering to their feet, wading birds. In the brackish water at the edges of estuaries, the taller water plants may be standing in water at high tide, as shown on page 152, and surrounded by exposed mud at low tide.

Long term, most ponds and lakes are temporary habitats for water plants as they are gradually filled in by the accumulating remains of the plants, beginning from the shallower margins and extending to the deeper central parts. When the water table drops

A cattail, *Typha orientalis,* showing leaves and the distinctive inflorescence. Small male flowers are attached to the spine-like tip, with densely crowded female flowers below.

A rush (*Juncus*), reflected in the still water of a pond.

below the surface of the resulting swamp, shrubs can invade, eventually followed by trees where the climate is suitable. All the stages in this sequence can be observed in the innumerable ponds and lakes in northern North America, left behind as the ice sheet retreated.

Mangroves and other trees of watery habitats

In books on water plants written by temperate-zone botanists, tropical mangroves often receive no mention. They are however, just as specialized to cope with the excess of water in their habitats as the many temperate herbaceous water plants are in theirs. Mangroves mostly grow in mud where the sea is shallow, in tropical estuaries and inlets. Altogether there are about 54 species in 20 genera, belonging to 16 families, so the mangrove life style has evolved independently a number of times (Hogarth 1999). Mangroves are generally small trees, but they can be reduced to shrub dimensions where salinity is very high or other factors limit growth.

Apart from young mangroves in canopy gaps, there is no undergrowth. Vines rooted above high tide level, epiphytes (including orchids and ferns), and mistletoe parasites can be common, though, and are often the same as those found in forests on dry land. Unlike the mangroves themselves, these associated plants do not have to cope with excess salinity and lack of oxygen in the water. The mud is exposed at low tide, and at high tide the lower trunks and branches of the trees are submerged. The limited amount of oxygen in the substrate is near the surface of the mud, so mangrove roots spread widely but do not run deep. However, the oxygen that is obtained from the mud, or from the seawater at high tide, is far from sufficient; the main air supply comes from "breathing roots" that function at low tide.

In species of *Rhizophora*, aerial roots originate from the trunks as much as 2 m (6 1/2 feet) above the base of the tree and then arch downward to enter the mud, where extensive, shallow branching takes place. The first arching root or prop root usually gives rise to a succession of other such roots that, in combination with those of other plants of the same species, form almost impenetrable tangles. The prop roots provide most of the support for the trunks, but they also have extensive air chamber systems, often beginning just above where a root enters the mud. Air enters the chambers via pustules of loose corky cells (lenticels), and oxygen diffuses from where it is in high concentration at the entry level to where it is in lower concentration in the buried roots.

When the aerial roots are flooded at high tide, the corky lenticels are able to prevent water from entering the air chambers. It is also thought that air is sucked in quite strongly when the aerial roots are first exposed at low tide. The theory is that the oxygen in the buried roots at high tide is steadily depleted by respiration and only partly replaced by the carbon dioxide by-product. In contrast to oxygen, carbon dioxide is readily soluble in water, and most of it diffuses out from the roots. As a result, the gas in the

A mangrove, *Rhizophora,* with downward-arching prop roots. New Caledonia.

air chambers changes from being under pressure to being under tension, and at low tide the air is initially sucked into the aerial roots.

In some species of other mangrove genera, shallow roots that spread from the base of the trunk have upper sides that extend into the air. In other species, such roots grow up into the air at intervals and loop down again. As they become woody, these breathing roots, or knees, extend upward, sometimes as much as 1 m (39 inches) or more. The widespread genus *Avicennia* is even more specialized. Its shallow, extending roots give rise from their upper sides to vertical, finger-like roots that stand as much as 30 cm (12 inches) above the mud. These breathing roots are an impressive sight in their thousands when exposed at low tide. It has been estimated that a single *Avicennia* tree can produce more than 10,000 breathing roots.

The other big problem that mangroves face is an excess of salt in their habitat. Most are able to keep most of the salt from entering their roots, but some salt intake is unavoidable and it gradually builds up in tissues. The response to that problem is to move salt into the bark, whose cells are dead when mature, or into aging leaves that take the salt with them when they drop off. Some mangroves, too, have special glands in their leaves that excrete a concentrated salty solution, which dries out and blows or washes away.

The flowers of mangroves are varied. Some are pollinated by wind, others by birds, bats, or a full range of insects. Much more distinctive are the fruits, usually containing a single large seed well provided with food reserves. These seeds are remarkable in that there is no period of dormancy—they germinate while still attached to the tree and are able to draw nutriment from their parent. In some rhizophoras the seedlings can attain a length of 30 cm (12 inches) before they drop into the water. The smaller seedlings of avicennias sink after a few days and anchor themselves with roots, so they do not get too far from home, but those of the rhizophoras float around for about a month before settling into position. They can travel kilometers or miles during this time. It is doubtful whether mangrove seedlings can successfully travel great distances. If they go too far they reach the open sea where they are less likely to find suitable habitats and are more likely to be damaged by wave action.

Mangrove forests provide a habitat for many animals, notably snakes, lizards, crocodiles, bats, birds of many kinds, including waders, and fish, among which mudskippers are the most remarkable. A mudskipper breathes in air, and skips across the mud using its fins, which it also uses to climb trees. Among invertebrates, crabs are conspicuous, also barnacles, and among insects, mosquitoes are often uncomfortably abundant.

A scene in a low mangrove forest of *Avicennia marina* at low tide. The exposed mud is covered with many finger-like breathing roots intermingled with mangrove seedlings. There is a tidal channel in the background.

Thin plank buttresses of *Sloanea koghiensis*. New Caledonia.

Periodically flooded freshwater swamps in the tropics and some warm temperate localities also provide a home for sometimes large trees with modifications similar to those of the mangroves. Some, such as screw pines (*Pandanus*), have stilt roots; others have loop roots or knees—the bald cypress (*Taxodium distichum*) of the southeastern United States being the best-known example, though some question whether these actually take in air (Attenborough 1995); and other trees have erect breathing roots, branched or unbranched.

A striking feature of some of the trees of freshwater swamps is the formation of plank buttresses at the bases of their trunks that also extend partway along large horizontal roots. These buttresses are often quite thin, and because they grow out to fill in the angle between trunk and root they are basically triangular in shape. In some trees they are enormous, extending 9 m (30 feet) or more up the trunks and out along the roots. Buttresses are best developed on the tallest trees in the swamps, and it is thought that they provide additional physical support for the trunks in the far from solid substrate. Plank buttresses greatly increase the surface area of the lower trunks and exposed roots, so they may also play a role in the aeration of the submerged roots. It is interesting to note that where some of the swamp trees grow on better-drained sites, plank buttresses and breathing roots are developed only weakly if at all.

Plants of river flood zones

Plants in flood zones form quite distinctive communities in and near streams, mostly in the tropics (van Steenis 1981). They are shrubs that grow on islands in the streambed or, where the streams are bordered by cliffs on one or both sides, on the lower parts of the cliffs up to the limit of the more frequent floods. The shrubs are streamlined to avoid damage from the turbulent floodwaters, and this is usually achieved by the leaves being tough in texture and long and narrow in form. Sometimes the stems, too, are narrow and flattened.

A much more extensive type of river flooding, both in time and space, is found along the Amazon. There, floodplains can extend as far as 80 km (50 miles) from the river. Where the soil consists of fertile silt, there are tall trees, many strongly buttressed, as well as vines and epiphytes. One of the trees in this forest type is the rubber tree (*Hevea brasiliensis*). During the flood-free season the ground is densely covered with gingers and similar plants. Where the soil consists of infertile sand, the trees are shorter; many belong to the Myrtaceae, including the aptly named *Eugenia inundata* (Prance and Lovejoy 1985).

Rainfall in the headwaters of the Amazon is generally seasonal, and during the drier season from June to October the floodplains have little or no standing water. During the rainy season from December to May they can be inundated to a depth of 12 m (40 feet), so it is possible to canoe among the crowns of the shorter trees. The remarkable thing is that this depth of water persists for 5 months or more, so the trees must have some as yet unknown means of preventing the death of their root systems from lack of oxygen. The trees drop their floating fruits into the water, where they are avidly sought by fish, and it is claimed that some seeds will germinate only after they have passed through the digestive system of a fish. The floodplain forests are known as várzea and have species different from those of the general rain forest on well-drained sites.

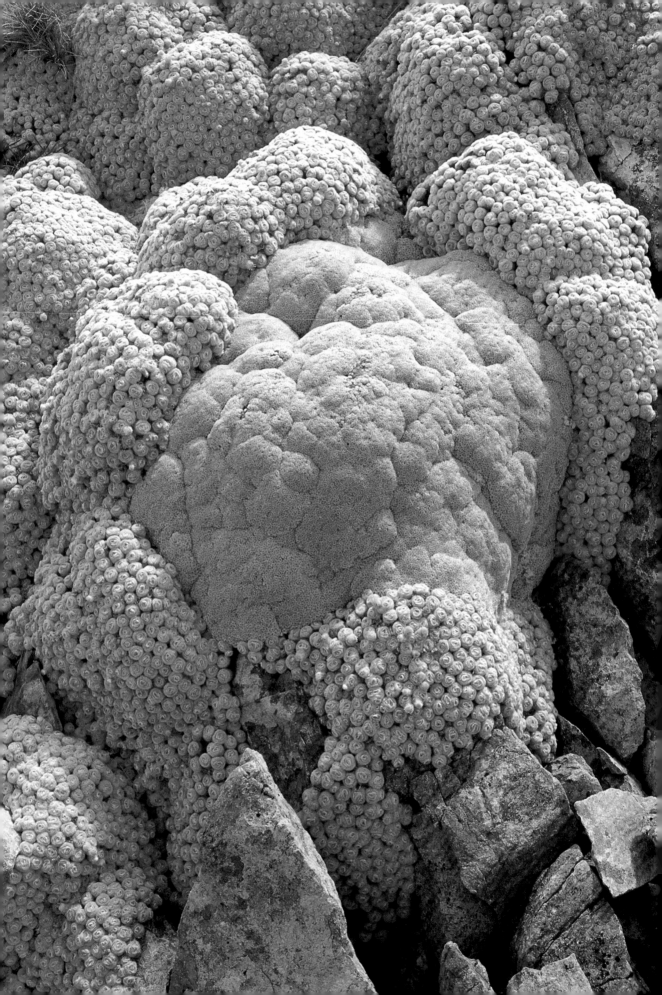

CHAPTER SIX

Too Cold for Trees

◆◆◆

Mountain and Arctic Plants

Most mountains are formed where the world's crustal plates push against each other. We live in a time when crustal movements are particularly active, so high mountain ranges are widespread at plate boundaries throughout the world. North and South America are advancing westward against the Pacific Plate, and the result is an almost continuous complex of mountain ranges through western North America, Central America, and the particularly high Andes of South America. On the other side of the Pacific, interaction between the Indian–Australian and Pacific Plates has formed the Southern Alps of New Zealand and the high mountains of New Guinea and other mountains in Southeast Asia. India itself is forming the highest mountains of all, the Himalaya, as it pushes into the Eurasian Plate. Finally, the northward movement of Africa has given us the Atlas Mountains in Morocco, several ranges in Spain, the Swiss Alps, and a complex of mountain ranges in southeastern Europe and the Middle East.

Volcanoes are often associated with these mountain ranges, but there are also isolated volcanic mountains away from crustal plate margins that form at hot spots where molten magma comes to the surface. Notable examples are the Hawaiian and other

Two cushion plants growing together: a dense, gray *Raoulia eximia* is surrounded by a yellow *Haastia pulvinaris* (both Asteraceae), which has much stouter twigs and some flower heads. New Zealand.

high Pacific islands, the Canary Islands, and on continents, the east-central African mountains and Yellowstone in Wyoming.

Going up a mountain, the air steadily thins and the mean annual temperature drops by 6.5°C (12°F) per 1,000 m (3,300 feet). At the height where the mean temperature of the warmest month is 10°C (50°F), the trees mostly stop as it is no longer warm enough in the growing season for them to grow and reproduce. This is known as the tree line, which is the lower limit of the realm of alpine plants. The tree line can be as high as 5,000 m (16,400 feet) in the equatorial Andes, gradually lowering to sea level at about 70° north in the Arctic.

An apparent anomaly is that some mountains at similar latitudes can have tree lines at quite different elevations. Land heats up much more in the summer growing season than does the sea, so on a mountain on a continent the 10°C (50°F) isotherm for the warmest month is much higher than it is on a mountain at the same latitude on an is-land, where the summer heat is moderated by the surrounding sea. As an example, at 42° south in New Zealand the tree line is at 1,500 m (4,900 feet); in the Rocky Moun-tains of Colorado at 40° north it is at 3,100 m (10,200 feet).

With what special conditions do alpine plants have to cope? Well, cold temperatures to begin with, particularly during winter for mountains of temperate latitudes. The cold slows growth or even stops it at times of frost and snow.

On many mountains, moisture is not a problem. As wind is lifted up mountain slopes, it cools and the water vapor it contains precipitates into rain. So going up a mountain there are steadily decreasing temperatures and steadily increasing rainfall. However, if there is a prevailing wind direction, as is often the case, most of the rain or snow is dropped on the windward side and the winds are relatively dry when they reach the lee side. On particularly high mountains, the higher elevations on the windward side also receive little precipitation. Rainfall increases up to a certain height on this side, but with the winds after this point having lost most of their moisture, conditions now become steadily drier. In the high tropical mountains of central Africa, New Guinea, and the northern Andes, precipitation decreases above 2,000–3,000 m (6,600–9,800 feet).

With the thinner atmosphere, sunlight is very intense at higher altitudes, as pale-skinned people find to their cost if they do not protect themselves against the sun. Also, ultraviolet light is very intense, which could lead to deleterious mutations in al-pine plants, though in many, coverings of hairs or ultraviolet-absorbing pigments act as a screen. The thin air does not absorb much of the heat from the sun, but the intense

Southern beech (*Nothofagus fusca, N. menziesii,* and *N. solandri* var. *cliffortioides*) forest at 42° south in New Zealand. There is a well-defined tree line at 1,500 m (4,900 feet).

An ancient bristlecone pine (*Pinus longaeva*) and younger trees at about 37° north and 3,300 m (10,800 feet) in the White Mountains, California.

rays can raise the temperature of the ground very considerably in summer, especially where it is rocky, and this in turn warms the layer of air nearest the ground to a level conducive to plant growth. When skies are clear on the other hand, this daytime heat is quickly lost at night, and frost often follows, even in the warmer growing season.

On many ridges and slopes the soil is very thin as a result of rainwash and gravity. Even where there is a reasonable depth of soil on gentler slopes, it is generally infertile as a result of the cold, which slows microbial breakdown of litter and perhaps also slows the chemical breakdown of the rocks. In hollows on the other hand, peat can accumulate to considerable depths, though many alpine plants are not suited to these acidic, waterlogged conditions.

Violent winds can also be a growth-restricting factor for alpine plants, both by intensifying the effect of cold temperatures and by causing mechanical damage. All these are problems faced by cold-tolerant plants at all latitudes, but there are also some problems that are peculiar to temperate, polar, and tropical latitudes (Wielgolaski 1997).

Alpine plants of temperate regions

A feature strongly limiting plants in temperate mountains is the short growing season, which ranges from about 2 to 4 months between snowmelt in spring and the first snowfall in fall. As a result, alpine plants are mostly low shrubs or herbaceous perennials (Zwinger and Willard 1972, Dawson 1988, Dawson and Lucas 1996). The leisurely sequence available to annuals at lower elevations, of germination in spring, flowering in later spring and summer, and seed dispersal in fall, is not possible above tree line. The few alpine annuals are mostly small plants that can devote most of their energy to reproducing as quickly as possible. In this way alpine annuals are similar to the more abundant desert annuals, or ephemerals, but those grow when abundant moisture is temporarily available, and the warm temperatures facilitate rapid growth and reproduction.

To make the most of the short growing season, most alpine plants form their flower buds during the previous season. These remain dormant until warming weather in the spring. The alpines also store food reserves in roots or rhizomes, enabling a quick start when conditions become favorable.

Shrubland and herb-field—The zone of colorful alpine flowers

In the northern temperate zone the trees at tree line are typically conifers, belonging to several genera, including firs (*Abies*), hemlocks (*Tsuga*), junipers (*Juniperus*), larches (*Larix*), pines (*Pinus*), and spruces (*Picea*). In the southern hemisphere the trees are more often flowering plants, not conifers, and notably species of southern beeches (*Nothofagus*) in South America and Australasia.

In some places the tree line is sharply defined, but in others, stunted, windswept, widely spaced trees struggle upward for a limited distance. More often the first zone above tree line is dominated by shrubs. Here the heath family (Ericaceae) is prominent, including dwarf rhododendrons, but there are many other families represented. Alpine heaths are also found in the southern hemisphere along with species of Epacridaceae (now included in Ericaceae) in Australasia. There may also be dwarf conifers, mostly junipers in the northern hemisphere and species of Podocarpaceae in the southern.

The next zone upward is the herb-field or alpine meadow. This community is a closed cover of mostly short sedges and grasses with their inconspicuous, wind-pollinated flowers, and a wide array of species with larger, often brightly colored flowers that are insect-pollinated. During spring and summer the latter can form eye-catching displays over the mountain slopes. In the northern hemisphere many genera familiar to gardeners are represented, including *Anemone*, columbines (*Aquilegia*), *Epilobium*, *Gentiana*, buttercups (*Ranunculus*), *Saxifraga*, and violets (*Viola*). Some herb-field plants die

Mountain shrubland in New Zealand, including brownish *Dracophyllum longifolium* (Ericaceae–Epacridaceae) and grayish green *Phyllocladus alpinus* (Podocarpaceae).

Ranunculus lyallii in an herb-field. New Zealand.

down in winter and resprout from bulbs or rhizomes. Others are evergreen, especially those with rosettes of leaves, or with tufted leaves, as in the sedges and grasses.

Some herb-fields in the mountains of the southern hemisphere are dominated by large tussock grasses, each often 1 m (39 inches) high and wide or more. It is estimated that individual tussocks may live for more than a century. A mountainside closely patterned with these tussocks is an attractive sight, especially when restless winds toss them like waves of the sea.

Southern herb-field plants that are not grasses have to be quite tall where the tussocks are dense, but smaller species are also present where the tussocks are more widely spaced. A number of genera are shared with northern hemisphere mountains, including forget-me-nots (*Myosotis*), *Epilobium*, *Gentiana*, *Ranunculus*, and *Viola*. Other genera are southern only, though some of those, including *Hebe* and *Leptinella*, have northern relatives (*Veronica* and *Cotula*, respectively).

Fells and screes

As we climb above the herb-field, the going for plants gets tougher. The temperature drops, the winter snowfall is deeper and takes longer to melt in spring, the winds are more violent, the soils thinner, the sunlight more intense, and at times moisture for plant roots can be in short supply. As a result, on these fells the plants are often low and scattered, and there is much exposed rock. At these higher elevations the water for the plants mostly comes from snowmelt. Snow is most abundant on lee slopes as it is often blown away on windward slopes, which are drier during summer as a result.

On sloping terrain, where plant roots penetrate into crevices, there are scattered rosette plants, some prostrate shrubs, and tufts of grasses and sedges, but the most distinctive and specialized growth forms are the cushion plants. These may be herbaceous perennials up to about 20 cm (8 inches) in diameter, among which species of *Saxifraga* and *Silene* are prominent, or shrubs that may attain enormous dimensions, from 1 m (39 inches) to several meters or yards in diameter. Some of the largest of these can be found in the Andes, where they mostly belong to the carrot family (Apiaceae), and in New Zealand, where they belong to the daisy family (Asteraceae) as well as the Apiaceae.

Cushion plants are very freely branched, and the ultimate branchlets are finger-like and pressed tightly together side by side with only the tips visible at the smooth, rounded surface of the cushion. In the large cushions, the densely leafy twigs are sometimes so tightly compressed that their outlines at the surface are hexagonal (see page 178). Such a cushion is almost as hard as a rock and can be stood on without causing any damage. Other cushion plants have densely compacted leaf rosettes.

Cushion plants are ideally suited to surviving the rigors of high elevations. Their smooth, rounded surfaces are not easily damaged by wind, nor can wind penetrate into the interior to cause chilling, drying, or mechanical damage. The air within the cush-

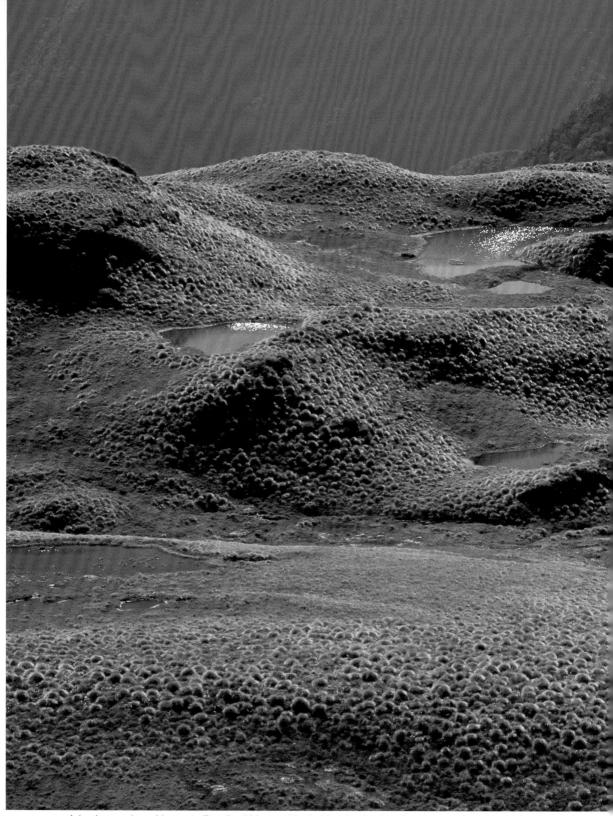

A landscape shaped by ice in Fiordland National Park, New Zealand, with a cover of large tussock grasses belonging to the genus *Chionochloa*. The dark vegetation near the tarns is alpine bog.

ion is almost a closed system, and on a sunny day its temperature can be many degrees higher than that of the external air. The dead leaves below the surface persist, so some nutrient recycling can take place, and the leaves can also absorb and retain water, especially when they are densely hairy. The larger forms of cushion plant in New Zealand have densely woolly leaves; this and their rounded shape led to them being referred to as "vegetable sheep." In these, the dead interior leaves break down into a water-retentive mass between the tortuous branches that is like shredded blotting paper. In densely compacted cushions the leaves are unable to expand, so they form permanent buds. In season, a flower arises from the center of each such bud.

Large rock outcrops, especially if they are in groups, are a more favorable habitat for fell plants. Here, there can be shelter from wind and some accumulation of soil. As a result there is a wider range of plants growing at their best. On plateaus and broadly rounded ridges some soil is able to build up, and the surface may have a largely complete cover of very small plants only a few centimeters or an inch or more high; this is sometimes called alpine tundra. With the shearing effect of the winds, taller plants are not be able to survive, but close to the ground the wind speed is reduced. Lichens are common, rosette plants, too, and small cushion and mat plants. There may be dwarf shrubs, including rhododendrons and willows (*Salix*), these surviving the wind by being two-dimensional and closely pressed to the ground. Sometimes the original roots and lower stems of these shrubs die off, and the plants cling to life by forming roots on their still leafy twigs.

What is known as patterned ground may develop on these level surfaces by the action of frost, which is frequent and severe. The water in the soil turns to ice, which expands to push the ice–stony soil mass upward and outward to form mounds that are sometimes known as "frost boils." The mound centers are more or less equidistant. With each frost the mounds push against each other, and as with the cushion plant twigs, they tend to assume polygonal shapes bounded by hollows. The larger stones pushed up by the ice slide down into the hollows. This stirring of the soil by ice interferes with root development, but small plants with shallow roots survive reasonably well.

Where an area of patterned ground adjoins a steeper slope, the soil, loosened by ice expansion and lubricated by the water of the daytime thaw, slowly oozes down the slope, drawing the polygons out into elongated stripes separated by stony hollows. This process is known as solifluction.

Screes provide a remarkable habitat for certain, very specialized plants. In most young, steep mountains of the world, where the rocks fragment readily with weathering, the angular debris often builds up into enormous aprons, or screes, poised at the steep angle of rest. They sometimes extend through 1,000 meters (3,300 feet) of elevation. While the fell-field is clearly a difficult habitat for plants, scree seems to be im-

Patterned ground on the Old Man Range, New Zealand.

possible. Not only are plants likely to be buried or uprooted by movement of the scree, but there appears to be no soil, no water, and the rocks become so hot with the intense sunlight that it is hard to imagine that any plants could become established, let alone survive.

Getting out onto a scree is no easy task. The shingle slides with every step, and the experience is similar to walking along the steep side of a sand hill—but if you tumble, landing on angular stones is much worse than landing on sand. As you gradually leave solid rock farther behind, the scree may seem at first to be completely plantless, then you spot one plant, then another, and another. They are often the same color as the stones, often fleshy in texture, and tend to be scattered fairly evenly several meters or yards apart. Several species are usually present. To find out how they are able to survive it is necessary to excavate around them. This requires much patience as stones from above constantly slide into the cavity. If you are eventually successful you will find that at about 20–30 cm (8–12 inches) deep there is a base layer of wet sandy silt where the plant roots, or rhizomes with roots, are embedded. The moisture comes from snowmelt or rain that sinks down between the stones. Most scree plants die down during winter; in spring, leaves and inflorescences grow up between the stones to the surface. There the leaves cope with the problem of excessive water loss from the heat of the stones on a sunny day by having a dense woolly covering of hairs or by being fleshy and storing water.

Scree gradually creeps downslope, and the plants as a result become aligned in the same direction. The roots extend upslope sometimes for considerable distances, and the stems grow downslope. Probably each crop of leaves pushes through the stones a little below the position of the previous year. There still remains the problem of sudden and extensive movement of the stones. This can happen at snowmelt in the spring when the stone–soil interface becomes well lubricated with water and the stony layer suddenly slides on the more stable soil layer, or it can be caused by boulders falling from rocky crags above the scree. Even then, many of the plants are able to survive as a result of the leaves and inflorescences having only slender or brittle attachments to the rootstocks. When the stony layer moves abruptly, a plant is not uprooted; rather, its upper part shears off and the rootstock or rhizome is able to form new leaves and inflorescences, though there is sometimes a delay until the next season.

The majority of mountain plants of more stable habitats could not survive, let alone reproduce, in this challenging habitat. Nevertheless, the scree plants of a particular region are generally related to, and probably derived from, species of more stable habitats in the same region.

Mount Baldy, New Zealand, mantled by screes.

Notothlaspi rosulatum (Brassicaceae) with a cone-like arrangement of flattened capsules, on scree. New Zealand.

Leptinella dendyi (Asteraceae) on scree. New Zealand.

Lignocarpa carnosula (Apiaceae) excavated from scree. Normally, only the much-divided leaf blades at the top appear at the surface. The leaf stalks have delicate attachments to the just visible stem. New Zealand.

Snowbanks and alpine bogs

Snowbanks at higher elevations are another special habitat for plants. Snow lies in deep hollows, generally on the moister, shadier slopes, and because it is so deep it persists well into summer. The disadvantage of this for plants is that the growing season is very short, a few months for plants near the periphery of the snow patch, where the snow is shallow and melts first, but perhaps only a month at the center, or no time at all if the summer has been cool. However, there are advantages, too. In winter the snow cover protects the plants from wind and maintains somewhat warmer temperatures than in the open air. During summer there is more shelter from gales, and on the concave slopes a deeper soil builds up that has a steady if cold supply of water from the gradually melting snow.

Some of the earliest snowbank species to appear actually open their flowers beneath the thinning snow, then push through it, gaining a head start on the growing season. Prominent here are two genera of the Ranunculaceae, *Caltha* and *Ranunculus*, which are represented by different species in snowbanks in a number of places throughout the world. Inward from this outer group there are concentric zones of species that correlate with the reducing length of the growing season. These form a complete cover of mats, small cushions, rosettes, and a turf of grasses and sedges. At the center there are mostly only hardy mosses and lichens, which can remain alive even when their part of the snowbank does not melt before the end of summer.

On some mountains, alpine bogs form in hollows of varied extent and depth in level terrain. They are best developed where rainfall and snowmelt are plentiful but

Psychrophila obtusa, a close relative of *Caltha.* New Zealand.

An alpine bog with tarns in the Old Man Range, New Zealand.

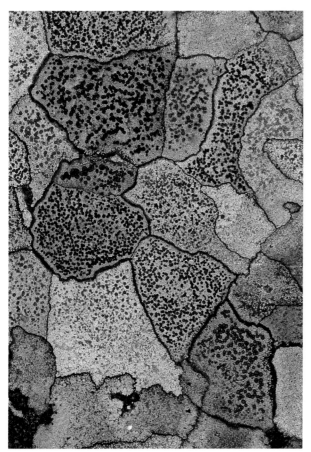
Artistically patterned crustose lichens on an alpine rock.

where water also drains in from surrounding slopes. The water table is close to the surface, and often there are also scattered ponds or tarns. The dominant plants in these bogs are mostly mosses, belonging to many genera. Among them are species of peat moss (*Sphagnum*), which are very water absorbent by virtue of having large, empty cells, scattered among normal cells, that can hold considerable quantities of water. The mosses tend to grow up into hummocks, somewhat drier on their crests, on which flowering plants can then establish. These include small shrubs (heaths and heath relatives, and dwarf willows in the northern hemisphere), rosette plants, and small, tufted grasses and sedges. The substrate below the living surface is very acidic; this and the cold temperatures lead to very slow decay of dead plant parts. As a result the dead material or peat steadily accumulates to a considerable depth, and the surface of the bog gradually becomes higher. In this way some hollows can be completely filled in, and the surface becomes sufficiently well drained to support species from better-drained sites.

On some mountains in the southern hemisphere, cushion plants are prominent in alpine bogs. Some, mostly sedges, are quite small. Others are large, such as species of *Donatia* in New Zealand and southern South America. The cushions of this genus are dense and very hard, and sometimes provide a substrate for smaller rosette plants. Cushion plants are mostly species of well-drained, sometimes dry habitats, so it is difficult to understand what advantage this growth habit could have in a waterlogged situation.

Plants virtually disappear when the zone of permanent snow is reached, but there is still some exposed rock in places and a few hardy flowering plants are able to wedge themselves into crevices. Lichens can be quite common, too, and after flowering plants give up, some lichens continue on to the highest rocks.

Arctic tundra

The Arctic tundra, beyond the limit of trees in high northern latitudes, borders the Arctic Ocean and ranges from about 60° to 70° north, or 80° north on some island groups (Wielgolaski 1997). During the last glacial period the present location of the tundra was occupied by an ice sheet that extended from polar regions far to the south. In middle northern latitudes south of the ice, the cold climates of the time would have induced tundra vegetation in many places, both on the plains and the mountains. With the coming of warmer times the ice retreated, and the tundra followed it northward. Tundra in middle latitudes was replaced by forest and grassland except at higher elevations in the mountains. It is not surprising then that there are strong similarities between the alpine vegetation of lower latitudes and the tundra of high latitudes. Indeed, many species are shared between the two regions, and botanists recognize one Arctic-alpine flora.

Despite these similarities, the polar environment differs from the alpine environment in several respects. Because of the ice sheet, the polar terrain is a low-lying pattern of broad rises and hollows. Beneath the upper layer of peat or soil there is a permanently frozen subsoil known as permafrost. Sometimes on slopes the upper layer, which thaws during the growing season, slides off the permafrost, exposing the ice. Permafrost is localized and uncommon in the mountains farther south. Permafrost also underlies the forest near its edge, and the short conifers there develop a shallow root system above it.

Sunlight is less intense toward the pole than in the mountains because of the denser air at the low elevation and the low angle of the sun, even at midsummer. The growing season is short, but this is compensated to some extent by the long hours of daylight.

The types of vegetation closer to the pole are similar to some of those in the mountains. In the depressions there are innumerable lakes surrounded by bogs that are vastly more extensive than in the mountains. The plants of the bogs include grasses and sedges, mosses (including *Sphagnum*), lichens, and sometimes dwarf willows and some heaths. In better-drained areas there can be low shrubby vegetation near the latitudinal tree limit, with birches (*Betula*) and willows (*Salix*) up to 60 cm (24 inches) high and an understory of heath species, grasses, and other flowering plants up to 20 cm (8 inches) high. The ground is covered with mosses and lichens. Farther north only the heath layer continues, gradually giving way to an herb-field of grasses, sedges, and a wide array of herbaceous flowering plants, including geophytes, that provide a showy display in summer. In the high Arctic there is a transition to a sparse vegetation similar to fell-field, where cushion plants, mostly species of mountain avens (*Dryas*), are conspicuous. In many places, frost-induced soil polygons are strongly developed and provide a striking sight, particularly from the air.

At the other end of the world the largely ice-covered Antarctic Continent is centered on the South Pole and extends to between 80° and 63° south. There are only two flowering plants, a small grass (*Deschampsia antarctica*) and a chickweed relative (*Colobanthus quitensis*), and they are restricted to the Antarctic Peninsula. There are mosses and lichens, too, on the Antarctic Peninsula and on limited areas of exposed rock closer to the pole.

Alpine plants of tropical mountains

Mountains high enough to have alpine vegetation in the tropics are found in the Andes of northern South America, on New Guinea and some Indonesian mountains, in east-central Africa, and on the Hawaiian Islands (Rundel et al. 1994). Climatically, there are a number of differences between the tropical mountains and those at higher latitudes. With the higher temperatures in the tropics, alpine conditions are restricted to quite high elevations—above about 4,000 m (13,100 feet) in Kenya, Peru, and New Guinea —so the air is thin and sunlight particularly intense. More importantly, there are no seasons near the equator, even in the high mountains, so the growing season for alpine plants is year-round. There is, however, a big difference between daytime and nighttime temperatures. During the day, temperatures can be quite warm, but on a clear night in the thin air the heat rapidly dissipates and frosts can be frequent year-round.

On these tropical mountains the zone above tree line is mostly occupied by grasses, some of large tussock form, and thick-leaved evergreen shrubs. In the central African mountains and the Peruvian Andes particularly, there are also large, rosette-leaved plants without trunks, or with quite massive unbranched or little-branched trunks. The leaves are sometimes extremely woolly and white or silvery. The old leaves often persist as an insulating layer, at least on the youngest parts of the trunks. These unusual plants give a very distinctive aspect to this type of tropical alpine vegetation.

In the northern Andes the genera involved are *Puya* of the Bromeliaceae, *Espeletia* of the Asteraceae, and lupins (*Lupinus*) of the Fabaceae. In central Africa, there are giant lobelias, and tree senecios and *Carduus* of the Asteraceae. The only species of this form in New Guinea is a tree fern, *Cyathea atrox*, well above the range of other tree ferns. In Hawaii the well-known silversword (*Argyroxiphium*) of the Asteraceae forms large, silvery rosettes, though it does not have a significant trunk. In the Canary Islands north of the Tropic of Cancer, two species of *Echium* (Boraginaceae) are large alpine rosette plants, and in New Zealand south of the Tropic of Capricorn, *Aciphylla* (Apiaceae; page 8) forms large, spiny rosettes without trunks in the mountains, so this growth form is not entirely confined to tropical mountains.

Many of these large rosette plants have equally large inflorescences that are strik-

Puya fosteriana in cultivation with a dense, elongate, inflorescence.

David Minja with a "giant daisy" (*Senecio kilimanjari*) on Mount Kilimanjaro, Tanzania, with huge rosettes of thick leaves and skirts of persistent, dead leaves.

ingly elongate and unbranched, with many densely packed flowers. Included here are puyas, lobelias, silverswords, echiums, and aciphyllas. These inflorescences may be resistant to wind damage, and the crowding of the flowers may enable some retention of daytime warmth during the cold nights. Being so conspicuous, the tall inflorescences would be easily located by pollinators, though at higher elevations, where pollinators are fewer, some of the rosette species are wind-pollinated. Some species with single rosettes die after flowering; those with several rosettes may die completely, or only the rosettes that flower die.

The dense covering of hairs on the flowers, bracts, and leaves of some of the rosette plants may retain warmth; this has been shown to be true in the case of the densely woolly floral bracts of puyas. The hairs also act as a screen against ultraviolet rays. The numerous, densely crowded, broadly based leaves of a rosette surround the immature leaves at the center and afford them some protection. In the lobelias, senecios, and espeletias, however, there is a further specialization. At night the mature leaves of a rosette curve inward, enclosing the conical bud at the center and protecting it from frost. Sunlight in the morning stimulates the leaves to spread apart again. The large, tussocky habit of some of the grasses also has a warmth-conserving function as it has been shown that the interiors of their densely packed bases are several degrees warmer than the surrounding air.

Although the giant rosette plants dominate locally, there is also a ground cover of prostrate shrubs, small grasses, and perennial herbaceous plants. At the upper limit for plants, only small grasses, small herbaceous plants, and lichens remain.

Trees that shut down during severe continental winters

Trees that go dormant in winter are able to grow actively during summer, which can be quite hot in continental climates, and in places in middle latitudes uncomfortably humid as well. The winters are cold, and often dry or too cold for water to flow. If those conditions persisted year-round, it really would be too cold for trees. Climates that swing from one extreme to another are most fully expressed on the large northern continents. In middle latitudes the mostly flowering trees lose their leaves during winter. At higher latitudes the dominant conifers are mostly evergreen with small, tough, cold-resistant leaves that are narrow and needle- or scale-like (Eyre 1968).

Deciduous forests

Almost all flowering trees and shrubs have a weak layer of cells, an abscission layer, in the leaf stalks near where they attach to the stems. When leaves fall, they separate from the plant at this weak layer. Although the leaves of some evergreens can last for several years, those of the deciduous trees of northern temperate forests last one growing season only; there are few winter-deciduous trees in the southern hemisphere. In fall, as the weather cools, the leaves drop away, leaving the trees with bare branches. Before they drop, useful nutrients are moved into the stem, and the chlorophyll breaks down and no longer masks the red, yellow, and brown accessory pigments that provide the brilliant fall displays.

Leaf fall in deciduous forests does not result from temperatures declining to a critical level, which would vary from season to season, but is triggered when day length shortens to a critical point. The shortening days cause chemical changes in the leaves, resulting in leaf fall at about the same time each year. That this is so is demonstrated when a deciduous tree has a branch growing close to a street lamp. Days are artificially lengthened for such a branch, and it retains its leaves, despite increasing cold, long after the rest of the tree has become leafless. Temperature, however, can influence the timing of leaf fall to some extent. The process leading to leaf fall, once triggered by declining day length, can be hastened by an early cold snap.

What is the advantage of this fairly precise timing of leaf fall and dormancy? If

Fruits and leaves of *Liquidambar styraciflua* in fall.

declining temperature were the determining factor, during an unusually warm early winter the trees would retain their leaves; then, if a sudden "big freeze" were to follow, the trees would suffer a drastic setback. Their leaves would be killed, but more importantly the thin sap of the active tissues of stems and roots would likely freeze, causing cells to die. The concentrated sap of dormant trees is much more resistant to freezing.

Among smaller plants on the forest floor in these forests, the shrubs are also often deciduous, and the herbaceous plants die down to food-storing roots, bulbs, or rhizomes. In early spring, before the trees have come into leaf and the forest floor is still well lit, these small plants quickly form new leaves and flowers. Many of them provide very attractive, often massed displays and include bluebell (*Hyacinthoides non-scripta*) and trilliums among many others. There may also be annual herbs that complete their life cycle in one growing season, surviving winter in the form of seeds. These

Leafless aspens, *Populus tremuloides*, during winter.

A red-flowered species of *Trillium* with broad, mottled leaves.

New spring growth of an elm (*Ulmus*) with some bud scales still persisting.

seeds will not germinate until they have been subjected to several months of winter cold, which ensures that seedlings will not appear until conditions are favorable in the spring.

Trunks and branches of deciduous trees are well protected by a layer of corky bark. The delicate twig tips, with their immature leaves for the next season, are protected and insulated by many closely overlapping bud scales. These seal off a space around the young leaves, keeping them moist and also enabling them, by metabolic processes however minimal, to keep the temperature within the bud at a sufficient level to prevent freezing.

The state of winter dormancy in these trees is not easily broken. A brief mild spell in winter is not sufficient, and fortunately so, as a flush of new leaves would only be killed by the return of winter cold. It has been found that dormancy is broken only after a sufficient period of cold temperatures, in some cases several months below 10°C (50°F). Following this, with rising temperatures in spring and sometimes triggered by increasing day length, the apparently dead trees of these northern forests come back to life in a relatively short space of time. It is at this time, too, and into early summer that flowering is concentrated, allowing several months for the development of fruits and the dispersal of seeds.

High-latitude coniferous forests

In Siberia, northern Europe, and northern North America, mostly in sparsely populated areas, there are vast extents of coniferous forests, known as taiga, occupying much of the terrain scraped flat by ice sheets during the last glacial period. In North America these high-latitude coniferous forests are continuous with similar forests at higher elevations in the north–south mountain ranges.

Where these forests have been locally destroyed, by fire and gales in pre-human times and by fire and felling since then, the pioneers are deciduous flowering trees—species of birch (*Betula*) and poplar (*Populus*). These grow quickly but are eventually shaded out by the much taller conifers. The conifers outcompete the flowering deciduous trees as a result of their tolerance of shallow, infertile, often poorly drained soils, which are frozen in the winter and in some cases overlie permafrost in the short summer.

The conifers are species of fir (*Abies*), larch (*Larix*), pine (*Pinus*), and spruce (*Picea*). Only the last is deciduous, and its species favor swampy sites. Pines are found on better-drained sandy soils, though there are some small species on swampy sites, and the other genera are mostly intermediate in their requirements.

Summers are short in these higher latitudes, and the evergreens have the advantage of being able to start photosynthesizing as soon as the weather begins to warm. For deciduous trees there is a delay of several weeks as the new leaves unfold and become functional. There are no scaly, overwintering buds in conifers, but the small, narrow leaves are densely crowded, especially at the twig tips, so this provides reasonable insulation for the growing points. Also, snow on flattened branches, as frequently illustrated on Christmas cards, is good insulation.

These coniferous forests are not rich in species. Sometimes over considerable areas there is only one species of tree, and with the deep shade cast by the canopy there are few or no smaller plants on the forest floor. Instead, there is a deep litter of needle-shaped leaves and dead, decaying wood. In eastern Asia and eastern North America, however, the forests are somewhat more diverse, with more tree species and a few herbaceous and shrubby ground plants.

CHAPTER SEVEN

A Love-Hate Relationship

◆ ◆ ◆

Plants and Animals

The Bible says, on "a day of darkness and of gloominess . . . the land is as the garden of Eden before them, and behind them a desolate wilderness; yea, and nothing shall escape them" (Joel 2). The reference is to a plague of locusts sent by Jehovah as one of his 10 punishments for wayward mortals. Locusts are several species of cricket that still swarm and destroy plants from time to time, though at least the causes seem to be natural (Chapman 1976). If in a particular season there have been unusually good rains in the drought-prone places where these locusts breed, plant growth is prolific and the locusts feed and reproduce enthusiastically. They can produce several generations of offspring in a short period of time. The local supply of plant food soon runs out, and the locusts then form themselves into dense swarms, which fly, often great distances, in search of edible plants. One such swarm in eastern Africa was described as being more than 30 m (100 feet) deep on a front 1.6 km (1 mile) wide that took 9 hours to pass by. Such swarms blot out the sun, and if crops are encountered the locusts descend and quickly strip them of everything edible before passing on. This is an extreme case, but a wide range of animals have been using plants as their larder for so many millions of years that it is perhaps surprising that any plants still exist.

A cabbage tree moth on a dead leaf of a cabbage tree (*Cordyline australis*). New Zealand.

Plants under attack

The parts eaten by animals, to the detriment or sometimes the death of the plants, are often leaves but also young stems and buds, flowers, green and ripe fruits, seeds, roots, and even the wood of trunks and branches (Crawley 1983). In the latter case, termites and the larvae of some beetles chew their way into the wood, gradually boring out a network of tunnels. These wood borers are not able to digest the cellulose of the wood themselves, and this task is left to the bacteria and protozoans that inhabit their digestive systems. A small proportion of the sugars resulting from this process is food for the microorganisms, and the rest provides energy for the hidden tunnelers to continue with their task. The mammals known as ruminants, which include many large and familiar animals from domestic cows to free-ranging giraffes, also utilize microorganisms to break down cellulose. Ruminants have several stomachs of which the first in line is the rumen. Well-chewed plant material enters the rumen, and the microorganisms break down the cellulose molecules into their sugar components. Animals that cannot make use of microorganisms in this way digest the other organic compounds of plant material and excrete the cellulose.

A gum emperor moth caterpillar dining on a *Eucalyptus* leaf.

Some animals that eat plants chew their way, including slugs and snails, and among a multitude of insects, grasshoppers, ants, weevils, beetles, and the larvae of moths, butterflies, and flies. Larvae often chew leaves in from the margins and sometimes roll them up or hold them together in clusters with web-like threads so that the larvae are screened from predators as they feed.

Adult insects of some species deposit their eggs within leaf, young stem, and immature fruit tissues, where they develop into larvae. The larvae of leaf miners gradually eat their way through the inner leaf tissues, forming a sometimes complex pattern of tunnels visible externally. A larva that develops inside a young stem secretes a chemical that induces the stem cells to proliferate into a gall, which provides a renewable source of food as the larva enlarges. The codling moth caterpillar is the best known of burrowers into fruit. The young caterpillar penetrates the skin of an apple and eats its way to the core. Anyone who bites into such an apple without looking first is in for an unpleasant surprise.

Some wood-boring larvae, too, derive their nutriment from soft tissues. They bore into the wood only to provide a safe place for their development into adult moths. The puriri moth in New Zealand is an example. The young larva burrows into the trunk of a puriri (*Vitex lucens*), or several other trees, first upward at an inclination to the vertical, then vertically downward. The sharp angle in the tunnel presumably prevents access to probing bird beaks, or stops flooding by rain. The larva then eats away a diamond-shaped area of bark and outer sapwood around the opening to the tunnel, and the edges of the scar form a renewing callus that provides food for the caterpillar for as long as 5 years. The feeding area is concealed by a sheet of silk and plant debris. The caterpillar eventually metamorphoses into the bright green moth with a wingspan up to 15 cm (6 inches). The adult moth does not feed and, after mating and laying eggs, dies within a few days.

Leaf-cutting ants illustrate a special case of herbivory. They cut out pieces of leaves much larger than themselves and carry them, held aloft like flags, to their nests. They

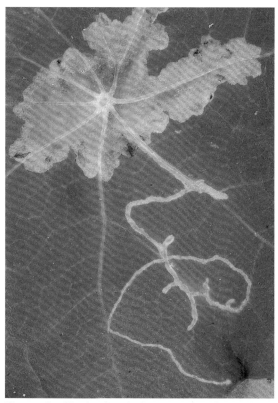

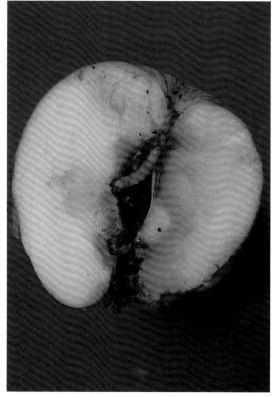

The result of feeding by a leaf-mining caterpillar inside a nasturtium (*Tropaeolum majus*) leaf.

An apple cut in half to reveal a codling moth caterpillar.

A camouflaged burrow occupied by a puriri moth caterpillar.

The entrance to a vacated burrow of a puriri moth caterpillar.

A puriri moth, which has a wing span of 15 cm (6 inches).

do not eat the leaf tissue but use it to make fungus gardens and feed on the fungal growth. They still depend on plants for their nutrition, but at secondhand.

Sucking insects are more precise and specialized in the way they obtain food from plants. Their mouthparts are modified into slender needle-like tubes that they insert into living tissues and suck out the highly nutritious cell contents. In this way they avoid having to ingest bulky cellulose cell walls that they are unable to digest. Insects that feed in this way are well known to gardeners and include aphids, psyllids, whiteflies, scale insects, and bugs. Mites also have sucking mouthparts.

The often much larger vertebrates include a number of species that eat a range of plant parts similar to that of the invertebrates. Among the herbivorous vertebrates are lizards, birds, and a variety of mammals, including bats, mice, squirrels, marsupials (such as the Australian possums introduced into New Zealand, which have done much damage to the forests), primates, goats, cows, and at the biggest end of the scale, elephants. Some mammals, including ourselves, are omnivores, eating both plants and animals. Individually, because of their larger size, a vertebrate consumes much more plant material than an individual invertebrate, but because of their large numbers, invertebrates are equally or more destructive, especially when conditions are favorable.

How plants survive the onslaught

Plants avail themselves of a variety of defenses against getting eaten (Crawley 1983, Howe and Westley 1988). The surface layer of cells, or epidermis, of leaves and young stems is the first line of defense against small invertebrates. A surface waxy layer, sometimes very thick, is indigestible and difficult to penetrate. Hairs, which are outgrowths from epidermal cells, are also very effective. These may be soft but so abundant that small invertebrates are unable to penetrate through the blanket-like layer they form. Other hairs are more aggressive: short, stiff, sharply pointed, and sometimes hooked. They can damage the more delicate invertebrates. Sticky glandular hairs are also a common defense. These hairs are generally multicellular, with rounded tips that exude a sticky glue. Small animals are trapped by this glue, and if they cannot disentangle themselves, they die.

Surface defenses against larger vertebrates are much more evident and daunting as they involve sharp points that can do much damage to the soft flesh of herbivorous mammals. Prickles are hard, surface outgrowths, narrowing to sharp points, and they are sometimes hooked to penetrate readily, as those who prune roses or gather blackberries become painfully aware. Thorns are short, highly modified, lateral stems, as in the shrub japonica (*Chaenomeles japonica*) and the vine *Bougainvillea*. The backward-angled thorns of the latter are also used for climbing. Spines are modified leaves or parts of leaves. In holly (*Ilex*) these are derived from the marginal teeth of the leaves, as they are in species of *Agave*. However, those of agaves can be much more damaging as they are narrowly attenuated and seem to be as hard as

Leaves of an *Agave* with impressive marginal spines. The leaves are patterned with impressions of the margins and spines of older leaves.

steel. In desert cacti, the most heavily armed of plants to protect their precious stores of water from thirsty animals, the leaves are entirely modified into spines. In some species there are also backward-curved barbs at the tips of the spines, which anchor themselves in flesh like fishhooks.

Many plants also have chemical defenses against hungry animals. Some of these interfere with the their digestive processes; others are poisonous. A number of chemical compounds in plants interfere with digestion by binding with proteins to render them indigestible, or by binding with enzymes so that they become unable to carry out their role in digestion. The major compounds here are lignins, which harden the cell walls of wood in particular, and brown-colored tannins, which are dissolved in the cell protoplasm. These groups of chemicals are widespread among plants.

Many plants also counter animal attack with poisons or by having unpleasant tastes, particularly in new growth before tannins and lignins have formed. Literally tens of thousands of different poisons and distasteful compounds are found in plants. Immature fruits, too, often taste hot, bitter, or sour. Eating of such fruits and dispersal of their immature seeds would be no use to the plants. When the seeds are mature the fruits change from camouflage green to brighter colors; the unpleasant tastes disappear and are replaced by harmless and nutritious sugars and other compounds. However, some ripe and brightly colored fruits are poisonous to people and other mammals, and also to parrots and some other birds. These animals crush and kill seeds when they eat smaller fleshy fruits, which is not desirable from the plant's point of view. Where poisons are present in berries, they are usually confined to the seeds, and the seed crushers learn to avoid them. Most birds do not crush seeds; they digest the nutritious fleshy tissues and pass the seeds without harm to themselves or the seeds.

Some animals have evolved that are immune to the poisons of particular plants. The immune animal in such a case has a distinct advantage over its relatives. For example, the mustard-type poisons of the cabbage family (Brassicaceae) are toxic to most butterfly caterpillars, one of the exceptions being the cabbage white butterfly. As a result, among butterflies, the cabbage white has almost exclusive access to that plant family as a source of food.

Some plants that are in fact palatable resemble or mimic particular toxic plants and thus are also off the menu for animals. Some animals that are immune to a particular plant toxin store it in their bodies, and carnivores learn to avoid them, too. For example, some beetles and bugs feed on the spurge family (Euphorbiaceae) and are immune to the toxin in the milky latex. These insects are conspicuously colored, which is a keep-away signal to other animals. Some animals mimic parts of plants to hide from their predators. Some moths have wings colored and patterned so that they are almost invisible on tree bark or dead leaves. Some caterpillars and adult stick insects mimic twigs, and most remarkable of all, the wings of some insects look exactly like leaves,

A small columnar, Mexican cactus, *Neobuxbaumia euphorbioides,* with long spines on the margins of the stem ribs.

Two small shrubs, *Pseudowintera colorata* (Winteraceae; left) and *Alseuosmia pusilla* (Alseuosmiaceae; right) with very similar leaves, often red and sometimes with yellow patches. *Pseudowintera* has a hot peppery taste and is avoided by herbivores. Its look-alike, *Alseuosmia,* often grows with it and is also avoided. The lowermost leaf of the *Pseudowintera* has been turned over to show the white underside, a feature that distinguishes it from *Alseuosmia,* the upper left leaf of which has also been turned over. New Zealand.

either green, or brown and dead (page 206). They may even have the typical leaf vein pattern with a midrib and secondary veins.

Ants, once again, play a special role for some plants (Huxley and Cutler 1991). Notable are some trees of the pea family (Fabaceae), which as well as having nectaries in their flowers also bear them on leafy stems, leaf stalks, and elsewhere. This is the case with a number of species of *Acacia* and *Paraserianthes,* whose foliage is palatable to browsing animals. Stinging ants are attracted to the nectar or sugary tissues of the extrafloral nectaries, and sometimes to nodule-like oil bodies, and they attack any would-be browsers. Some acacias are also armed with daunting thorns. In some, these are large and the ants hollow them out to provide accommodation. They come and go through a small opening in each thorn.

Some plants, notably the nettles (*Urtica*), have specialized stinging hairs. These contain a fluid under pressure, and when an animal brushes one of them, the delicate tip is removed and the sharp point then exposed sinks into flesh, injecting the stinging fluid as if from a hypodermic needle.

There are other invertebrates that studies suggest play a role somewhat similar to that of the stinging ants, but instead of stinging and driving away browsing mammals, they attack and eat small invertebrates that feed on leaves, or they eat the filaments of parasitic fungi that start to grow on the leaves. These useful invertebrates gain a feeding site, and the plants also provide them with a place to live where they can hide from their own predators and lay their eggs. The shelters provided are known as domatia, which are found on the leaves of a wide range of woody flowering plants. Domatia are located on the undersides of leaves, singly in the angles where secondary veins meet the midrib. In some large tropical leaves there are also domatia in the angles of higher-order veins. They are small hollows that range, depending on the species, from open and saucer-shaped, to flask-shaped with a pinhole-like opening to the outside. In many cases they are lined with hairs. Some domatia are more pouch-like with a sort of roof over the vein angle that is open toward the leaf margins.

The function of the domatia has long been a puzzle, even though the name means "little house." Studies in South Korea (O'Dowd and Pemberton 1998) and eastern North America (Pemberton and Turner 1989) have shown that a number of species of mites inhabit domatia. Some feed on herbivores such as whiteflies and spider mites, and others on fungal filaments. Some other small invertebrates provide a similar service to plants with domatia, including thrips, small bugs, and lacewings. The first two also help themselves to some of the plants' juices. However, this proposed function of domatia needs to be investigated in other parts of the world, as casual inspections of species with domatia often fail to reveal any tiny inhabitants.

A close view of the tip of a *Paraserianthes lophantha* shoot. There is a green-colored nectary on the leaf stalk at upper left.

Stinging hairs of the giant nettle *Urtica ferox*. New Zealand.

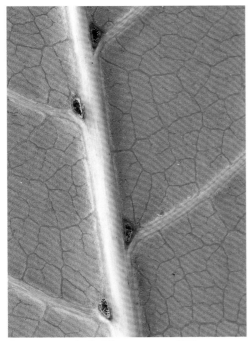

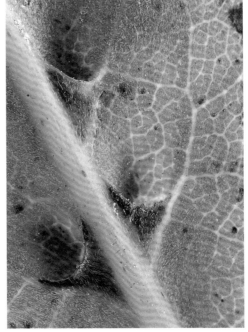

Domatia on a leaf of *Coprosma grandifolia* (Rubiaceae). New Zealand.

Pouch-like domatia of *Elaeocarpus dentatus* (Elaeocarpaceae). New Zealand.

How seed plants reproduce

In the majority of animals there are males that provide sperm cells and females that provide eggs for reproduction, so self-fertilization is not possible. A sperm and an egg fuse together, becoming the first cell of a new individual. Half the chromosomes, with their controlling genes, come from one parent, and a matching but not identical set from the other parent. Apart from the early splitting of an embryo to form identical twins, it is not possible in nature for higher animals to produce exact replicas or clones of themselves. Very controversially, it has been found possible to clone many animal species artificially, and potentially humans, but this has not happened independently in nature.

Plants are much more diverse in the ways they reproduce themselves, and some do so in several different ways. Among seed plants, the cone bearers produce pollen and ovules in cones that are mostly dense aggregations of firm or woody scales attached to elongated axes. There are separate pollen cones and seed cones, sometimes on the same tree, sometimes on different trees. Each pollen grain eventually forms two sperms, and each ovule at maturity contains two eggs or sometimes more. Cone-bearing seed plants once dominated the world's vegetation. Nowadays the familiar conifers are their main group with about 550 species, followed by the very different cycads with their large, palm-like leaves with almost 300 species.

Monterey pine, *Pinus radiata*, with a green seed cone from the previous season and elongated clusters of pollen cones releasing pollen.

In the conifers, pollination is by wind, and pollen is dispersed in great quantities, usually in spring. Very few of the pollen grains bring about fertilization, so this could be considered a wasteful method. It has been generally believed that cycads are also wind-pollinated. More recently, it has been suggested that beetles and small bees are in fact the usual pollinators, with wind also playing a role (Jones 1993). As an example, in *Zamia furfuracea* of Mexico the larvae of a small weevil feed on parts of

A grove of the conifer *Araucaria columnaris* on New Caledonia.

developing pollen cones. The adults emerge when the pollen is being released and carry some of it with them when they are attracted to the nectar drops at the tips of the ovules of seed cones (Proctor et al. 1996, 370).

The ovule-bearing cone scales of conifers and the comparable, sometimes leaf-like appendages of some cycads do not enclose the ovules, so a successful pollen grain may come into direct contact with an ovule. In some conifers it becomes attached to a sticky drop of nectar protruding from the pore leading to the egg. The nectar provides some of the nutriment for the pollen grain to produce a pollen tube that conveys the two sperms the short distance to fuse with eggs. In other conifers the ovules do not have nectar drops, and the pollen grain extends a pollen tube, sometimes for some distance, to reach an ovule. Strangely, in cycads and the distinctive *Ginkgo* the sperms are able to swim, which they do briefly in a small amount of liq-

The cycad *Encephalartos ferox* with a large, brightly colored seed cone.

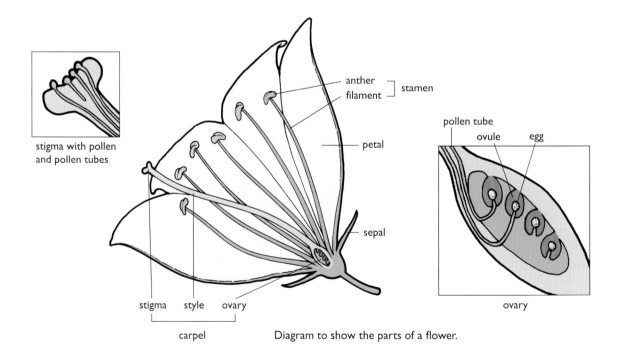

stigma with pollen and pollen tubes

Diagram to show the parts of a flower.

uid in a hollow at the tip of the ovule. This seems to be the persistence of a primitive, ancestral pattern.

Almost 100 million years ago flowering plants displaced the cone-bearing seed plants as the dominant group in world vegetation. They are much more diverse in their forms and functions than the cone bearers and much more numerous with more than 400,000 species spread throughout the world. A major difference between flowers and seed cones is that in a flower the sometimes leaf-like appendages at the center (the carpels) that bear the ovules are folded so that their margins meet and fuse. This provides a closed container, or ovary, that protects the ovules and later the seeds from chewing insects and other animals as well as cold and drought. In some more advanced flowering plants the ovary, too, is protected. Here the sepals, petals, and stamens are attached to the rim of a tubular structure, which is often fused to the ovary so that visitors to a flower have no internal access to it. At the top of the ovary there is usually an erect stalk or style that is tipped by a variously shaped stigma whose sticky, sugary exudate both traps pollen grains and provides much of the energy for the pollen tubes to grow down the style to convey sperms to the ovules. In the flowers of some species, the stigma does not form an exudate.

More primitive flowers are considered to be those where the parts are numerous, symmetrically arranged, and separate from each other (for example, *Ranunculus*). An advanced flower has few parts, often asymmetrically arranged, and fused together in various ways (for example, *Tecomanthe*, page 220). The advanced features are adaptations to animals as pollinators.

There is also an important difference between cone-bearing and flowering seed plants in the way in which nutriment is provided in the seed, to give the embryo a good start in life. In seed cones the nutritive tissue is formed before fertilization takes place, so if fertilization does not happen then the food supply, considerable in the case of cycads, is wasted. In flowering plants, nutritive tissue is not formed until a sperm has fused with an egg. In this case the second sperm delivered by a pollen tube fuses with a special nucleus associated with the egg, and the combined nucleus then rapidly divides

A symmetrical flower of *Ranunculus lyallii* with numerous petals, stamens, and carpels, the last attached to a dome-like axis at the center of the flower.

Asymmetrical flowers of *Tecomanthe speciosa* with partly fused sepals and petals, only four stamens, and a single style from a fusion of two carpels.

to form the nutritive tissue. The food stored in the nutritive tissue is often in the form of densely packed starch grains, but also as protein granules or oils. This is clearly a more efficient system than that of cone-bearing seed plants as nutritive tissue is only formed if needed.

The complexities of flower pollination

A difference from conifers is that most flowers are pollinated by insects, and some by birds or other animals (Proctor et al. 1996). This is considered to be more effective than wind pollination as the pollinating agents carry pollen directly from flower to flower, so there is no need to produce it in the wasteful quantities required for successful pollination by wind.

We can only speculate about how pollination by animals came about. Reproductive processes are energy demanding, so in flowers the pollen, ovules, and seeds are rich in nutrients and are therefore sought by plant-eating animals. A useful side effect of this, though, is that the animals unintentionally transport pollen from flower to flower. Flowering plants have evolved to maximize this benefit, to exact payment in a sense, for the food they provide. Initially, this food would have been pollen, sugary stigma exudates, and the less accessible ovules and seeds, and feeding on these parts would have interfered with the reproduction of the plants. Later, flowering plants evolved that were able to produce an abundant sugary fluid or nectar, similar to the stigma exudate, from flower parts modified as nectaries. The sole function of nectar in flowers is as a food for pollinators, both to encourage visits and to discourage the eating of reproductive structures. Some insects do take pollen as food, though there is always sufficient leftover for pollination. Bees, for instance, take nectar to make honey, and also pollen, which is a more balanced food as it contains proteins and amino acids as well as sugars.

Animal-pollinated flowers signal their presence to prospective pollinators by colored petals or other flower parts and by pleasant or in some cases, to us, unpleasant aromas. The flowers of some species, particularly those with small, open flowers crowded in groups, are visited by a wide range of pollinators. Others are visited by particular animal groups or in some cases, particular animal species. The advantage of this is that an exclusive pollinator or group of related pollinators actively seek out their target species, so pollination is more reliably achieved. This is a pattern in which long-tongued insects such as moths, butterflies, and bees, and long-beaked birds are strongly represented. The flowers concerned are often shaped to conform to the body of the pollinator, and the nectar is concealed at the bases of flowers of tubular form, such as those of fuchsias and the New Zealand *Phormium*, or at the ends of nectar-secreting spurs (in nasturtiums, *Tropaeolum*, for example), where it can only be reached by tongues or beaks of appropriate length. Nectar robbers though can circumvent this by pushing their tongues through or between the petal bases to gain access to the nectar. Even some exclusive pollinators do this to save themselves the bother of pushing into the flowers.

Tubular flowers of *Phormium cookianum*.

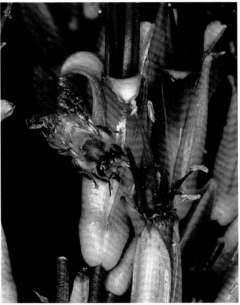

A bee with its tongue inserted between the petal bases of a *Phormium* flower to steal nectar.

The disadvantage of relying on just one pollinator, however, is that if the latter is reduced in numbers by unfavorable weather, many flowers will not set seed. If the pollinator is wiped out by disease or predation, then the plant can survive only if some individuals are able to self-fertilize or reproduce vegetatively.

In flowering plants the stamens that produce the sperm-forming pollen grains are usually in the same flowers as the ovary that encloses the ovules. Each ovule contains one egg. In a bisexual flower, then, the simplest way for pollination to take place is for the pollen of that flower to be deposited onto the stigma of the ovary or ovaries of the same flower, resulting in self-fertilization. Self-fertilization is obligate in a minority of species but also occurs from time to time in species that are normally cross-pollinated.

The buds of some self-pollinating flowers never open, and the pollen is deposited directly on the stigma of each flower. In other self-pollinating species the flowers do open but are smaller and less attractive than those of their cross-pollinating relatives, and the pollen is released near the stigmas.

Self-pollination is particularly common among annuals, especially the short-lived ephemerals. Habitual selfing is a quicker and more reliable method of producing abundant seed, before their short lives end, than crossing, which depends on pollinators that sometimes may be in short supply as a result of inclement weather or disease. Habitual selfing is less common among perennials as, if there is an unfavorable season with little or no seed production, that can be redressed in subsequent favorable seasons.

The offspring resulting from self-fertilization have the same genetic constitution as the parent, though there may be differences in the way the individual genes function as a result of chromosomal rearrangements during the cell divisions that form the sperms and eggs, and after a sperm fuses with an egg. After about 10 generations of selfing, the offspring are then essentially clones of the parents for generation after generation.

In other plants the offspring are exact clones even though the flowers fully open and appear quite normal. In many members of the citrus fruit family (Rutaceae), eggs in the ovules are formed in the normal way, but the cell that becomes the embryo is an ordinary cell of the ovule that does not fuse with a sperm. This cell has exactly the same genetic composition as the parent plant and becomes an exact replica of it. This type of reproduction, where an embryo is formed without fertilization, is termed apomixis.

In another, more widely occurring type of apomixis, the cell giving rise directly to a new plant is either the egg cell or a sister cell of the egg. This type of apomixis is common in a number of genera such as blackberry (*Rubus*), dandelion (*Taraxacum*), and hawkweed (*Hieracium*) in northern temperate regions, where thousands of apomictic clones have been named as separate species. In these genera the apomictic groups have arisen from sterile hybrids between sexually reproducing species. Only those hybrids that could reproduce by apomixis were able to clone into large populations. Occasionally, normal fertilization does take place within a cloned population, and because of chromosomal rearrangements during this process, the offspring are slightly but consistently different from their parents and thus mimic the kinds of differences seen between species. In the cloning forms of *Rubus,* and many other flowering plants exhibiting a similar pattern, seeds do not develop until the flower has been pollinated and a pollen tube has conveyed two sperms to an ovule, one of which fuses with a special cell, triggering the formation of nutritive tissue. So a sperm is not required to initiate an embryo but is required to initiate its food supply.

Plants can also clone or be cloned from organs other than those of the flower. This is known as vegetative reproduction. Artificial cloning by cuttings or, more recently, tissue culture is extensively practiced by horticulturists, and it is fortunate that such practices are not considered morally objectionable, as they are with animal cloning.

Many plants clone vegetatively as well as reproduce sexually, and some reproduce only vegetatively. With vegetative reproduction, plants are able to spread quickly into new ground when conditions are favorable. Gardeners are often told, "It is a very attractive plant, but if you don't control it, it will take over your whole garden."

A common method of vegetative reproduction is by horizontal stems that spread above (stolons) or below (rhizomes) the ground. The strawberry (*Fragaria*) provides a familiar example of spreading by stolons. At the tip of each stolon a new leaf rosette and a cluster of roots are formed. When this has anchored in the soil, it gives rise to a new stolon, and so on. The new rosettes function pretty much as independent plants and become fully independent when the stolons decay. The Japanese anemone (*Anemone hupehensis*) is an example of an aggressive rhizome spreader.

Some plants, including some trees, can produce leafy shoots from far-spreading roots as a method of cloning. Some succulents, such as *Kalanchoe fedtschenkoi*, form plantlets at the margins of the leaves, as does the nonsucculent fern *Asplenium bulbiferum* on the upper surfaces of its fronds.

A number of perennial herbaceous plants, the geophytes (Chapter 2), survive severe winters or seasonal drought by

A frond of *Asplenium bulbiferum* bearing plantlets.

dying down to food storage organs: bulbs with fleshy scale leaves; corms that are short, erect, swollen stems; rhizomes, which are short horizontal stems; and root tubers. These give rise to new leaves and flowers in the favorable season, and before they die down they form a number of new bulbs, corms, or rhizomes. Over the years this results in close clumps of plants that can be easily divided for propagation in gardens. In some, tubers form at the tips of long rhizomes, as in the potato (*Solanum tuberosum*), and more widely spaced new individuals are a result.

Another mode of vegetative reproduction is found in a wide range of plants. Some or all the flowers in an inflorescence are replaced by little bulbils or plantlets that drop or blow off and become independent plants. In alpine vegetation, where pollination may be inadequate when the weather is bad during the short growing season, a number of grasses and other herbaceous plants regularly produce plantlets in place of flowers, as do some weedy species of *Allium* at lower elevations. The large rosette succulent *Furcraea foetida*, native to South America, with its tall, much-branched flowering stalks, is perhaps the most striking example of this mode of reproduction.

Although self-pollination and vegetative cloning are widespread, the majority of flowering plants have evolved sometimes elaborate means of ensuring or encouraging cross-pollination. Why is cross-pollination so important? If a species is perfectly adapted to a particular habitat and climate it would seem that any variation would be a disadvantage and that selfing or cloning would be the norm. However, particularly over the past few million years, habitats have changed drastically many times, as a long series of glacial periods have alternated with much warmer interglacials. With such changes some unvarying species would have become extinct. In species that had at least some outcrossing, there would have been a residual, variable, outcrossing group, some plants of which would be suited to the new conditions. With continuing trends toward hotter or colder, wetter or drier, there would be a stepwise selection of variants of variants deriving from the original species.

Part of an inflorescence of *Furcraea foetida* in which flowers have been replaced by plantlets.

Variable outcrossing species are also better able to cope with fungal diseases and herbivores, which themselves vary. An outcrossing plant species may be susceptible to a particular variant of a fungal disease. If conditions are favorable for the fungus, most of the plants may die, but there are likely to be some that have resistance and so the species is saved from extinction. If later the new version of the plant species is susceptible to a new variant of the fungus, the game begins again.

Another disadvantage of long-term selfing arises when a particular site or gene on a chromosome undergoes a change or mutation. Although sometimes a mutation may improve the fitness of a plant to a particular habitat, the change generally results in the mutated gene's malfunctioning in greater or lesser degree. As there are always two chromosomes of each type, one from each parent, a normal gene on one chromosome, which matches a mutated gene on the other, often dominates and suppresses its faulty partner. In an inbreeding species, however, the chance of a plant's inheriting a double dose of a faulty gene is quite high. The result can be lethal, or if not the plant may exhibit impaired growth. On the other hand, in an outcrossing species the chance that a plant with a faulty gene will cross with an unrelated plant with the same faulty gene is very remote.

Invariability is the best recipe for a species to expand its populations in its preferred habitats, but at least some variability is insurance for long-term survival should these habitats change or disappear. This is why flower modifications for cross-pollination are found in so many plant families. Such modifications are known as cross-pollination mechanisms, and it is sometimes wrongly assumed that they all ensure that only cross-pollination takes place. To illustrate that this is not always so, consider *Iris*. The flower of *Iris* is very distinctive as the styles have three branches, each of which is similar in color and form to a petal. The underside of each petaloid style is closely pressed to a true petal. At the tip of a petaloid style, on its underside, there is a stigma, which covers the upper surface of a membranous flap. The latter is attached in such a way that when an insect pushes its head between the style arm and petal, the flap folds back, exposing the stigmatic surface. If the insect has come from a flower of another plant of the same species and picked up pollen, some of it will be deposited on the stigma, and cross-pollination will result. When the insect pushes its head farther in, so that its tongue can reach the nectar, its head will encounter the stamen pressed up against the style arm and pick up pollen. The action of backing out of the flower will close the membranous stigma flap, so self-pollination is unlikely to happen. However, if the same insect then moves to a different

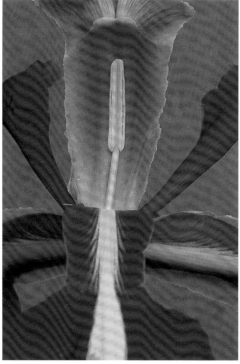

An *Iris* flower with one petal pulled down, away from a petaloid style, revealing a large stamen and above its tip the small membranous flap that is stigmatic over its upper surface.

style in the same flower or to a different flower on the same plant, self-pollination will result. The insect may visit several flowers on the same plant before moving on to another plant, so self- may outnumber cross-pollinations.

Other plants have different devices. In flowers of some species the stamens are mature and release pollen some time before the style extends and the stigmas are receptive (for example, *Pelargonium*). Once all the pollen is gone, the stamens move away from the elongating style. An insect bringing pollen from one plant to another will bring about cross-pollination if it settles on a flower at the receptive-stigma stage. If there is sufficient pollen still adhering to the insect from the first plant and it then visits a few more stigma-receptive flowers, further cross-pollinations will result. However, an insect is likely to self-pollinate any stigma-receptive flowers it visits if it has visited a pollen-stage flower on the same plant first. Strangely, it has been found that most species with this pattern of reproduction are self-incompatible, that is, the stigmas and styles reject self-pollen. As this effectively excludes selfing, it is difficult to understand what purpose the time difference between pollen and stigma maturation could possibly have. One suggestion is that if maturation coincided in time, small stigmas might be so covered with incompatible self-pollen that pollen from other plants would have no access to them (Lloyd and Webb 1986).

In the *Pelargonium* flower on the right, the anthers are releasing pollen and the style is still short. On the left, the anthers have shriveled and the several stigmas have spread apart from each other and are receptive.

A smaller number of species of some genera have a similar but reverse system with the stigmas receptive before the stamens release their pollen. In most of these, however, the plants are self-compatible. Once again, this mechanism brings about only some cross-pollination.

The most elaborately modified flowers of all are those of orchids. The often striking forms, colors, and sometimes the fragrances of these flowers make them much admired and widely cultivated. Although the parts of the flowers vary widely in size and shape, they mostly follow the same basic pattern: six flower segments (sepals and petals) of which the lowermost at maturity is modified as a landing stage or labellum for pollinators and, at the center of each flower, a less conspicuous but very distinctive structure called the column. This is a fusion of a style and stigma with a single functional stamen. The anthers, which form the pollen, are always situated above the stigma on the column, and the flowers are so arranged that the pollinator goes past the stigma first and deposits any pollen it may have, and then past the anthers, where pollen (in masses called pollinia) adheres to the insect before it leaves the flower.

Again, there can be selfing between different flowers of the same plant, but because of the stigma–anther arrangement in orchids and the pollen being mostly dispersed in sticky clumps, it might be assumed that pollination of an orchid flower by its own pollen would be virtually impossible. This is not always so. In some orchids, if no pollinator visits then the flowers can self-pollinate by the pollinia falling onto the stigma or by pollen tubes penetrating down to it. In the chlorophyll-lacking genus *Gastrodia*, it is even reported that in *G. cunninghamii* of New Zealand the tip of the column curves over to place the pollinia against the stigma. This has also been reported for orchids in other parts of the world. Some orchids always self-pollinate. Most orchids, though, are pollinated by a wide range of insects and birds, and the adaptations of their flowers relative to the pollinators are equally varied.

Pterostylis is an orchid genus with about 150 species in Australia, New Guinea, New Caledonia, and New Zealand. The flowers are distinctive in having green and white segments that are often drawn out into long, pink to red, antenna-like tips. The upper sepal and two petals are aggregated into downward-curving hoods, hence the common name greenhood

A close view of the center of a flower of the orchid *Zygopetalum*. The labellum leads up to the column. The anther cap has been removed to reveal the two pollen masses, or pollinia. The stigma is hidden in the cavity below the anther.

A cut-open flower of *Pterostylis banksii* in side view. The vertical labellum is on the left. It has a stalk-like prolongation below its point of attachment, which is brush-like at its tip. This stalk may prevent the labellum from swinging in too far. The column is on the right with the swelling of the stigma partway up, and at the top, one of the two wings and the yellow pollinia.

A *Pterostylis banksii* flower viewed from below, showing the protruding tip of the labellum at center.

orchids. The pollinators are ants and small species of the fly group of insects (Diptera), and often a species is pollinated by only one species of pollinator. The labellums of *Pterostylis* flowers are sensitive to touch, and when a pollinator lands on one it quickly swings upward from a more or less horizontal to a vertical position. The pollinator is thus contained in a tube formed by the labellum and two wings, one on each side of the column, and if it has brought pollinia from another flower, these will stick to the stigma. The only way out for the insect is to clamber up the column, where it picks up pollinia before escaping. Even with this ingenious system, cross-pollination only results if the pollinator then goes to a flower of a different plant.

The labellum returns to the horizontal position after an hour or so, and the trap is set again, so if no pollen was brought the first time, there is another chance. Perhaps the hooded form of the flowers prevents the labellums from being triggered by raindrops or other falling objects.

What attracts pollinators to *Pterostylis* flowers? There is no nectar reward, but some species have glands that secrete aromas similar to the pheromones produced by female pollinators to attract males of their species. This is deceitful but effective. The attraction of other species of *Pterostylis* is unclear. In New Zealand about half the 24 or so species of *Pterostylis* are self-pollinating, a much higher percentage than elsewhere. Some of these species are shared with Australia and their regular pollinators are not present in New Zealand, so only plants able to self, and their progeny, have been able to survive. *Pterostylis* also reproduces vegetatively by short to long rhizomes that enlarge into food-storing tubers.

A wide range of other orchids, unrelated to *Pterostylis*, also attract male pollinators. They are more specialized in this respect because as well as giving off odors similar to those of the females of the species, they resemble them in form and coloration. The males attempt to copulate with the orchid flowers (pseudocopulation), and if the pollinator has come from another flower of the same species, pollination is achieved. The pollinators are mostly bees and wasps. This phenomenon was first observed in North African and European orchids of the genus *Ophrys* but is now known in unrelated genera in eastern Australia and South Africa, so the deceit has evolved a number of times. Orchids in general, however, do provide a food reward, mostly nectar, for visitors.

The Orchidaceae is not the only family to include species that deceive pollinators by offering a reward that is not delivered. In the other families that stand out in this respect there are species that attract certain flies and wasps that normally lay their eggs in rotting flesh, dung, or fungus fruiting bodies. The flowers that attract these pollinators exude appropriate odors but provide no sustenance for developing larvae.

In the arum lily family (Araceae) the "flowers" are actually inflorescences. What appears to be a single large petal is in fact a modified leaf, the spathe, which partly encloses a central column (for example, in *Philodendron*). The column in most aroids has a zone of small, crowded female flowers, reduced to ovaries and stigmas, at the base and above that a zone of equally reduced and crowded male flowers, which may extend right to the tip. Sometimes the upper end of the column is finger-like and sterile. In some particularly foul-smelling species of *Arum* the spathe is a dark, meaty red, often blotched with white. In other species it is pale to white, so these have to rely solely on their odors to attract pollinators.

A *Philodendron* cultivar with a bright red spathe. The crowded male flowers are on the exposed part of the column. The female flowers are hidden by the lower part of the spathe.

The unpleasant odors are only produced during the first day of opening, which is when the stigmas of the female flowers are receptive. Beetles or flies attracted to the inflorescences land on the open upper part of the spathe or on the tip of the column. Both these parts are extremely slippery, and the insects fall down into the lower tube-like part of the spathe. Larger insects are stopped by a zone of bristles, but smaller ones tumble through right to the bottom. If some of the insects have brought pollen from another flower, then during their scrambling around some of this will attach to the stigmas. The stigmas soon shrivel, so self-pollination cannot take place when pollen is later released to shower down on the trapped insects. On the second day the bristles shrivel and the unrewarded pollinators escape, bearing good loads of pollen. During the first day of opening, the columns generate much heat, probably not for the comfort of the pollinators but rather to maximize evaporation of the compounds providing the odors.

The most spectacular of the aroids, *Amorphophallus titanum*, has a similar pollination system. This species comes from Malaya and is remarkable for the great size of the inflorescence, up to 2 m (6 1/2 feet) high and about 1 m (39 inches) wide, as well as for the repulsive smell, which has led to the common name corpse flower.

Species of Dutchman's-pipe (*Aristolochia*, of the Aristolochiaceae) have smelly "trap flowers" that are even more elaborate than those of the Araceae.

Stapelia (of the Apocynaceae, including Asclepiadaceae), illustrated on page 99, is a cactus-like genus of southern Africa. The wide, shallow flowers are often meat red, with long hairs giving a resemblance to the skin of mammals. Again, the odors given off are like those of rotting meat or dung. Pollinators such as blowflies lay their eggs near the center of a flower, where they pick up the sticky pollen masses typical of this family. One of the most notable carrion flowers is that of the strange parasite *Rafflesia* (Rafflesiaceae), shown on page 55.

Flowers that attract the small flies known as fungus gnats give off a mushroom aroma and sometimes have structures that resemble a fungus. In *Arisarum proboscidium* of the Araceae, the top of the column is enlarged into a spongy white mass that looks very like fungal tissue. Fungus gnats lay their eggs in this tissue and often fall from the slippery inner surface of the spathe to the base of the column, where they may bring about pollination. *Aristolochia arborea* takes fungal mimicry even further. Here there is a structure standing above the entrance to the trap, which resembles a mushroom, complete with gills beneath the cap. Fungus gnats try to lay eggs on the gills, but these are so slippery that they often lose their grip and fall into the trap.

In contrast, however, there are two well-known cases in which particular insects lay their eggs in the flowers of particular plants—yuccas and figs—with a successful result for both parties. Yucca moths, which are mostly species of *Tegeticula*, pollinate just one species of *Yucca* (Agavaceae) or sometimes a group of related species. A female yucca moth enters a large, typically only partly open, yucca flower, climbs up several anthers, and gathers pollen, which it shapes into a lump and carries to a flower in another inflorescence. At the pollen stage the stigmas of a flower are no longer receptive, so it seeks out a flower where they are. It then pushes its ovipositor into the ovary, laying one egg in each of the three compartments, and moves to the group of three stigmas at the top and deposits the pollen. Fertilization follows, and the ovary enlarges and the ovules develop into seeds. The moth eggs hatch into larvae, which feed on some of the developing seeds. Before the seeds are fully mature the larvae emerge and change into pupae in the ground. Adult moths appear in spring when the yuccas are coming into flower. Some other small moths take advantage of the yucca moths' efforts and also lay eggs in *Yucca* ovaries but provide no service in return.

Fig wasps are an even more complex story. The genus *Ficus* (Moraceae), which includes trees and vines, is a large genus of about 800 species throughout the tropics with some species in warm temperate regions. The very small male, female, and neuter (sterile female) flowers are crowded on an axis, which, in the course of development, essentially turns inside out, forming a flask-like structure, or syconium, lined with flowers. The syconium opens to the outside by a small terminal opening, which is partly blocked by small scales. It matures into the distinctive fig fruit.

In most cases a species of wasp and a species of fig have an exclusive relationship. There are several different patterns, but probably the simplest is where there are two types of syconium borne by different trees. In one type there are neuter flowers and male flowers with the latter grouped around the exit from the syconium. A visiting, fertilized female wasp pushes its way into the syconium and deposits one egg into each of several neuter flowers, as well as a drop of a secretion that stimulates the ovary of the flower to enlarge into a gall, which provides food for the larva. This achieved, the female wasp dies. The larvae develop into male and female wasps. The rather stunted males emerge first, bore into the ovaries occupied by the females, fertilize them, then die. The females emerge when the male flowers are releasing pollen and pick up pollen as they push their way out of the syconium. If a female then goes to the second type of syconium on a different tree, which contains only female flowers, it will pollinate those flowers, and seeds will be formed. If it goes to another syconium of the first type, it will lay eggs in the neuter flowers and the cycle will begin

A syconium of *Ficus dammaropsis*.

again. In other figs the two types of syconium are found on the same tree, and in some there is only one type of syconium, enclosing male, female, and neuter flowers.

The preceding examples are samplings from a kaleidoscope of patterns where most of the species are both self- and cross-pollinated. We now turn to the opposite extreme, from the exclusively or predominantly selfing or cloning species we first considered to those where only cross-pollination is possible.

Where there are male and female flowers on different plants, a pattern known as dioecism or dioecy, cross-pollination is ensured. Perhaps 10% of the world's flowering species are dioecious with the highest percentages in tropical trees and the species of some isolated islands. Many families include some dioecious species, so the pattern has evolved many times.

In some cases the flowers appear to be bisexual, but the stamens of the female flowers do not produce viable pollen, and in the ovaries of male flowers the ovules abort. Mostly though, the nonfunctional stamens and ovaries are visibly reduced and in extreme cases are mere rudiments. A disadvantage of this pattern is said to be that only some plants can produce seeds. However, the comparable pattern in higher animals seems to work very well and even leads to problems of overpopulation from time to time. Dioecious species would also seem to be at a disadvantage in spreading to new localities. A single seed would not be able to found a new population. This might not apply to berry-fruited, dioecious plants, however. Birds usually swallow a number of berries, each of which may contain a number of seeds, so a single bird could deposit a group of seeds of such a species with a good chance that both male and female plants would be represented.

Some dioecious plants are wind-pollinated, but most are insect-pollinated. Male flowers are often larger and showier than the females. It is suggested that pollinators would tend to visit male flowers first and then carry pollen to the female flowers.

Two other patterns are related to dioecy, but in both some self-pollination occurs. In gynodioecy, populations of the species exhibiting the pattern have some plants with female flowers and the others with bisexual flowers. As the female flowers can only cross-pollinate and the bisexual flowers may cross- or self-pollinate, cross-pollination probably predominates. Gynodioecious species are found in many families. Monoecy is where there are male and female flowers only, as in dioecy, but they occur in separate clusters on the same plants. Only a few plant groups have this condition, though they can be conspicuous in the northern hemisphere where a number of monoecious tree species dominate large areas of vegetation. Wind pollination is the rule, and the small flowers are crowded in erect spikes or hanging catkins.

Wind-pollinated trees, mostly of the northern hemisphere, including beeches (*Fagus*), birches (*Betula*), and oaks (*Quercus*), are monoecious, as is the sedge genus *Carex* and a number of wind-pollinated aquatic plants. In many monoecious species, because the stigmas of the female flowers are receptive before the male flowers release their pollen, some cross-pollination is ensured, though self-pollination must also take place. Among cone-bearing seed plants, the conifers are predominantly monoecious, but with some dioecy. Cycads are entirely dioecious, though some individual cycads are known to have switched sex following trauma. *Ginkgo* is dioecious, with the sex of individuals controlled by a pair of sex chromosomes, as in humans.

There is no visual clue to a second and more common means of ensuring cross-pollination known as self-incompatibility. In self-incompatible plants, pollen of a plant is unable to fertilize the ovules of the same plant and often of its close relatives. Essentially, self-pollen is rejected by the stigma and style as a result of some chemical interaction. Sometimes the pollen grain is prevented from forming a pollen tube by the stigma; sometimes a pollen tube is formed but aborts in the style. More rarely, the pollen tube reaches an ovule and the ovule aborts. Self-incompatibility is widespread but it has not yet been quantified on a world basis. It is estimated that one-third of the flora of the British Isles is self-incompatible. Self-incompatibility is superior to dioecy in that all plants are capable of producing seeds.

Another pattern involving self-incompatibility, known as heterostyly, is puzzling. It has arisen in a number of families and is characterized by at least two different types of flower borne by different plants. In one type of flower the style is short, and the stigma is situated well below the anthers—a thrum flower. In the other type of flower the arrangement is reversed: the style is long and the stigma is in the position of the anthers in the first type of flower, and the anthers are in the position of its stigma—a pin flower.

The suggestion is that a pollinator visiting a pin flower would pick up pollen on its head, and if it then went to a thrum flower that pollen would be transferred from its head to the stigma and cross-pollination would be achieved. In the thrum

An alder, *Alnus glutinosa*, with hanging catkins of male flowers (right) and cone-like fruits of female flowers of the previous season.

flower, the pollen would be picked up much farther back on the pollinator's body and could only be transferred to pin flowers, and again cross-pollination would result. Some books state, or imply, that this system makes self-pollination impossible; others are more cautious and assert that though self-pollination is unlikely, it is not impossible.

The best-known example of heterostyly is the primrose (*Primula vulgaris*) and its relatives. The petals are fused together and in their lower parts form a narrow tube. In thrum flowers there is a conspicuous ring of anthers at the mouth of the tube, and the stigma is situated about halfway down; in pin flowers the anthers are about halfway down, and the prominent stigma is at the mouth of the tube.

A pollinator that comes first to a *Primula* pin flower pushes past the stigma at the entrance and, as it reaches down to the nectar at the base of the tube, picks up pollen on its head from the anthers deep within. As it backs out from the flower, what is to prevent self-pollen getting on the stigma? If the pollinator then goes to a different plant with thrum flowers, when it pushes through the anthers at the entrance it would pick up pollen from them on its head. On its head, then, it should have a mixture of pollen of the flower it is visiting as well as of the flower on another plant that it has come from. If this is the case then when its head encounters the stigma deep within the flower it is visiting, why do both self- and cross-pollination not result? Yet a study has shown that this cross-pollination system is more than 90% successful. The pollen grains of pin and thrum flowers can be distinguished. Those of pins are smaller than those of thrums, and it was found most of the pollen on each stigma was from a flower of the other type. All that is puzzling enough, but it has become even more so since it has been discovered that the great majority of species with this cross-pollination system, involving different flower types, are self-incompatible. The latter ensures that self-pollination cannot happen, so what is the point of having different flower types?

An opened thrum flower of *Primula vulgaris* on the left with a short style and the anthers at the mouth of the petal tube, and a pin flower on the right with a long style and the anthers partway down the petal tube.

In the preceding account of pollination mechanisms and methods of cloning without pollination, we have sampled a cross section of a bewildering array of patterns. Every possible means of ensuring successful reproduction, as well as survival in changing environments, seems to have been explored. Many flowering species employ several modes of reproduction in keeping with adage, "Don't put all your eggs in one basket." To give one example, the common violet (*Viola*) produces sweet-smelling flowers in spring. They are mostly visited by hoverflies with long proboscises that are able to reach the nectar in the quite long spur at the top of the flower. During summer and into fall a quite different type of flower is formed near the ground, where it is completely hidden by the foliage. These flowers never open and pollinate themselves. Quite large purplish capsules develop, packed with seeds. More seeds are produced in this way than by the insect-pollinated flowers, though at least some seeds of the latter, resulting from cross-pollination, provide some variability. The violet also spreads vegetatively by rooting stolons, forming extensive mats to the exclusion of other plants.

The pollinators

Pollination by animals predominates among flowering plants, but even in the more ancient cone-bearing seed plants, though wind pollination is the rule for conifers, insect pollination by beetles and moths is common among the cycads and the unusual Gnetales—*Gnetum,* which includes tropical vines, and the mostly desert-dwelling *Ephedra* and *Welwitschia mirabilis* (the last shown on page 97)—thought by some to be closely related to the ancestors of flowering plants. So when flowering plants first appear in the fossil record, during the Cretaceous period about 130 million years ago, insect pollinators of cone-bearing seed plants probably already existed and could have added pollen and sugary stigmatic secretions of flowers to their menu.

The ancestral flowering plants were quite diverse, and descendants of some of them exist today. They included water lilies, true lilies, the *Magnolia* family and relatives, saxifrages and related plants, and plane trees (*Platanus*). The latter are wind-pollinated, and if it is true that insect pollination was the original state for flowering plants, then the less common wind pollination must have originated quite early.

The insect fauna in the Cretaceous was less diverse than now, and highly specialized pollinators had not yet evolved. Pollinators would have been mostly unspecialized beetles and short-tongued flies and wasps. The fossil record of beetles goes back to about 100 million years before flowering plants came on to the scene, and they are now perhaps the largest group of organisms with about 350,000 species named and doubtless many others that have not been described. Some of the descendants of the earliest flowering plants, such as species of *Magnolia* and related genera and some water lilies, are still pollinated by beetles.

At the end of the Cretaceous, about 65 million years ago, came the extinction of the dinosaurs. A number of groups of cone-bearing seed plants also disappeared, but the flowering plants do not seem to have been much affected. Partly as a result of reduced competition from the former and of moister world climates, the flowering plants evolved rapidly over subsequent geological periods to attain the world dominance and the almost bewildering diversity we witness today.

Insects, too, have diversified extensively during this time, partly as a result of interactions with flowering plants. The flowers of some plants retained the simple form of their Cretaceous ancestors, which were open to many different visitors in search of food, and radially symmetrical with numerous sepals, petals, stamens, and ovaries, with no fusion between those parts (as in those of *Ranunculus*, shown on page 219). Among present-day plants, such as the magnolias, many of these primitive features have been retained. However, a number of new families of flowering plants arose with more specialized flowers where pollination is achieved more reliably by equally specialized pollinators. The flowers tend to have relatively few parts as well as fusion between the parts, particularly the sepals and petals (as in those of *Tecomanthe*, shown on page 220). The tubular form is often asymmetrical with an upper and lower lip, the larger lower one functioning as a landing stage for the pollinator. The flowers are shaped and the parts are arranged so that a particular group of pollinators, or even a particular pollinator, will bring about pollination most of the time. Nectar is often hidden deep within the flower so that it can only be reached by more advanced insects with long tongues, such as long-tongued wasps and bees, butterflies and moths, and long-proboscid flies, as well as long-beaked birds that evolved as pollinators more recently. The concealment of nectar is to prevent smaller insects, which are unlikely to bring about pollination, from stealing it.

Insects

Beetles were probably the first flower pollinators, but they now play a minor role. They seem not to have very discriminating color vision, so the flowers they pollinate are often pale or drab in color, and the beetles are attracted by odors instead. Some beetle flowers have reasonably pleasant fruity aromas and are visited for food; others have unpleasant rotting meat or dung smells and are visited in the vain hope of finding a suitable site for laying eggs. Magnoliaceae and other related primitive families, and water lilies, are mostly visited for pollen, but in some cases the beetles also eat reproductive structures and the destruction they cause often outweighs the gain from any pollination that may take place. In *Calycanthus* and some other genera there are sugary outgrowths that divert the beetles' attention from the more important reproductive parts. Evil-smelling flowers visited by some beetles include those of some species of the arum lily family (Araceae). Some groups of pollinating beetles originated during the expansion of flowering plants, and some of their species, as well as species of older beetle groups, take pollen and nectar from small open flowers crowded in dense, often flat heads, as in the carrot family (Apiaceae) and the daisy family (Asteraceae), whose dense heads of small flowers simulate single flowers.

The fly group of insects is large and diverse. Most flies have short tongues and take nectar and sometimes pollen from heads of small open flowers or short tubular flowers, where they must often compete with small beetles. The flower colors attractive to flies are yellow, pink, or white with sweet or, to our noses, often sickly sweet fragrances. Flies looking for a site to lay their eggs are attracted to brown to purplish flowers smelling of meat or dung. Some flies have evolved longer proboscises (mouthparts) and pollinate blue to purple flowers where the nectar is concealed in quite long tubes. These include bee flies and hoverflies. Some species of the latter are unusual in that they feed on the pollen of wind-pollinated grasses.

The related moths and butterflies are important flower pollinators. While their caterpillar larvae feed on a wide range of plant tissues, including leaves, stems, and buds, the adults ingest liquids only, particularly the nectar of flowers. They have long tongues, which are coiled into tight spirals when not in use. The flowers they pollinate have equally long tubes or nectar spurs, the record for the latter being 40 cm (16 inches) in *Angraecum sesquipedale,* an orchid in Madagascar pollinated by a hawk moth with a tongue of similar length.

Butterflies are mostly active during the day and are notable for the bright and attractive coloring of their wings. The flowers they visit in temperate regions are mostly

The flower-like inflorescence of an oxeye daisy (*Leucanthemum vulgare*) with disk florets at the center and ray florets, simulating petals, surrounding them. The visitor is a tiny longhorn beetle.

A blue moon butterfly visiting a flower.

blue or purple to deep pink and yellow, but many visit red flowers in warmer parts of the world. The fragrances of butterfly-pollinated flowers are sweet and pleasant.

Moths are mostly active at dusk or on moonlit nights, so it is not surprising that the flowers they visit are white or pale in color, making them easily located in the dim light. Their fragrance, too, can be extremely strong, so although sweet, it can be overpowering. In many cases the scent is only produced at night.

Bees and their relatives are major players in flower pollination, and of these the bees are especially important. They are red-green color-blind but are attracted to yellow, blue, purple, and ultraviolet flowers, or flowers with combinations of these colors. Often, there are stripes or lines of dots of contrasting colors leading the bees from the entrance to the nectar. These are known as honey guides and can be compared to the lines of lights that guide landing aircraft. Sometimes there are ultraviolet honey guides, visible to bees but not to us. Bee flowers are sweetly perfumed with a range of different scents.

Some bees have short tongues and mostly visit small open flowers, often in company with small flies and beetles. These are known as solitary bees, and they feed on both pollen and nectar. The social bees are a larger group, living in colonies that often occupy elaborately constructed nests. Both nectar and pollen are gathered and taken back to the nest in a nectar sac within the body of the bee and pollen sacs on its legs. These bees

Dodecatheon flowers with reflexed petals and the stamens in a conical arrangement for buzz pollination.

have long tongues, though not attaining the lengths of those of moths and butterflies, and pollinate larger flowers that have concealed nectar and petals fused into a tube, often two-lipped. Some bees only pollinate one plant species, locating the flowers by following the trail of specific scents. A number of honeybees and bumblebees are also skilled at stealing nectar without entering the flowers; they puncture the base of a flower or a nectar spur with their tongues.

Honeybees have one remarkable ability. One bee can encounter a plant or group of plants in flower. After collecting nectar and pollen, it flies back to the nest or hive and does a special little dance, which tells the other bees the direction and distance of the site. The dancer will have picked up some of the scent of the flowers, so the others will also know the species of the plants before they fly en masse to find them.

Some bee-pollinated flowers have an unusual form. They generally hang downward, and their petals are strongly bent upward away from the other parts, revealing a small group of large anthers tightly pressed together into a conical shape. Plants with this form of flower include shooting stars (*Dodecatheon*), some solanums, and borage (*Borago officinalis*). Bumblebees cling to the cones and set up a vibration that causes the dry pollen to shower from the anthers onto their bodies. This is known as buzz pollination.

Wasps are less important than bees as flower pollinators. They are mostly predators of other insects and spiders, but a number also visit flowers for nectar and pollen. Their tongues are mostly short, so like flies they frequent small open flowers or those where the nectar is shallowly contained. As with bees, some wasps are solitary and others are social, the latter often building elaborate nests with many small compartments.

Some social wasps exhibit a similar though less specialized behavior to that described for honeybees. An individual wasp that finds a good concentration of suitable flowers behaves in an agitated fashion on its return to the nest, then leads other wasps to the site.

Ants look quite different from bees and wasps but are related to them, and though some of them pollinate flowers, they are mostly too small to pollinate many flowers. However, they are strongly attracted to nectar and other sugary substances. It is suggested that the primary purpose of extrafloral nectaries on twigs and leaves below the flowers in some species is to divert multitudes of ants from taking flower nectar without bringing about pollination.

Thrips are very small insects and are usually regarded as pests because they suck juices from plants. Some, however, pollinate flowers of tropical trees, including species of the families Dipterocarpaceae and Annonaceae. The flowers are very small, white, and fragrant. The thrips visit them for pollen (Turner 2001).

Birds

Birds were paid little attention in early studies of pollination as there are no bird pollinators in Europe or temperate Asia. But birds are important pollinators in central and southern Africa, southern Asia, Australasia, and the Americas. In the Americas the great majority are hummingbirds, which hover as they take nectar. They are mostly small, and the smallest can be mistaken for some of the larger hovering insects. The greatest diversity of hummingbirds is in the northern Andes, but they are present far to the south in South America, and in North America they migrate as far north as Canada. Bird pollinators belong to different families elsewhere in the world and cannot hover, so they must perch on nearby stems or flowers to take nectar. Apart from the parrots known as lorikeets, which visit flowers mostly for pollen, pollinating birds seek nectar only and obtain proteins by eating insects.

Some pollinating birds have quite long beaks, 3 cm (1 1/4 inches) in some hummingbirds. All have tongues at least partly tubular, often forked, with brush-like tips to lap up the nectar. Birds have little or no sense of smell, so bird flowers are scentless, but unlike most insects, birds can distinguish red from green, so many of the flowers they visit are bright red and contrast strongly with the background of leaves. This is a clear signal to birds that is lost on insects. Some bird flowers are bright yellow, or red and yellow, and sometimes bright green, giving effects similar to those of gaudy tropical parrots. In some cases what appear to be brightly colored petals are brightly colored leaves

Tubular, densely crowded *Aloe* flowers.

surrounding clusters of flowers. Notable here are poinsettias (*Euphorbia pulcherrima*), bougainvilleas, and some rosette bromeliads.

The relatively small amount of nectar supplied in insect flowers would not be sufficient to sustain larger birds, so bird flowers are mostly quite large and often tubular to contain an abundant supply. The flower parts, too, are often robust to withstand beaks and claws. As noted, bees often steal nectar. This is even more common in birds, whose hard-pointed beaks easily punch holes into nectar stores. Dense crowding of flowers, as in aloes, largely prevents this behavior.

Bats

Bats are flying mammals with many species concentrated in a warm climate zone extending from the equator to about 30° north and south, and sometimes beyond. Insects and fruits figure prominently in the diet of bats, but also nectar and pollen, and even blood in some species.

There are two main bat groups: megabats and microbats. Megabats are found in

Africa, southern Asia, Australasia, and on islands of the Pacific and include the flying foxes, which are large, attaining a wingspan of 1.8 m (nearly 6 feet) in *Pteropus samoensis*. Flying foxes mostly eat fruit, but other and somewhat smaller megabats are important pollinators. Microbats, some of which are only a few centimeters or an inch or more long, are widespread in the bat zone of the world, including the Americas, but only those in the latter region are flower pollinators.

Megabats have large eyes and good vision, so they locate objects by vision or smell though some species have a limited ability to echolocate. Microbats have poor vision, so they largely depend on their sense of smell and their remarkable echolocation ability to find flowers.

Like most moths, bats are active at night, so there are similarities in the flowers the two visit. Bat flowers are often white or pale in color, though they are sometimes shades of green and purple; they open late in the day and produce copious amounts of nectar and pollen during the night, as well as heavy scents that are musky or fruity rather than sweet.

Like bird-pollinated flowers, the parts of bat-pollinated flowers (for example, those of saguaro, *Carnegiea gigantea*, shown on page 90) are robust to cope with the claws of the bats. Some bat flowers are wide open and cup-like, and the bats cling to the lower part of the cup as their tongues lap up nectar. A well-known example of this type of flower belongs to the cup-and-saucer vine (*Cobaea scandens*), a tropical liane grown as an ornamental in some warm temperate localities. A quite different and strange type of flower fits the bat like a face mask as it hovers near the flower. A more common type is tubular with long, projecting stamens; included here are agaves, some cacti, and some species of the banana genus *Musa*.

Both for bats that have good eyesight and those that do not, flowers are locatable most easily if they are clear of the foliage. This is achieved by cauliflory, in which flowers are borne on the trunks or main branches of trees, or by the flowers having long stalks and the inflorescences long axes, so that they hang down into the space below the forest canopy.

Syzygium acre with flowers arising directly from the slender trunk. New Caledonia.

Other mammals

More recently, it has been realized that a number of small nonflying mammals are also pollinators. In many cases the flowers concerned are primarily adapted to pollination by birds or bats but provide sufficient nectar and pollen to be a useful food source for the mammals. However, it seems clear now that in Australia, southern Africa, and northern South America there are plants that are primarily adapted to pollination by small marsupials and/or rodents.

In Australia the small marsupials known as honey possums and sugar gliders both take pollen and nectar from a number of species of Myrtaceae and Proteaceae. In *Banksia* and *Dryandra* of the latter family it has been found that some species are adapted to bird pollination and others to marsupial pollination, and some are visited by both birds and marsupials. The marsupial-pollinated flower heads are dull in color and have a scent, so they are similar to those of bat-pollinated flowers. Some of the plant species with these characteristics have tufts of leaves at ground level and inflorescences also seated on the ground. Others are bushes with the inflorescences concealed within the crown of the shrub. Of other shrub species with completely exposed flower heads, some have brightly colored flowers and no scent, which suggests bird pollination, and others have features suggesting marsupial pollination. Only among the marsupials, particularly the honey possum, are there visible adaptations for nectar feeding. The honey possum has a slender tube-like snout and an extensible tongue, which is brush-like at the tip. The palate is transversely ribbed to scrape nectar and pollen from the tongue.

Banksia repens with leaves and a flower head arising from a short underground stem. Western Australia.

In South Africa a number of species of *Protea* are pollinated by mice. The flower heads of these species are wider and flatter than those pollinated by birds, drab in color, and have a bat-flower scent and abundant nectar. The flower heads are formed near the center of the bushes and near the ground, where they are readily accessible to the mice.

In cloud forest high in the Andes, species of *Blakea*, belonging to the mostly showy-flowered Melastomataceae, are pollinated by small rodents. The flowers are hidden among the foliage and have green petals. Pollen is released and nectar produced during the night, which is when they are visited by the rodents.

At much lower elevations in the tropical rain forest of the Andes, some trees are thought to be pollinated by primates (for example, *Pseudobombax tomentosum*, by monkeys) and marsupials (for example, *Mabea occidentalis*, by the red woolly opossum). The conspicuous flowers, with the nectar in shallow petal cups, are in stalkless clusters a little way back from the tips of leafless branches. The flowers on such a branch open all at once, providing a good nectar supply for the pollinators.

Lizards

Reptiles are not notable as pollinators, but a study in New Zealand has shown that some native geckos and skinks regularly visit the flowers of several native plants for their nectar and bring about pollination (Whitaker 1987). These flowers are also visited by birds and in some cases insects, so the lizards are not the sole pollinators.

Scaly grass flowers with large, dangling anthers.

Wind

The conifers among the cone-bearing seed plants, but only a minority of flowering plants, are wind-pollinated. The latter include a number of genera of northern temperate trees, grasses—and sedges and rushes of similar form —and a scattering of species and genera in many other families. In spring, when one sees clouds of pollen rising from wind-pollinated trees and puddles yellow-rimmed with pine pollen, it might be assumed that wind pollination must be very effective despite the great wastage. In fact, it seems it is fully effective for only relatively short distances and is successful only where the plants concerned dominate the vegetation over extensive areas, and individual plants are never far from others of their species. This is the case with the conifers in their vast forests in higher-latitude northern temperate regions, the wind-pollinated flowering trees at lower northern latitudes, and the grasses of prairies and steppes, again mostly in the northern hemisphere.

Wind-pollinated flowers are strikingly different from animal-pollinated flowers. They have no need to attract pollinators, so they are small, often crowded together, with petals or similar parts lacking or scale-like, and often brown. There is no nectar. The anthers of the stamens are large, producing abundant pollen, and the filaments are often long and slender so that the anthers dangle from the flowers where the breezes can readily shake out the pollen. The stigmas, too, are distinctive, being relatively large and often feathery, to sift pollen from the air.

Water

Only a few species of aquatic plants have their pollen transported by water (Chapter 5, under "Submerged plants," page 160).

Dispersal of seeds and fruits

Botanically speaking, a fruit does not have to be fleshy and edible. It is an enlarged, seed-containing ovary, which at maturity may be fleshy or dry. A dry fruit may remain closed, when it is often small and seed-like, or split open to release the seeds. The fruit may be derived from the ovary of a single carpel or from the fused ovaries of a group of carpels. In most cases there are as many compartments in a fruit as there are carpels involved.

Fleshy fruits are often referred to as berries, but botanically this term is reserved for fruits in which the seeds are free within the flesh. In other fleshy fruits called drupes, the inner layer of the ovary wall is hardened into a stone-like layer, as in plums, peaches, and other stone fruits. The single seed, enclosed by the stone, is known as the kernel.

Dry fruits can be derived from a single carpel, which at maturity splits open along the line where its two margins originally met and fused at the bud stage of the flower, to release the seeds. This is a follicle, and some consider it to be the most primitive type of fruit. It is found in a number of relatively primitive families such as the Magnoliaceae and Ranunculaceae. The legume of the Fabaceae and other families is a variation on this, where there is an opening along the midrib of the leaf-like carpel as well as the margins. Some dry fruits, called achenes, derived from a single carpel do not open and contain a single seed. An example of a plant with achenes is the buttercup (*Ranunculus*). Achenes look like and function as seeds. On the other hand, capsules are dry fruits derived from several fused ovaries. At maturity the capsules generally split into a number of segments, equal in number to that of the carpels, to release the seeds.

Some fruits are derived from more than just the ovaries. Where there is a tubular upgrowth enclosing the ovary in some flowers, then this becomes part of the fruit. Examples of this among fleshy fruits are those of the fuchsias, and among dry fruits, those of the huge daisy family (Asteraceae). The individual fruits of the daisies can be interpreted as a type of achene, which also looks like and functions as a single seed. Some-

A woody capsule of *Xanthostemon* (Myrtaceae) that has split into five segments to release the seeds.

Left: Open, woody follicles of an Australian waratah (*Telopea*, Proteaceae) with the hard styles still attached above. At flowering, the two margins are fused together, and they split apart at the fruiting stage to release the seeds. The indentations are where the seeds were attached.

times in these cases the sepals of the flower persist and are modified for dispersal in various ways.

The agents of seed dispersal

As with pollination, birds are also important seed dispersers over a wide latitudinal range. In the tropics, monkeys, bats, and other mammals play an important role, as do rodents more widely. There are even fruit- and seed-eating fish in seasonally flooded forests along the Amazon and, more commonly, in low swamp vegetation throughout the world. Although playing a major role in pollination, insects, with the exception of ants, are minor players in seed dispersal. Dispersal of light seeds or fruits by wind is most common in temperate and colder regions but can also be found in the moist tropics among some of the taller, wind-exposed trees and plants that colonize canopy gaps and other open places (van der Pijl 1982, Estrada and Fleming 1986). Buoyant seeds and fruits are transported by water in freshwater lakes and rivers, and along seacoasts. A few plants eject their seeds violently, over mostly short distances.

Birds

Seed-dispersing birds range from many small species at all latitudes, through larger tropical birds, including the strange toucan and the flamboyant birds of paradise, to some of the even larger, flightless ratites of the southern hemisphere, notably the cassowary.

Some seeds or fruits with attaching devices can be transported on birds' feathers, or in the case of sticky seeds, such as those of *Pittosporum* and mistletoes, on their beaks as well. External attachment is more effective with mammals, with their hairy or furry coats. However, there is one tree genus, *Pisonia,* widespread through the Pacific islands, that seems depend on external attachment to bird plumage for its dispersal. At maturity the small, narrow fruits exude a very sticky glue over their surfaces that traps smaller birds, leading to their death. Larger birds are discomforted, no doubt, but they are still able to fly and can transport the fruits with their many contained seeds for considerable distances.

A much commoner means of external transport of seeds by birds involves very small seeds, without attaching devices, from a wide range of swamp and water plants. Wading birds that frequent wet habitats pick up mud on their feet, or even in their plumage if they crash-land. Such mud samples often contain many small seeds from a

The bird-catching tree *Pisonia brunoniana* with a feather adhering to a very sticky fruit.

range of species. A number of these birds are migratory over great distances, including between the northern and southern hemispheres. It is not surprising then that many swamp plant species are found throughout the world.

However, the most important means of seed dispersal by birds, everywhere from tropical rain forests to polar tundra, is by internal transport. Birds swallow the seeds within the flesh of fruits, or in some cases swallow dry seeds, and later excrete them in their dung at a new location (as in mistletoes, for example, Chapter 1, under "Hemiparasites—Mistletoes and their relatives," page 62). To resist the digestive juices, the seeds may have hard coats, or in the case of drupes, the stone protects the seed. Some pigeons and other larger birds can swallow relatively large fleshy fruits with single large seeds or stones, or large, free seeds with fleshy coats. These large seeds pass through the birds, losing their edible parts en route. Other birds strip the seeds of their edible parts then drop them, or after their crops have performed a similar task, regurgitate them. How far the seeds get depends on where the bird enjoys its meal. Some studies have shown that seeds that have passed through birds, and other animals, have a higher germination rate than those that have not, so that is an additional benefit.

Some birds, including parrots and finches, feed directly on seeds and destroy them in the process. However, some of the seeds are dropped intact, though this does not get them far from the parent plant, and a few others are inadvertently swallowed intact and may later be deposited some distance away. There is a similar pattern with smaller granivorous birds of temperate grasslands, which eat the small seeds of grasses, sedges, and other plants. Seeds germinated from the droppings of such birds show that the small proportion of the seeds swallowed intact is sufficient for effective dispersal of the plants concerned.

Some pigeons, jays, rooks, and other birds that eat and destroy larger seeds are in the habit of storing some seeds in caches in the soil for winter use. They carry the seeds in their beaks or regurgitate them. Some seeds get dropped on the way, not all are eaten during winter, and some caches are not relocated by the birds, so this an effective means of dispersal, particularly since the seeds are effectively planted in the soil. Pines, beeches, oaks, and other trees are dispersed in this way.

Plants that are adapted for internal bird dispersal have specialized fruits or seeds that are similar to bird-pollinated flowers in having showy colors. Berries or drupes are often bright red, black, an intense shade of blue or purple, or contrasting combinations of these. Some fruits that open at maturity stand out because of their bright contrasting colors. In some species of *Pittosporum* the open capsule valves have a red lining and enclose a yellow sticky fluid in which the shiny black seeds are embedded. Some large seeds that attract birds have red, fleshy coats (for example, the conifer *Prumnopitys ferrugineus*) or are partly enclosed by red, fleshy arils (for example, *Alectryon excelsum*). Even here there is deceit by plants: in *Abrus* the seeds have no fleshy

Red berries of *Syzygium maire*. New Zealand.

An open, two-valved capsule of *Pittosporum cornifolium* with black seeds embedded in a sticky yellow fluid. New Zealand.

Blue-purple berries of *Lobelia physaloides*. New Zealand.

Each of the furry capsules of *Alectryon excelsum* splits transversely to reveal a shiny black seed embedded in a convoluted red aril. New Zealand.

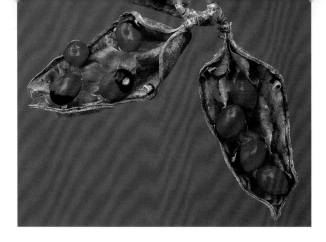

Open pods of *Abrus precatorius* with hard, smooth seeds, the red parts simulating arils and the black parts, enclosed seeds.

edible tissue at all. They are smooth and hard, and their upper two-thirds are bright red, simulating an aril, and the rest is jet-black, simulating an enclosed seed.

Mammals

Of seed-dispersing mammals, the bats, because of their ability to fly, poor vision in some, and nighttime foraging, are a special group. Fruit-eating bats are concentrated in the Old World, but some have also evolved in the New World. They cannot readily locate fruits by their color, so the fruits are inconspicuously green, yellowish, or whitish. The fruits generally have a strong odor of something fermenting or rancid, often similar to the bats' own odors, which enables them to be located at night. Obstacles in the way of the bats are reduced by the fruits' being borne on long stalks or stems hanging below tree foliage, as in the mango (*Mangifera*), or on the trunks of trees, as with some figs and many other species. Some smaller plants, too, have bat fruits, including some shrubby species of pepper (*Piper*), and wild bananas (*Musa*).

Bats generally take fruits back to their roosts, where they are safer from predators. With fruits with one or a few large seeds the fleshy tissue is eaten and the seeds discarded, whereas with fruits containing many small seeds, some of the seeds are spat out, and some of the rest pass through the bat unharmed.

Rodents, including mice, rats, and squirrels, eat seeds and destroy them, but as with some birds they also transport them and bury them for later use. Some of these seeds escape the sharp teeth of the rodents and eventually germinate. In temperate regions their main food supplies are acorns and large seeds of deciduous trees and conifers as well as the grains of grasses and small seeds. In the tropics, some squirrel species transport the acorns of tropical oaks and related genera, whereas others eat the flesh of fleshy fruits and discard the seeds. An interesting case is the Brazil nut (*Bertholletia excelsa*), in which the large seeds with their fleshy arils are contained in a woody fruit that can only be opened by the use of considerable force. A large rodent, the agouti, can open them, eats the arils, and buries the seeds as a reserve.

The mostly larger placental and marsupial mammals, except for primates, are also important seed dispersers, particularly the herbivores, but even some carnivores contribute by eating fruits from time to time. Fruit-eating non-primates do not have good color vision, so the larger fruits they favor are not visually conspicuous, but these mammals have a good sense of smell. However, the odors that attract them are often unpleasant to us. Because of their well-developed teeth, mammals mostly destroy seeds, but studies of their droppings show that a sufficient number get through unscathed.

The most notable of the mammal fruits is the durian (*Durio zibethinus*) of Southeast Asia. The large fruits when young are covered with heavy spines, presumably to prevent their being opened before they are ripe. When they are ripe they are green to brownish and so heavy that they often fall from the tree and break open. At this stage a strong and to most people repulsive smell is emitted, attracting mammals—from monkeys to elephants—from near and far to feast on the abundant white arils surrounding the seeds. Many people, if they can tolerate the smell, also find the durian delicious to eat.

Unlike birds, through which seeds can pass in half an hour to a few hours, mammals have long intestines and the passage takes at least a few hours, to weeks. Sometimes the seeds are in the gut so long that a few of them germinate and are then digested. This slow passage makes it more likely that the seeds will be deposited some distance from the parent plant.

The primates include monkeys and related animals such as ourselves. Unlike other mammals, primates have good color vision and a less well developed sense of smell, so they generally find their food visually. Most eat a wide variety of foods, of which fruits and seeds make an important contribution. Many of the fruits eaten by other animals are also consumed by primates, but some seem especially suited to them—ones that are large and hard, and contain large seeds embedded in fleshy tissue. With their fingers and teeth, primates are able to open these fruits to get at the edible interior. Mangosteen (*Garcinia mangostana*) fruits are an example, as well as large, indehiscent pods of the Fabaceae and several other families.

Transport of dry seeds and fruits attached externally to nonflying mammals is important for a minority of flowering plants. The species are mostly herbaceous and grow in open habitats such as tropical savannas and temperate grasslands, where small to large browsing mammals with hairy coats have long been the agents for transporting their seeds. These plants are generally regarded as weeds, and humans,

Durian (*Durio zibethinus*) fruits on sale in Singapore.

with land-clearing activities and domestic animals such as sheep and cattle, have greatly increased their ranges throughout the world. Small seeds are often abundant in mud sticking to the feet of terrestrial mammals and to the footwear of humans. Many weedy species have been transported far and wide by this means.

Other seeds and fruits have attachment devices. A number of small seeds produce a sticky mucilage when wet, including those of plantains (*Plantago*), some violet and rush species, and buffalo grass (*Paspalum*), in which the scales enclosing the seeds are very sticky even when dry. These seeds may attach to birds as well as mammals.

The seeds and seed-like fruits of other species have more elaborate modifications, mostly in the form of hooks and spines that can be uncomfortable or even painful for the unfortunate animals. Some of these plants are quite small, and some are familiar as weeds in gardens as well as in the wild. Species of *Galium* (cleavers or goosegrass) have slender trailing stems and small, rounded, seed-like fruitlets densely covered with small hooks that cling tenaciously, like Velcro, to clothing and fur. The fruitlets and associated scales of some grasses work their way into animal coats. The scales are sometimes hooked but are more often drawn out into slender thread-like awns that penetrate into

A close view of an *Uncinia uncinata* seed head, showing the distinctively hooked spines. New Zealand.

wool or woolen clothing. Many species of *Acaena* have four long spines at the top of the achene, each with a cluster of backward-curving hooks at the tip. These achenes, clustered together in rounded heads, attach themselves very effectively to clothing and can sometimes be a great problem for sheep farmers. In the largely southern hemisphere *Uncinia*, related to the more widespread sedge genus *Carex*, there is a single long spine attached to the side of the fruitlet that ends in a hook shaped like a shepherd's crook. Hairs can slip easily into the latter but become firmly wedged, a painful experience for those with hairy legs. In the tropics, some single-seeded pods of legumes have spines that penetrate into the feet of animals.

The sesame family (Pedaliaceae in the broad sense, including Martyniaceae) of the Americas, southern Asia, Australia, and subtropical Africa comprises quite large herbs with relatively large woody capsules impressively armed with spines and hooks. The latter attach to large browsing mammals and scatter seeds as the animals move around. Perhaps the most remarkable of these capsules are those of the mule-grab (*Proboscidea fragrans*) of Texas. The capsules, which fall to the ground when they are mature, have two, long, upward-curving horns. When a mule or other animal treads on such a capsule it tips upward and the sharp horns firmly attach to the leg, assisted by small hooks elsewhere. The capsules also attach to the tails of horses and mules when they brush against them.

Reptiles

It has been suggested that in the Age of Reptiles that preceded the present Age of Mammals, reptiles, including herbivorous dinosaurs, would have been dispersal agents for plants with seeds with fleshy coats. In confirmation of this, dinosaur fossils have been found with large, intact, fossil seeds from cone-bearing plants in their stomachs. Fossil dinosaur droppings also contain similar seeds. Descendants of the cone-bearing seed plants of that period, such as the cycads, still have large seeds with fleshy coats, but these are sometimes dispersed by large flightless birds such as the emu, not by reptiles. At the present day, though reptiles are no longer major players in seed dispersal, they probably are more significant than has been thought in the past.

On the Galápagos Islands, giant iguanas feed on cactus and other fruits, and the seeds in their droppings are viable. Tortoises have been noted to eat fallen fruits in several parts of the world, and in Malaysia they have been reported as eating the fruits of a swamp palm and some durian species. In the latter plants, the fruits are situated near the ground.

The same study that showed that some New Zealand species of geckos and skinks are pollinators also showed that they disperse the seeds, contained in berries, of other species. The seeds of some of these plants are also distributed by birds, but some may be primarily if not exclusively distributed by the lizards. The plant species concerned are of the distinctive divaricate form common in New Zealand, small-leaved and excessively twiggy, with the twigs densely interlaced (Chapter 1, under "Juvenile forms of vines and other plants," page 27). They have an abundance of small flowers and, later, berries, mostly borne toward the center of the shrubs. The berries would not be easily seen by birds but would be readily accessible to lizards moving around on the ground beneath the shrubs.

Insects

The only insects that play a significant role in seed dispersal are the ants. Ant seeds all have often conspicuous outgrowths known as elaiosomes, or oil bodies, that are derived from a wide range of seed and single-seeded fruit parts, including stalks and coats. The elaiosomes contain oils of various kinds, which are highly favored by ants as an energy-rich food. As ants are small, the seeds, too, are mostly small and mostly borne by shrubs and herbs in both temperate and tropical regions. Ants carry the seeds to their nests, dropping some on the way and also stopping to eat some of the oil bodies, then discarding their seeds.

A surprising range of plants have seeds with oil bodies, including species of *Primula*, forget-me-nots (*Myosotis*), *Veronica*, *Viola*, the sedge genus *Carex*, and a number of grasses. Familiar shrubs in the group of ant-dispersed plants are broom (*Cytisus scoparius*) and gorse (*Ulex europaea*).

Wind

A number of seeds or dry, one-seeded fruits are dispersed by wind. The simplest situation is where the seeds are minute and dust-like, so light that they can be carried by the winds for tremendous distances. They are produced in large numbers in capsules. All the species of the very large orchid family have dust-like seeds, but a number of other families are represented more modestly, including species of *Rhododendron* and some insectivorous (*Nepenthes* and *Sarracenia*) and parasitic (*Balanophora*) plants. The minute seeds of these plants also increase their buoyancy by having thin seed coats extended into wings of various shapes. Other unspecialized seeds much larger than these, though still small, and even quite large seeds can be transported great distances by the violent winds of storms and by the powerful uplifting force of localized whirlwinds or larger cyclones.

Another means of dispersal of unspecialized seeds is found in plants known as tumbleweeds, which, though having become part of the folklore of the Wild West, are also found widely distributed in open, drier places elsewhere in the world. The species are herbaceous and often annual, and when their capsules are ripe the whole plant (or in some just the inflorescences) dries up and becomes detached. If these tumbleweeds do not already have a spherical shape they curl up into that form. With a steady wind the tumbleweeds bounce across the open landscape, scattering seeds as they go, or release the seeds when they are moistened by rain.

The tumbleweed known from ancient times is the rose of Jericho (*Anastatica hierochuntica*) of the mustard family (Brassicaceae). The whole plant breaks away at ground level and rolls away. The seeds are not released until a wet hollow is encountered or it rains.

The seed heads of a number of grasses also function as tumbleweeds. The most striking examples are species of *Spinifex* in Southeast Asia and Australasia that inhabit coastal sand dunes. Their seed heads are aggregated into spherical groups, and some of the scales associated with the seeds are drawn out into long, stiff spines whose tips are also spherically arranged. When the heads separate from the rest of the plant, they, often in company with many others, bowl along the beach or over the dunes at quite remarkable speeds, dropping their fruitlets as they go. Only when they settle into a sand hollow do they come to rest, at least for a while.

As noted, most dust-like seeds have wing-like extensions of their coats. In tropical and temperate forests a number of mostly tree and vine species also have strongly winged but much larger seeds or single-seeded fruits. The wings of the fruits are mostly extensions of the fruit wall, or they are sepals, or less often petals, that have persisted from the flower and become greatly enlarged. The wings of seeds are extensions of the seed coat.

The fruits may have single terminal wings, as in the samaras of maples (*Acer*), or a rosette of terminal wings derived from the sepals or petals. Docks (*Rumex*) and other members of the buckwheat family (Polygonaceae) have strongly winged sepals, which mostly function in wind dispersal but in some species have hooks so they can be dispersed by animals as well. Others have some corky tissue, enabling them to float in water. Fruits of plants in other families have pairs of opposite lateral wings, as in the birches, or several lateral wings derived from the fruit wall.

Winged seeds are released from capsules, follicles, or cones. They may have single terminal wings, as in species of pine and other conifers, and banksias and other genera of Proteaceae. In other plants, tissue-paper-thin wings completely encircle the seed.

The notable family here is the *Catalpa* family (Bignoniaceae), which comprises mostly tropical woody vines and is especially abundant in tropical South America.

Winged seeds and fruits fall far short of the distances that dust seeds can attain. Those that have terminal wings slowly rotate downward whereas those with lateral wings gently float. If there is no wind, then they reach the ground near the parent plant; with a wind they are moved farther away, at first through the air and then along the ground. Observations have shown that, at most, distances of a few hundred meters or yards can be reached, though 2–3 km (1.25–2 miles) has been recorded for Scots pine (*Pinus sylvestris*) and a few other trees (Ridley 1930).

Plumed seeds or one-seeded fruits have dense tufts or coverings of soft silky hairs that act like parachutes, giving great air buoyancy (for example, those of *Stapelia*, shown on page 99). The seeds or fruits can be carried some distance by a wind gust, then settle on the ground, only to be lifted

Seed heads of *Spinifex hirsutus* that have come to rest together in a dune hollow.

up again by another gust. They can sometimes ascend to considerable heights, as can be observed in thistledown on a summer's day. It is clear that plumes are much more effective than wings for long-distance travel, sometimes several hundred kilometers or miles, rarely much more. A complicating factor, though, in determining the distances traveled is that the seeds can separate from the plumes during flight, and the latter, now lighter still, continue on alone. Sooner or later, rain is encountered, and the journey is over. Again, most of the species with plumed seeds or small fruits are herbs, and often weedy herbs, of open temperate and tropical habitats. However, there are also some trees and woody vines in warmer parts of the world. In a number of tall grasses the scales associated with the small, seed-like fruits form long, dense plumes of hairs for wind transport. Included here are the sugarcane genus *Saccharum*, and the pampas grasses (*Cortaderia*) of South America and Australasia.

In some species the hair plumes are borne by the persistent and elongated styles of

Cortaderia fulvida with an impressive array of fluffy seed heads growing on a river terrace. New Zealand.

the flowers. Well-known examples are some species of *Anemone*, water and wood avens (*Geum*), and most notably, all species of the widespread genus *Clematis*. Species in which the plumes are derived from sepals belong overwhelmingly to the huge family Asteraceae. The plumes, or pappus as it is termed in the daisy family, may arise directly from the top of the fruit, as in the sow thistles (*Sonchus*), or be carried on a long, slender stalk, looking something like an umbrella, as in the dandelions (*Taraxacum*) and many other genera.

In rather fewer plants the plumes grow out from the long stalks of the fruits, and the hairs are so long and abundant that they have the appearance of fluff. In cattails (*Typha*) the tiny and numerous flowers are distinctively crowded into dense heads. The minute fruits deriving from the female flowers are each released in a little ball of fluff that can blow for great distances.

Plumed seeds are formed in large numbers in elongated capsules. The plumes, often with very long hairs, are mostly at the tips of the seeds. The best-known examples are the widespread herbaceous species of willow herb (*Epilobium*). Many are weedy, and some are known as fireweeds as they are early colonizers after fire. The capsules gradually split open from the tips, slowly releasing the seeds over a number of days. The dogbane and milkweed family (Apocynaceae, including Asclepiadaceae), of which many species are woody vines in warmer regions, have similar capsules. *Tillandsia* and related genera of the Bromeliaceae have small seeds with hair plumes arising from the base.

Some of these seeds are known as woolly seeds and have dense hairs all over their surface. The hairs are often very long and entangled, and so look quite like wool. Two species are economically important. *Gossypium* is a shrub, widely cultivated for the abundant masses of soft hairs of the seeds, which are made into cotton cloth. *Eriodendron anfractuosum* is a tropical tree that is the source of kapok. The rather large capsules of these species release the wool and the seeds gradually. Poplars (*Populus*) and willows (*Salix*) also have woolly seeds. The seeds of the poplars, in particular, with their abundant white fluff, blow around on the ground and look like snow.

Water

Some examples of water-dispersed seeds have been considered in Chapter 5. However, water dispersal is not confined to permanently or frequently wet habitats. In drier places where seeds, and particularly small seeds, have been deposited by animals or the wind, they can be moved farther by rainwash, especially on slopes. Where seeds have been deposited by birds in a place unsuitable for establishment, such as a tree branch, then rain can wash them to the ground, though this would be no advantage for epiphytes. In a real downpour, leading to floods, then even large seeds can be moved a long way. Flooding rivers can carve into the alluvial soils of their banks, which contain seeds buried by earlier floods, and eventually some of them can end up on a new surface where they can germinate after the flood recedes. On the other hand, some seeds can be carried all the way to the sea, where with notable exceptions they are mostly killed by the salt water.

The seeds of some plants that rise from the water's edge, such as sedges and rushes, quickly sink to the bottom when they are scattered on the water. They germinate and form small plants that, being light, rise to the surface and may drift into shallows where their roots can anchor them. Other plants that grow in deeper water, such as water lilies, also have seeds that sink immediately, but the roots of their seedlings anchor themselves in the mud on the bottom. The seeds of mangrove trees and shrubs of muddy tropical shores germinate on the trees, and the sometimes quite heavy seedlings drop into the sea or into the mud at low tide. Some large seedlings have spear-like primary roots (for example, those of *Rhizophora*), which anchor them in the mud. If these and other less specialized seedlings drop into the sea, they float around for a while, carried by currents, until a low tide settles them on temporarily exposed mud.

Other plants in or near water have seeds or fruits modified for water dispersal. These float as a result of having corky or air-filled tissues. In single-seeded fruits the fruit wall may be light and corky, or a layer of the wall may be air-filled. The outstanding example is the coconut palm (*Cocos nucifera*), so widespread along tropical shores. The outermost layer of the fruit wall is thin and smooth; the middle layer is very wide and fibrous, and contains much air; and the innermost layer is the very hard shell. Coconuts drop or are washed into the sea and can travel great distances before they wash up on another shore and germinate.

Some floating fruits, particularly legume pods, contain many seeds, and buoyancy is provided by the air trapped between the wall of the fruit and the seeds. Many of these legumes grow along rivers or at the edges of lakes, and the pods drop into the water. In rivers, tumbling with stones can break open the pods and release the seeds, or the pods can eventually decay. The seeds of many species of the Fabaceae have thick, hard, waxy coats that can exclude water for some time. They can also float as a result of air trapped between the pair of seed leaves of the embryo. Again, tumbling in rivers can abrade the seed coats, allowing water to enter and germination to follow. If this does not happen, then seeds washed up on shore can eventually germinate when the seed coat decays, particularly at the thinner part where the seed stalk was attached.

Considerable numbers of these "drift seeds" can end up in the sea, where their impervious coats protect them from the salty water. They can be carried by currents for enormous distances. For example, the Gulf Stream carries a number of tropical seeds, mostly of legumes, to deposit them on European or even polar shores. Most often noted are the large seeds, called sea beans or nicker nuts, of two legumes: *Caesalpinia bonduc* and *Entada gigas*. The latter is a woody tropical vine that grows on the riverside, with pods about 1 m (39 inches) long. Some of these seeds have been found to be viable on cooler shores and have been germinated, but the species cannot establish itself in cool to cold higher-latitude climates.

Normally wind-dispersed seeds or fruits can end their journeys being conveyed on water if their wings or plumes of hairs float well. Some aquatic plants have floating fruits, armed with hooks and spines, that are reminiscent of those designed to attach to the coats of browsing animals. The water chestnut (*Trapa natans*) is the best known of these. It is usually suggested that such special features are to enable the fruits, after they have floated for a while, to entangle with other aquatic plants and germinate. It is also possible that the hooks and spines are devices that could attach to the feathers of ducks or to the coats of mammals visiting streams or ponds to drink.

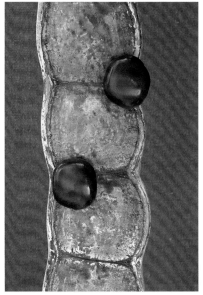

Part of a pod and seeds of *Entada gigas*. The pods are divided into one-seeded segments.

Explosive seed release

Some plants provide the energy for dispersing their seeds themselves, but the distances attained, though useful, are not great. The devices involved are varied and sometimes ingenious. The seeds are contained in capsules or pods. In some, the cells of the fruit walls die and dry, and a tension gradually develops as the drying progresses, to the point where the valves of the fruit suddenly separate and toss out the seeds. Familiar examples of this are gorse and broom, and in the heat of summer one can hear the small explosions and scattering of the seeds of these shrubs. The seeds are only thrown about 1 m (39 inches), but both *Ulex europaea* and *Cytisus scoparius* have seeds with oil bodies, so they may be transported farther by ants.

Other plants have capsules that are still living at maturity. The best known of these belong to the genus *Impatiens*, of which the cultivated forms with their brightly colored flowers are very popular. The capsules are fleshy and translucent, and the valves become so pumped up with water when mature that even the lightest touch will cause them to suddenly separate and coil up, with seeds flying in all directions. Mostly, the seeds travel only 1 m (39 inches) or so, but one taller species, *I. roylei* from the Himalaya, can toss them 5–6 m (16–20 feet).

Several species of violet are examples of a third group with explosive fruits. The three boat-like valves of the capsule separate widely from each other. Each contains many small, smooth seeds, and as the valves dry they shrink, gradually exerting increasing pressure on the seeds from opposing sides. One by one or a few at a time, the seeds are propelled away from the capsule. Squeezing an apple pip between finger and thumb produces a similar result.

We now come to the famous squirting cucumber (*Ecballium elaterium*), an herb that grows on dry sites around the Mediterranean. The fruit is about 5 cm (2 inches) long, with its stalk extending a short way into it like a plug. As the fruit matures, the mucilage within gradually builds up a considerable pressure, and eventually the plug gives way and the cucumber shoots away like a rocket, with mucilage and seeds squirting out as it travels. The seeds are generally propelled about 2 m (6 1/2 feet), though 6 m (20 feet) was recorded on one occasion.

The tables turned—Plants that eat animals

Plants that derive nourishment from animals are mostly called insectivorous, but also sometimes carnivorous, conjuring up images of the man-eating plants erroneously reported to exist in earlier times. Insectivorous plants belong to 15 genera distributed among five families, so as with other lifestyles, this one, too, has evolved independently several times, and there are several different methods these plants employ for trapping and digesting small animals (Juniper et al. 1989). Insectivorous plants mostly grow in swampy or marshy places where nutrients, particularly those containing nitrogen—an important component of proteins—are in short supply. There is plenty of nitrogen gas in the air, but plants are unable to utilize it in this form, so most have to obtain it, directly or indirectly, from certain species of bacteria that can. For insectivorous plants, the sources of nitrogen are the proteins of animals they digest.

In pitcher plants the traps are leaves formed into tubes or pitchers, sometimes termed pitfalls as the insects fall in and cannot get out. *Nepenthes* is the largest genus of pitcher plants with about 80 species in Southeast Asia, tropical Australasia, the Seychelles, and Madagascar. They are climbing plants with leaf tips converted into twining tendrils. The leaf blades are narrow and in some species as long as 1 m (39 inches). The vertically oriented pitchers develop from the tips of tendrils of some of the leaves. They are mostly narrow and tubular, with an upward-angled lid attached at one side of the opening at the top. They may be completely red or have red stripes and patches near the opening and on the lid, so they have something of the appearance of a flower. This may be an attractant for insects, but more significantly there are many glandular hairs secreting nectar over the lids and on the inside of the pitcher near the opening. The underside of a lid is covered with downward-directed hairs, which nudge the supping insect toward the opening. Seated on the edge of the latter is a ring of tissue that overlaps the rim to the inside and the outside. This ring has conspicuous radial ridges, each ending in a downward-curved spine that overhangs the interior of the pitcher. Alternating with the spines are prominent nectar glands. Insects that reach these glands

Nepenthes vieillardii with some of the leaves ending in pitchers. New Caledonia.

may then fall over the edge into the depths. If they manage to get to the underside of the overhang, the spines make it difficult for them to escape, and they then find themselves on a smooth, slippery surface from which they often fall into the fluid at the base of the pitcher. Often below the slippery layer there is another zone of downward-angled hairs, so the pitcher is very like a prison with a series of fences. The fluid-filled digesting zone has many glandular hairs that secrete acids and enzymes, which kill and digest the insects.

In young pitchers the edge of the lid is attached to the opening by enmeshed hairs. Even at this stage the lower part of the pitcher is filled with liquid. It has been suggested that the variously angled lids at maturity act as umbrellas, preventing rainwater from diluting the digesting fluid, but they are probably only partly effective in this respect.

The insects trapped are often ants, but other small animals are trapped, too. Large *Nepenthes* pitchers, up to 1 m (39 inches) in height in some species, have been found to contain mice, frogs, and other animals of similar size. This is true also of species of *Sarracenia* in North America that have large pitchers. *Sarracenia* does not climb, however, and the leaves and pitchers are in tufts or rosettes. Some mosquitoes, gnats, and flies lay their eggs at the edges of the openings of *Nepenthes*, and when they hatch, the larvae drop into the digesting fluid, to which they are immune, and feed on dead insects.

Darlingtonia californica is found in coastal and mountain marshes in northern California and southwestern Oregon. It, too, is tufted rather than climbing, but it is distinctive in appearance as the pitcher is curved over at the top, giving it a cobra-like appearance. This shape probably ensures that rain cannot enter the pitcher. Unlike *Nepenthes* and *Sarracenia*, it appears that in *Darlingtonia* the breakdown of captured insects is achieved by bacterial action alone.

Sundews are described as having flypaper traps. The leaves are densely set with stalked, rounded glands that exude a sticky fluid. Insects mistake the fluid for nectar, become firmly stuck, and the leaves slowly roll up, enclosing them. The many species of *Drosera* are found throughout the world. In some, the spoon-shaped leaves are in neat rosettes that when red in color have a flower-like appearance. This and the glistening nectar-like drops on the many stalked glands make them very attractive to insects. Other sundews are taller and branched, with leaves ranging from long and narrow, sometimes forked, to broad and shield-shaped. Once an insect becomes entangled in the sticky glue of the glands, the leaves slowly close, and glands of a second type, without stalks, exude a digestive fluid.

Triphyophyllum peltatum uses a method of trapping insects similar to that of *Drosera* at one stage of its growth. It is found in the rain forests of West Africa. Young plants form a rosette of normal leaves, followed by smaller leaves with stalked, insect-trapping glands. In the third stage of growth the stem tip elongates and climbs to the tops of trees, 30 m (100 feet) or more above the ground, where its flowers are produced. The climbing organs are pairs of curved hooks at the leaf tips. The large seeds are flattened disks with wide wings for wind dispersal.

The Venus flytrap (*Dionaea muscipula*) is the most exciting of the insectivorous plants because of the way it snaps shut when stimulated and its prison-like appearance. It is widely cultivated for this reason, but in nature it is restricted to a small area in North and South Carolina. The two lobes of each leaf blade normally spread widely apart, with long spines along their margins. The leaves are attractively colored in shades of red, and a zone just inside the upper margins have many nectar-secreting glands that attract insects and other small animals. The remainder of the upper surfaces has glands of a different type that secrete a digestive fluid when required. In this digestive zone are six narrow hairs in two groups, three on each lobe. These are sensitive. If a falling leaf or the like touches a hair, there is no reaction; if an insect, or finger, touches one hair twice in quick succession, or two hairs in quick succession, the lobes of the leaf quickly close and the marginal spines intermesh.

The mechanism of this closing movement is still not fully understood despite the observations and experiments of a number of botanists from Charles Darwin onward. It seems that the stimulated hairs trigger an electric charge that generates an acid within the cells on the undersides of the leaf lobes. The walls of these cells are under pressure from their contents, and as the acidity weakens the bonding of their cellulose molecules there is a sudden increase in cell size and an equally sudden partial closure of the leaf. The leaf continues to close more gradually, and the marginal nectar-secreting strips press closely together, forming a seal to prevent the leakage of digestive fluid. The inner parts of the lobes do not make contact and form a sort of stomach cavity. After everything has been extracted from the prey, the leaf opens gradually 5–10 days later. The opening movement results from an expansion

Several insects have been trapped by the sticky glands on the leaves of *Drosera arcturi*. New Zealand.

A Venus flytrap (*Dionaea muscipula*) waiting for a victim.

of cells on the upper sides of the leaves, though it is not clear how this is triggered. The enlargement of the cells cannot be reversed, and after three openings and closings activity ceases and the leaf dies. If the leaf is deliberately stimulated to close with a piece of leaf or something else inedible, the plant is not entirely fooled. No digestive fluid is produced, and the leaf opens again after a day or so. Small animals such as ants can escape from the trap, but those 1 cm (3/8 inch) long or more cannot.

Aldrovanda vesiculosa is related to *Dionaea* and was once widespread in the warmer parts of Europe, Asia, Africa, and Australia. Its traps are similar to those of *Dionaea*, but the the plant is a floating aquatic.

The final type of insectivorous plant is different from the rest in that the traps are submerged in water. These are the bladderworts (*Utricularia*), several hundred species of which are found worldwide. Most are submerged freshwater aquatics, lacking roots but with slender, much-branched stems and much-divided leaves with many narrow segments. The abundant bladder traps are attached to the leaf segments. Another group of species grows in wet, marshy sites, with some stems penetrating into the soil where the bladders function in the water that fills the spaces between the soil particles. The most unusual species grow as epiphytes in the American tropics, either in wet moss cushions or the water tanks of bromeliad epiphytes. Some bladderworts spread from leaf rosette to leaf rosette of a bromeliad by means of stolons. The leaves of epiphytic bladderworts that are exposed to the air are undivided and can be quite broad.

With so many species there is considerable variation in the details of the bladders, but the basic pattern is the same. Working out just how they function, though, has been difficult as the bladders are very small, 0.5–5 mm (1/64–3/16 inch) long, and only work under water. They are more or less pear-shaped with a lid or door at the narrow end. There are special glands on the inner surface of a bladder that connect through to the outer surface and expel water. This results in a strong suction within the bladder. When a small aquatic animal touches sensitive, external hairs on the lower part of the door, the latter suddenly opens, and water—with the animal—is sucked in. With the internal water pressure restored, the door quickly closes. The bladders suck in a wide range of very small animals, from minute amoebas to water fleas and small insect larvae, particularly those of mosquitoes. Small tadpoles and even very young fish can also be devoured. In these cases, the tail is first sucked in and the wider part of the body temporarily blocks the entrance. Digestion begins with the tail, and the rest of the body is slowly pulled in. Only when the hapless animal is fully inside the bladder can the water pressure equalize and the door close.

The flowers of utricularias, standing above the water in the case of the aquatic species, are often brightly colored and attractive, particularly so in the epiphytes. The flowers of the latter are as much as 5 cm (2 inches) in diameter.

CHAPTER EIGHT

Mostly Hidden Relationships

◆◆◆

Plants, Fungi, and Bacteria

Fungi and bacteria used to be classified as plants largely because their cells are enclosed by firm walls. Now, it has been concluded that these groups are quite distinct from each other and from plants. The fungi constitute a kingdom of their own, and the bacteria another. The latter differ from both fungi and plants in that their cells do not have nuclei (groups of chromosomes, made up of strands of DNA, enclosed by a membrane). Bacterial cells do have DNA, but it is not organized into chromosomes and is not enclosed by a membrane.

Fungi

Perhaps the biggest difference between fungi and plants is that fungi do not have chlorophyll and so, like the animals, depend directly or indirectly on plants for their food. Mostly they are hidden organisms, made up of pale, cobweb-like, branching filaments in the soil or, less often, water, under bark, or inside plants and sometimes animals (Carlile and Watkinson 1994). Reproduction is mostly by small, single-celled spores, produced in great quantity, that are spread far and wide, and are always present in the air.

Some fungi do become clearly visible when they form fruiting bodies, which grow out from the substrate in which the filaments develop. The fruiting bodies are made up

A foliose lichen, *Pseudocyphellaria homoeophylla,* with the spore cups of the fungal partner. New Zealand.

of densely compacted filaments, and at maturity they produce spores in enormous numbers. Some of the fruiting bodies are made more conspicuous by bright, attractive colors. The best-known fungi are the mushroom or gill fungi, in which spores are formed on the gills on the underside of the umbrella-like cap. In other groups the spores are formed in cup- to flask-like structures or over the whole surface of branched or unbranched fruiting bodies.

Many fungi grow on the dead remains of plants, particularly where these accumulate on the floor of a forest. Using enzymes, fungi break down the carbohydrates, proteins, and other compounds remaining in the litter to obtain energy. The carbon dioxide released goes back into the air, and the sulfates, nitrates, and other mineral nutrients are released into the soil, then recycle back into plants. These litter-decomposing fungi, in association with bacteria, are critically important for life on Earth as without them dead plant and animal remains would steadily accumulate to overwhelming depths. More and more nutrients and carbon would become locked up in the increasing litter, and eventually, life of any kind would become impossible.

To gardeners and farmers, many fungi are bad news because they parasitize plants, stunting their growth and sometimes killing them. Common among these are the mildews, rusts, blights, rots, wilts, and smuts. Some fungal diseases of plants have changed the course of history, as happened with the devastating potato blight in Ireland, which resulted in widespread starvation and mass emigration.

A cup fungus, *Peziza*.

Some parasitic fungi enter the aboveground parts of plants. Their spores settle on the plant surface, and each germinates by sending out a slender tubular filament. This must find a way to get through the outermost layer of cells or epidermis and into the interior of the plant. There are several ways this is done.

On the undersides of leaves there are many breathing pores or stomata, and some fungi use these as entry points. Once they have gained access, their filaments spread and branch through the extensive air spaces within the leaves. Where a filament makes contact with a cell, an outgrowth penetrates the cell wall and swells up at the tip to form a haustorium, which feeds by breaking down the organic molecules of the cell with enzymes and absorbing the simpler components. Some nutrients are taken up from the moist exterior surfaces of the plant cells within the leaf; some parasitic fungi obtain all their nutrients in this way.

Other pathogenic fungi penetrate directly through the wall of an epidermal cell. The tip of the filament enlarges into a flat disk that firmly adheres to the leaf surface. What is known as an infection peg develops from the center of this, which must now penetrate a waxy surface layer (the cuticle), then the outer cellulose wall of the epidermal cell, to reach the living interior. Sometimes the disk builds up a considerable internal pressure that forces the peg through like a hypodermic syringe, or enzymes are secreted that locally dissolve the cuticle and cell wall. In some cases, the fungal filament branches within the epidermal cell but goes no farther, as with powdery mildews; in others it spreads from cell to cell. Other fungi penetrate the epidermis between the walls, where adjacent cells are in contact, and their filaments then spread through the interior air spaces.

Plants have developed a number of defenses against parasitic fungi. Sometimes a cell that is invaded will quickly die, along with adjacent cells, even before the infection peg has breached the wall. If the fungus can only survive in living host cells, then it will be stopped and die. In other cases the cell wall adds new layers of cellulose, sometimes impregnated with fungus-inhibiting lignins and tannins, in front of the advancing peg

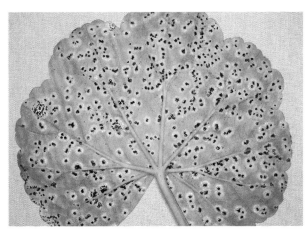

Rust pustules on the underside of a *Pelargonium* leaf.

Left: A powdery mildew on a forget-me-not (*Myosotis*).

tip. This may cause the pathogen to halt and die when it runs out of energy. The presence of the fungus may also trigger the formation of compounds, known as phytoalexins, that are toxic to fungi, though some fungi have enzymes that break these down and render them harmless. These defenses are not always fully effective. If conditions are warm and moist—very favorable for fungal growth—they may sometimes be breached. Often, plants heavily infected by a fungus eventually die.

Parasitic fungi spread to other plants by means of spores of various types. Those whose filaments spread over the leaf surface with the haustoria penetrating only into epidermal cells (the powdery mildews) form their spores externally. In most other fungi the filaments extend deep into the interior of the host plant. The spores are formed from clusters of filaments, and the spore mass eventually breaks through the plant epidermis. The many species of rust fungi exhibit this pattern. The best known of the rusts is wheat rust (*Puccinia graminis*), which although it does not kill the host plant stunts its growth and reduces the production of wheat grains. It has a complex life cycle and what follows is a simplified account.

During the growing season of wheat (*Triticum*), the rust spores produced are thin-walled and blow away to infect other plants. These spores are red, which gave rise to the common name of the fungus. Toward the end of the growing season, when it is cooler, different spores are produced that are black and thick-walled. These are able to survive through winter on the wheat stubble or on the ground. In early spring they germinate, forming small, thin-walled spores that blow onto the leaves of barberry shrubs (*Berberis*), if any have been unwisely allowed to grow in the vicinity. Rust filaments spread through the barberry leaves, and after a fairly complex process of sexual reproduction, thin-walled spores are produced that infect young wheat plants. As far back as 1660, wheat farmers in Germany concluded that barberry bushes surrounding their fields had something to do with the disease attacking their wheat. They persuaded the authorities to eradicate the barberry, and the problem was largely solved.

A number of parasitic fungi have thick-walled dormant spores, segments of filaments, or other structures that enable them to survive an unfavorable season or a period when a suitable host is not available. In the soil the story is largely different. The fungal spores are not moved around as they are in the air, so most persist as thick-walled resting spores and only become active when a plant root grows nearby. Exudates from growing roots rouse the spores into activity. Some form thin-walled spores that actively swim by means of mobile, hair-like appendages, and others are stimulated to germinate and send a filament toward the root. In addition, fungal filaments already present in the soil send filaments toward the root. Once again the root epidermis has to be penetrated, though in this case there are no stomata to make the task easier. Roots have no cuticle, however, so entry is not too difficult.

Some soil fungi are pathogenic to plants, causing them to wilt and die, but many others are beneficial. Invasion of plant roots by the latter does not trigger any of the defensive reactions just described. This is because the plant has some means of distinguishing friend from foe. The beneficial fungi still take sugars from the roots, but in return they provide an abundant water and soil nutrient supply, particularly nitrates and phosphates, for the plant through their far-reaching filaments. This relationship is known as a mycorrhiza, "fungus root." If anything, the plants probably benefit more than the fungi, so the latter can be partially excused for the parasitic behavior of some of their other species. Mycorrhizas are not rare or occasional but regularly occur in about 90% of seed plants and many other plants. If plants are grown where mycorrhizal fungi are not present, their growth is stunted or they die. This is also a relationship of long standing between plants and fungi—in microscopic sections of well-preserved, 400-million-year-old fossils of long-extinct swamp plants, fungal filaments very similar to those of present-day mycorrhizal fungi can be clearly seen.

In some plants the fungal filaments form a thick sleeve around the root tip, with some filaments extending out into the soil and others into the root between the epidermal cells. No haustoria are formed. An infected root forks several times, forming a distinctive cluster of short roots without root hairs. Plants with this type of mycorrhiza are trees, including pines and oaks. The fungi have large fruiting bodies, including truffles and others of mushroom form. These appear on the ground above the host roots.

Most mycorrhizas do not have a sleeve of filaments on the roots. A fungal filament penetrates through the wall of an epidermal cell, then both through and between interior cells. There are two types of haustoria penetrating into cells: balloon-like, and branched like a shrub. The fungi in this case do not form conspicuous fruiting bodies.

A variant of this pattern is found in the heath family (Ericaceae) and related families. The fungal haustoria are coiled bundles of filaments, almost completely filling some cells. Orchids are a special case. They all have mycorrhizal fungi, but it seems that the fungus gets little or no benefit from the relationship. Orchids have minute seeds consisting of a few cells with little in the way of food reserves. They will not germinate beyond an early stage unless they are invaded by particular fungi. The latter are able to break down organic compounds in leaf litter to release sugars, which are provided to the very small, young orchid. Later, most orchids form chlorophyll and so can feed themselves, but the fungus generally persists. Some orchids never form chlorophyll, so they depend entirely on the fungus, and as seen in Chapter 1 under "Indirect parasites—The mycotrophs," page 60, the fungus is sometimes connected to the roots of green plants, where it gains a sugar supply for itself and the mycotrophic plant. Within the orchid tissue the fungal filaments form coils within cells, but after a few days each coil is broken down and digested by the orchid.

Lichens

Lichens are very unusual. They are basically fungi, and most belong to the cup fungi, which form their spores in cup-like structures, but a minority belong to the mushroom group (Purvis 2000). Like fungi in general they are unable to manufacture their own food, but they learned a trick, probably many millions of years ago, that enables them to overcome this problem very successfully. They entrap simple, unicellular green algae or filamentous blue-green bacteria within their tissues and help themselves to the sugars and other compounds they manufacture. This is an enormous advantage for the fungal component, but as the alga or bacterium has to supply the fungus as well as itself with food, it is difficult to see how they gain much advantage.

Some of the algae and blue-green bacteria can live separately, but there are others that are only found in association with lichenized fungi. None of the lichen fungi are found living independently. For a lichen to develop, the first filaments of a germinating spore need to wrap themselves around a photosynthetic partner without delay. The

Two different crustose lichens growing on a rock.

cells of the latter, as the fungus enlarges, divide repeatedly and generally form a clearly defined layer within the fungus. This arrangement means that lichens function in much the same way as green plants do. Indeed, lichens can grow in extreme habitats that are beyond the tolerance of plants, such as hot desert rocks and frozen Antarctic rocks. In Antarctica they can survive temperatures as low as −200°C (−330°F).

Lichens can be conveniently grouped according to their form: crustose, foliose, or fruticose. Crustose lichens form circular patches that press close to their substrate: tree trunks, logs, rocks, and even glass. They are attached by fungal filaments, often so intimately that they cannot be detached without taking some of the substrate. The attaching filaments secrete acids that dissolve the surface of rocks and release mineral nutrients required by the lichen. By this means some crustose lichens become so firmly etched into rocks that rock and lichen are virtually one. The extreme in this respect are the Antarctic lichens. The lichen filaments, with their food-supplying partners, work their way between the grains of the granite and form a layer parallel to the rock surface. So, going inward from the surface there is first a translucent rock layer, which allows enough light to pass for photosynthesis, then the lichen layer.

Foliose lichens have a leafy look (see page 266). They are mostly broad and flat, and attached to the substrate at one or several points. Most grow in moist, shady places, and those of drier sites can sometimes dry up and become quite brittle, only to revive when it rains. Much-branched fruticose (shrubby) lichens may grow erect on the ground or on logs, or hang in curtains on twigs (see page 274).

Sometimes lichens contain both algae and blue-green bacteria. An interesting pattern has been observed in deep, narrow ravines in New Zealand and Scotland. In New Zealand a species of *Sticta* grows on the walls of ravines from top to bottom. In going from the better-lit upper parts down to darker levels, there is a gradual change in the form of the lichen from foliose to fruticose, and a gradual change of the photosynthetic component from an alga to a more shade-tolerant blue-green bacterium. The two forms had been regarded as species of different genera. Many other examples of this phenomenon are now known.

Lichens are often gray, the color of the fungal component, though when wet the green of the alga or bacterium shows through. Some species are more brightly colored, and even when the general color is gray the spore-producing structures may be red, yellow, brown, or black. These lichen pigments can be extracted and used as dyes for wool.

As well as reproducing by spores, many lichens reproduce vegetatively, either by portions breaking away or by specialized clusters of algal cells wrapped around by a few fungal filaments, which detach from the lichen and are washed or blown away. These cell clusters are either outgrowths from the surface or form in the interior and escape through crevices. Some species reproduce entirely in these ways.

A tree branch with a fruticose lichen above and below, and
a crustose lichen between, with fungal fruiting bodies.

Bacteria

Bacterial cells are much smaller than those of plants. Many bacteria occur as single cells, ranging in shape from spherical to narrow and elongated, and some are able to swim with motile hairs attached singly, or in tufts at their ends or all over their exterior surface. Other bacteria cluster in groups or are joined end to end in filaments.

Most bacteria, in collaboration with many fungi, feed on the organic compounds of dead plants and animals (Bisset 1970). Unlike fungi, however, some bacteria have photosynthetic pigments similar to those of plants. This enables them to manufacture their own food as plants do, and they have probably been doing so since long before plants came into existence. Fossils of bacteria have been found in rocks several thousand million years old.

Reproduction of bacteria is mostly by simple cell division, though in some, cells linked in groups in a filament become rounded and separate into small spores that are spread by the wind. To survive unfavorable conditions, many bacteria form special thick-walled cells that in some cases can survive temperatures near boiling and well below freezing.

Blue-green bacteria (formerly known as blue-green algae) are a special group. They are all photosynthetic and contain chlorophyll, but also other pigments, some of which are blue but others purple, brown, or red. Some species are single-celled, but many form long filaments. A distinctive characteristic is the enclosing of the cells and filaments in a thick layer of a jelly-like material. Some of the blue-green and other bacteria in the soil are able to absorb atmospheric nitrogen and convert it, by a process known as nitrogen fixing, into compounds that plants can use. Plants obtain these compounds, released into the soil when the bacteria die, mostly via mycorrhizal fungi, but some obtain them from nitrogen-fixing blue-greens living in their tissues—such plants include a number of liverworts, the floating water fern *Azolla*, species of *Gunnera*, and cycads, which have special roots whose tips (where the bacteria are found) emerge above the ground.

The legume family (Fabaceae) is notable for the association its roots have with a nitrogen-fixing bacterium, *Rhizobium*. The relationship develops when a *Rhizobium* cell attaches itself near the tip of a root hair, dissolves a hole in the root hair wall by means of an enzyme, then enters. It divides to form a line of cells extending to the base of the root hair, which then penetrate interior cells. The bacteria stimulate root cells to divide, and the result is a nodule or tuber several millimeters or fractions of an inch long, quite like a rice grain in size and shape. These nodules can be easily seen when pea or bean plants are uprooted. The bacteria in the nodules provide a much better supply of nitrogenous compounds than is available in many soils, and as a result the legume family is notable for being able to thrive in very infertile soils. When the legumes die, the nodules break down and the nitrogenous compounds gradually leach out and improve the soil, which is then able to support a wider range of plants, including many that are unable to form bacterial nodules.

Unfortunately, not all bacteria are so helpful to plants as those just described. There are fewer plant diseases caused by bacteria than those caused by fungi, but bacterial infections in wet weather can spread very rapidly and cause sudden and dramatic damage. Bacteria often enter through wounds. Some cause soft rot, in which fleshy roots and tubers are reduced to a slimy, smelly mess; others result in unsightly galls, or black spots of dead cells.

Viruses

This is probably the appropriate place to say something about the enigmatic viruses—enigmatic because it is difficult to say whether they are living or nonliving, and some say they straddle the boundary of both states. Essentially, viruses appear to be bits of DNA enclosed by protein coats. They are even smaller than bacteria, and it was not possible to see them until the electron microscope was invented (Levine 1992). As far as plants, animals, and bacteria are concerned, there is little that is good about them. They can only continue to exist by invading living cells and taking them over. The organisms infected may be reduced in vigor or so severely affected that they die. Many human diseases are caused by viruses, ranging from nonfatal colds and flu to crippling poliomyelitis and usually fatal AIDS and smallpox, which have killed millions in epidemics.

Often a virus is restricted to one host species and sometimes to particular organs. Hosts produce antibodies to combat the viruses, but in many cases this is in vain. If a host does survive, then it continues to produce antibodies and is immune to attack. An injection of inactivated virus can induce antibodies, and vaccination for many viral diseases is now widespread. There are rare cases in which a virus that causes a nonfatal illness can give immunity to a related, often fatal virus. The best-known example is cowpox. During smallpox epidemics in the Middle Ages it was noted that milkmaids rarely contracted the disease. This was because they often contracted cowpox from the cows they milked. Cowpox was not a serious illness, but the antibodies it induced were also effective against smallpox.

Viral diseases of plants are mostly transferred from plant to plant by sucking insects, particularly aphids, though other animals (mites, nematodes) are sometimes the vectors. Viruses may also be transferred by naturally occurring grafts between the roots of an infected and uninfected plant of the same species. If a virus is not placed by a vector directly into the cell protoplasm, it must get through the plasma membrane. Often, the protein coats of viruses are studded with spikes, and these attach to the plasma membrane, which stretches inward and breaks to release the virus into the cell. The virus then takes over the functions of the cell, inducing it to copy the viral genetic material many times and provide the materials for new protein coats. Following this, the cell usually dies, and often the mass of new viral particles so stretches the cell membrane that it bursts, releasing viruses to infect new cells. Viruses may also spread from cell to cell of a plant through interconnecting protoplasmic strands, especially in the phloem.

Unlike many animal viruses, numerous plant viruses attack a wide range of plants. "Some plants are badly affected by viral diseases whereas others are not. Some infected plants don't show much difference in growth, vigor or flowering. Others may decline rapidly and may die within two or three years" (Lucas 1998).

CHAPTER NINE

Plant Evolution Through the Ages

♦♦♦

An Overview

Undoubtedly, the oldest organisms are bacteria. Fossils of them, including blue-greens, have been found in rocks 3,000 million years old. The bacteria at this time were unicellular, but filamentous forms have been found in rocks about 2,000 million years old. Some of these are very similar to blue-green bacteria of today. The first plant fossils are simple unicells belonging to the algae. These have been found in rocks about 1,000 million years old. So, there was an inconceivably long period of time of about 2,500 million years when living organisms were very small and simple but probably often abundant in the seas, as some of their descendants are in the oceans today. A by-product of photosynthesis is oxygen, and photosynthetic bacteria, along with the first algae, were the first to begin adding oxygen to the atmosphere—a necessity for most living things.

Following this long period of slow evolution, we come to a time when life began to diversify and organisms became larger and more complex. This began about 544 million years ago, and the first era, the Paleozoic, extended to 248 million years ago. During the first period of the Paleozoic, the Cambrian, life was still largely restricted to the sea, with perhaps some algae and lichens in moist places on land. In the sea, the animals were all invertebrates. The algae were still represented by unicellular and filamentous forms, but also by larger, multicellular species. Today, three groups of algae are recognized. They all have chlorophyll, but some have other pigments as well. The green

Lycopodium scariosum with spore-producing cones. New Zealand.

279

algae do not have additional pigments, the brown algae have an additional brown pigment, and the red algae a red and sometimes a blue pigment. Fossils of the Cambrian indicate that these three groups were present then. From them have evolved the sometimes very large seaweeds of rocky coasts today.

By the middle of the Paleozoic, about the Devonian period, vertebrates (mostly fish) had evolved in the sea, and the first animals and plants began to establish on land. During most of the Paleozoic era, climates seem to have been at least mild and moist, the land areas low-lying, and the seas shallow. This means that there would have been a gradual transition from shallow sea to swampy land.

Moving onto the land was a very big step. In the sea there is an abundant water supply. Plants can take it in over their entire surfaces, and with always-submerged species there is no loss of water by evaporation. At low tide some seaweeds are exposed to the air, but this does not last long, and many keep moist with a covering of mucilage.

The first land plants known from fossils were simple in their organization and had modifications to conserve their more limited water supply—they are still utilized by the much more complex land plants of today. A waxy layer or cuticle covering the exposed plant surfaces largely prevents water loss by evaporation. However, access to essential gases from the air, such as oxygen and carbon dioxide, is still necessary, and this takes place through scattered small pores, or stomata. This inevitably entails some water loss, but if a plant's water content falls to a critical level, the stomata can temporarily close.

The early land plants grew in swamps. Some of their branches were below the swamp surface; others extended up to 0.5 m (19 inches) above it, away from the source of water. This aerial growth was made possible by a plumbing system in the interior of the stems where pipe-like series of empty cells (xylem) conveyed water to the higher parts. It is uncertain whether there were also cells (phloem) that conveyed sugars photosynthesized in sunlight to the stems in the darkness of the swamp. Plants that have the ability to transport water and sugars internally are known as vascular plants. Ferns and related groups that reproduce by spores are the most primitive of the vascular plants, and conifers and flowering plants—reproducing by relatively large, multicellular seeds—the most advanced.

With these modifications, new horizons opened for plants. Within the swamps and on higher, drier terrain there would have been many different unoccupied habitats. This is the type of situation that sets the stage for evolution to speed up. The first small swamp plants gave rise to larger, more complex swamp plants, and also to more drought-tolerant variants that could establish in unoccupied habitats on better-drained slopes. During the Carboniferous period that followed the Devonian, land plants burgeoned, culminating in swamp forests that included trees up to 50 m (160 feet) high that had well-developed though not very extensive water- and sugar-conducting tissues, and thickened outer tissues for support. These trees belonged to two main groups, which on the forest floor were represented by much smaller species. Descendants of the latter still exist today with several of the genera, such as *Lycopodium* (club mosses, page 278), *Selaginella* (spike mosses), and *Equisetum* (horsetails, page 282), widespread and well known.

There were ferns, too, at this time, and seed ferns. Because of their much-divided fronds, fossils of the seed ferns were initially identified as ferns until their seed-like structures were noted. They were mostly like tree ferns in form and possibly ancestral to the cycads. There were few true tree ferns. The earliest conifers also appeared about this time. The dead remains of these forests built up into deep layers of peat that eventually turned to coal, the origin of the name Carboniferous. Carboniferous coal in the northern hemisphere had a considerable influence on the course of human history as it provided the energy for the industrial revolution. The land animals at this time were mostly invertebrates, with a diverse array of insects. There were a few reptile vertebrates, but they played a minor role.

But the earliest, small, vascular plants of the Devonian were unlikely to have been the first land plants as they were already extensively modified for life on land. Because of the similarity of pigments, the first land colonizers would have been derived from the green algae of the sea and may have included flat, sheet-like forms like some green algae, or tufts of branching filaments like others. These would have grown close to the surface of the swamp and been inundated by flooding from time to time. Unfortunately, soft-tissued plants often decay before they can become fossilized, and there is no fossil evidence for the presence of such delicate plants at this time.

However, there are scattered fossils from the Devonian onward of small, soft-tissued plants, some sheet-like and others with stems bearing rows of small leaves, that may be closer to the green algae than to the early vascular plants. Some of these are very similar to the liverworts of today. There are also fossils of small, leafy plants that have been identified as mosses, and some of these, too, are similar to modern forms.

There are many species of liverworts and mosses in the world today, but they are small, low-growing plants and are mostly restricted to shady, wet places. They are not as well adapted as vascular plants to drier conditions. Their waxy cuticles are generally quite thin, and in leafy forms the leaves are often only one cell thick except for a thicker midrib. In these leaves there are no stomata—if they were present, they would be holes right through the leaf, which would serve no purpose. In thicker tissues there are a few cases of stomata or other types of pore that perform the same function of restricting water loss by evaporation. So for the most part, liverworts and mosses absorb water and essential gases all over their surfaces. Some liverworts form a flat sheet of cells, or thallus, pressed close to the ground and absorb water through their undersides, and the more numerous leafy liverworts and the mosses often grow in low cushions or dense

An *Equisetum* with tiered lateral branches.

clumps that retain water like a sponge. A few mosses have erect stems 5–10 cm (2–4 inches) high, sometimes more, and at the center of the stems there are elongate cells that resemble the water- and sugar-conducting cells of vascular plants and may function in a similar way.

Another reason that liverworts and mosses grow in moist places is that, like the algae, they have swimming sperms, so there must be enough water sufficiently often for them to swim to the eggs. Ferns and the related club moss and horsetail groups also have swimming sperms, so they, too, are mostly found in wetter, shady places even though their well-developed conducting systems enabled some of them to become trees in the past. As we shall see, the seed plants overcame this problem and so were able to spread into virtually all land habitats.

By the end of the Paleozoic, during the Permian period, world climates underwent a dramatic change. There was a severe ice age similar to that of recent geological times, extensive deserts developed, and there was much volcanism. There is evidence of high temperatures, too, so perhaps there were wide climatic swings. The species of the swamp forests were not suited to these conditions, and many became extinct. The conifers, which were a minor component of those forests, seemed to have been hardier and moved into the land areas abandoned by the ferns and related groups. They were

The thallus of a liverwort, *Monoclea forsteri*. New Zealand.

able to grow in quite dry sites because conifers do not have swimming sperms. Their pollen grains are carried by wind to the vicinity of eggs, and each grain sends out a pollen tube to convey a sperm to an egg. Extinctions among plants were moderate and gradual. In animals the extinctions were dramatic with 95% of marine species and 70% of all terrestrial families disappearing.

As the climate improved during the following Mesozoic era, the conifers underwent rapid evolution into a diversity of forms and dominated the vegetation of the world. At the same time, reptiles were undergoing what has been termed an "evolution explosion," which led to the most unusual group of animals, the dinosaurs. The Mesozoic is divided into three periods spanning the time from 248 million to 65 million years ago. At the end of the last period, the Cretaceous, there was again a time of widespread extinctions, which has been ascribed to climate change brought about by the Earth's being struck by a large meteorite. The dinosaurs in particular and many conifer groups became extinct. Birds and small mammals originated earlier but had played a minor role. They survived quite well and became dominant and diverse during the following Cenozoic era, which brings us to the present day.

Early flowering plants had appeared before the calamity, too, and many survived, though the reasons for that are not clear. During the Cenozoic they had their turn of rapid evolution and quickly became the overwhelmingly dominant plant group. Today, flowering plants are the most diverse of any of the plant groups, with trees, shrubs, herbs, vines, epiphytes, parasites, and even insectivores. Some of their success may result from their efficient reproduction with greater protection for parts leading to seed formation in the flower, greater protection for seeds in the fruits, and greater effectiveness in pollination and seed dispersal through the use of insects, birds, and other animals as transporters.

The ferns, and perhaps other early plant groups to a lesser extent, underwent a resurgence during the Cenozoic. Some ancient fern groups such as tree ferns (for example, *Cyathea, Dicksonia,* and *Todea*) and king ferns (*Angiopteris* and *Marattia*) survive, but most present-day ferns evolved during the Cenozoic in response to the mild, moist conditions provided by the luxuriant forests of flowering plants. Among invertebrates, insects, too, underwent a great diversification, in part because of their interaction with flowering plants as pollinators.

The early and middle parts of the Cenozoic era were mostly warm and moist, and the land areas of the world would have been largely forest-covered. From about 7 million years ago a cooling trend began that culminated in the Ice Age of the last 2.5 million years. The cooling was accompanied by expansion of deserts and the formation of high mountain ranges in the west in the Americas, in southern Europe, southern Asia, and Australasia. With the climatic deterioration, forests gradually disappeared in some areas because of decreasing temperature or rainfall, though tropical rain forests have probably not been greatly affected. We consider some examples of plant adaptations to these changes.

Australia is now a largely dry continent, but until the climatic cooling it was mostly forest-covered even in the now driest central parts. With greater aridity, closed-canopy forests gradually contracted and new, open habitats came into existence, with few plants able to occupy them. This led to a great burst of speciation, or adaptive radiation, of certain genera that had been playing a minor role in locally dry and infertile sites. The outstanding example is *Eucalyptus*, whose species, often with attractively patterned trunks and colorful flowers, are the backdrop to every Australian scene except in the driest places. There are about 500 species of *Eucalyptus*, with newly discerned ones added from time to time. Other members of the family Myrtaceae are also prominent, including the bottlebrushes (*Callistemon* and *Melaleuca*) and many other genera. The wattles (*Acacia*) have numbers of species comparable to *Eucalyptus*, and some of them can grow in the driest places. Among other families, the southern family Proteaceae is represented by *Banksia* and other genera.

Colder temperatures led to increasingly severe winters in temperate and polar regions, particularly in the extensive land areas of the northern hemisphere. The commonest adaptation to this climate pattern was for plants to become inactive in winter. Many flowering trees and shrubs, including oaks (*Quercus*), beeches (*Fagus*), and birches (*Betula*), became deciduous or had done so earlier at high latitudes in warmer times, losing their leaves before winter and protecting the growing points of their branches with overlapping scales. At even colder latitudes, species-poor forests were dominated by hardy conifers tolerant of cold, infertile soils. The conifers had small needle-like or scaly leaves and were mostly evergreen. In more open places, or in the forest understory, herbaceous plants evolved that died before the onset of winter, surviving as seeds in the soil (annuals) or dying down to soil level to regrow from food-storing bulbs, corms, or rhizomes in spring (herbaceous perennials). During the Ice Age there has been a succession of glacials alternating with warmer interglacials. During the glacials, ice sheets often extended southward, eliminating vegetation, which was replaced when the ice retreated.

Another situation in which unoccupied habitats come into existence is when volcanic islands rise above the sea at some distance from existing land. When the lava has cooled, habitats become available for plants, but the only way they can get there is by their seeds or spores crossing the often wide, ocean gaps from vegetated lands. Some plant groups have a better chance of doing this than others. Ferns, mosses, and liverworts, with their microscopic spores, can achieve it easily, and ferns in particular are well represented on moist, isolated islands. Seashore plants in the tropics, with floating seeds or fruits, are also long-distance travelers, which is why the same seashore species are found on just about every shore in the tropical Pacific. Plants with berries that are carried internally or seeds that attach externally to birds, and small seeds carried by wind, make the journey less often, but given enough time they can get there. At the other end of the scale, conifers and some flowering trees that have rather large, dry seeds or fruits are not found on isolated islands. As far as animals are concerned, those that fly, such as birds and insects, are well represented and often make the journey by being swept along by gales or hurricanes. There would have to be pretty powerful winds to carry in nonflying mammals, so until our species arrived on the scene, there were no mammals on isolated islands.

The most famous of the isolated oceanic islands are the Galápagos Islands, situated on the equator almost 1,000 km (600 miles) west of Ecuador. It was from his observations here in 1835 that Charles Darwin was led to formulate the theory of evolution by natural selection. Because of the cold Humboldt Current, temperatures and rainfall are not as high as might be expected. At lower elevations it is quite dry, with tree-like cacti (*Jasminocereus* and several species of *Opuntia*) prominent, but higher in the mountains there is dense cloud forest. Animals of special interest for evolution are finches, commonly known as Darwin's finches:

> The diversity of beak structure and feeding habits within this group is remarkable. The individual species feed in a variety of ways with each specialized in a particular way. Some eat seeds, some eat insects, some remove ticks from tortoises, some eat leaves, some eat flowers, some drink blood from seabirds, and there are two species that use twigs or cactus spines to extract insect larvae from holes in the dead branches of trees. Together, they fill the roles of seven different families of South American mainland birds. (Jackson 1985)

The colonizing finches would have come from South America and, like finches in general, would have mostly fed on seeds and at times on small invertebrates. If there were few or no other land birds, there would have been other types of food available that were not being utilized. In these circumstances, variants within the initial finch population, with different sizes and shapes of beaks enabling them to utilize foods other than seeds, would be able to adopt different lifestyles without competition. On their continent of origin such variants could also arise, but they would have to compete with other kinds of birds even better adapted to particular types of food.

The volcanic Hawaiian Islands are larger, higher, and even more isolated than the Galápagos. They are about 3,300 km (2,100 miles) from North America and about 7,000 km (4,400 miles) from Asia and Australia. The current larger islands in the group have formed over the past several million years, but there are eroded remains of other islands, the oldest of which may be 27 million years old. So there has been a long period of time for plants and animals to cross the very wide gaps, and a number have, though still with the exceptions of mammals and conifers. About 1,000 species of native flowering plants are in Hawaii, more than 90% of which are found nowhere else. It has been estimated that this flora has been derived by adaptive radiation from 272 colonizing species (Sohmer and Gustafson 1987).

A good example of adaptive radiation is a group of genera in Hawaii belonging to the daisy family (Asteraceae) that are related to the tarweeds of California and Mexico. The original tarweed colonist has radiated into species that are found in almost all habitats in Hawaii, from the lowlands to the mountains. Some species are prostrate in growth, others are shrubby, and some are small trees. The most spectacular species is the silversword (*Argyroxiphium sandwicense*) with its large, rounded tufts of narrow, silvery leaves and its huge, dense heads of red flowers.

Another example involves several genera of the bellflower and *Lobelia* family (Campanulaceae). The species are herbs to unbranched trees with terminal tufts of long, narrow leaves. The unusually long flowers are white to purple, and curved and tubular. They are pollinated by a number of species of birds known as honeycreepers, whose beaks are long and curved, matching the flowers they visit. Unfortunately, a number of the plants and birds have become rare or extinct since human arrival.

A final example is the genus *Metrosideros*, whose species and varieties in Hawaii are widespread from low to high elevations. Many are notable as early colonizers of lava flows, and their often bright red, long-stamened flowers are a striking sight. Once again, there is a wide range in growth form, from trees up to 25 m (82 feet) tall to rounded cushions in alpine bogs. The genus is also represented on many other high volcanic islands in the Pacific as well as having a strong representation on the continental-type islands of New Zealand and New Caledonia. DNA studies show that the *Metrosideros* species of French Polynesia and Hawaii are either identical, for the chromosome sites ana-

A Hawaiian *Trematolobelia* with a slender trunk and terminal clusters of flowers.

lyzed, to the New Zealand *M. excelsa* or are very close to it (Wright et al. 2000). *Metrosideros excelsa* is found along the northern coasts of New Zealand and is also a lava colonizer. In Hawaii, some of the trees on lava flows look very similar to *M. excelsa*, but other species differ considerably in leaf form, flowers, and growth habit. The seeds in *Metrosideros* capsules are small, thread-like, and probably wind-dispersed. It is suggested that seeds of *M. excelsa* reached French Polynesia during a glacial period of the Ice Age when the west-wind belt would have moved closer to the equator. It is speculated that seeds from French Polynesia could have been carried across the equator to Hawaii by rising equatorial air currents that descend at about the latitude of Hawaii. Adaptive radiation has taken place in French Polynesia as well as in Hawaii.

Natural hybridization between species and varieties of several genera in Hawaii is quite common, which might suggest that although adaptive radiation has resulted in considerable morphological and ecological differences, the species concerned remain genetically quite similar. Adaptive radiation has also occurred on isolated islands of a

The long-stamened flowers of *Metrosideros excelsa*.

different type. This is where mountains have arisen, either by crustal folding or volcanism, in forested regions. If the mountains are high enough, the upper parts are too cold for trees and new habitats come into existence. This has happened in New Zealand (Dawson 1988), which is separated from its nearest neighbor, Australia, by the Tasman Sea, 1,600 km (990 miles) wide. DNA studies show that some alpine genera in New Zealand, with many diverse species, are probably derived from a single immigrant species. An example is the horticulturally well-known genus *Hebe* (Plantaginaceae) with about 100 species ranging from small shrubs to small trees. It is suggested that "the New Zealand hebes are descendants of a small founder population that may have been derived from a single seed" (Wagstaff et al. 2002). The oldest *Hebe* fossils in New Zealand are pre–Ice Age, about 4 million years old, when alpine habitats were developing. The most primitive species now are above tree line, and the more advanced, larger species are mostly in open lowland habitats. Other alpine species belong to forest genera, for example *Coprosma* (Rubiaceae), which is also quite well represented in Hawaii. The ancestors of these alpine species did not have to arrive by long-distance dispersal—they were already present in the New Zealand forests.

As in Hawaii, natural hybridization is quite frequent in New Zealand. Populations of natural hybrids are even more variable than populations of species that can only outcross, and it has been suggested that natural hybrids play an important role in the occupying of new, isolated habitats and in the evolution of new species (Rattenbury 1962, Arnold 1997).

Our human species has appeared at one of those widely separated times in the Earth's history when the climate fluctuates wildly and the land is unstable. It would have been more comfortable to have appeared in one of the longer, more stable and more genial periods, but perhaps the present is more interesting and challenging, giving us the best opportunity to understand what life, in all its forms, is about. The currently dominant forms of life—mammals, birds, fishes, insects, and flowering plants—seem to be coping with the difficult times quite well, and in fact they may suffer more from our depredations than from the vagaries of nature.

Glossary

♦ ♦ ♦

achene Small dry fruit that functions as a seed. It contains a single seed that is not released.

algae (singular, alga; adjective, algal) Mostly aquatic, oldest, and most primitive plant group, comprising diverse but mostly unspecialized growth forms.

anther See stamen.

apomixis (adjective, apomictic) Development of a seed from a cell that has not fused with a sperm.

aril Edible fleshy outgrowth from the base of a seed that partly encloses it.

berry Fleshy fruit containing one or more seeds.

cambium (adjective, cambial) Thin layer of delicate cells between the conducting tissues, xylem and phloem, in stems and roots, which divides seasonally or year-round to form new xylem to the inside and new phloem to the outside. Another cambium renews the cork layer of woody plants.

capsule Dry fruit derived from two or more fused ovaries that usually splits open at maturity to release the seeds.

carpel Appendage(s) at the center of a flower bearing the ovules, which when fertilized develop into seeds. A carpel is more or less leaf-like, and as it develops it folds along its midrib so that its two margins meet and fuse, resulting in an enclosed space or ovary that protects the ovules. There is often a stalk or style extending from the tip of an ovary, ending in a usually sticky stigma, that receives the pollen from the same or another flower. Pollen tubes grow down the style to the ovules to bring about fertilization.

cauliflory Production of flowers on the trunks and more slender stems of some woody plants, especially in the tropics.

chlorophyll Complex molecule, mostly in the leaves of plants, that is able to capture the energy of sunlight, which the plant uses to combine water and carbon dioxide to form sugars.

chromosomes Mostly rod-like structures within cell nuclei. Each species has a certain number of them per nucleus, from two to hundreds, and a certain range of sizes and shapes. Chromosomes are in matching pairs, one of each pair from the male parent, the other from the female. Chromosomes are composed of coiled, very long DNA molecules, which control cell functions and development.

column Generally referring to a structure at the center of orchid flowers that is a fusion of a single functional stamen and a style and stigma. The column plays an important role in orchid cross-pollination mechanisms.

cone A cone has an elongated axis to which are attached many crowded, scaly or woody appendages that bear reproductive organs. In *Equisetum, Lycopodium,* and related genera, these organs produce microscopic, single-celled spores, and in the cone-bearing seed plants there are both pollen cones and seed cones.

conifer (adjective, coniferous) Largest group of cone-bearing seed plants, with mostly needle or scale leaves.

cork Outermost stem and root layer of trees, shrubs, and woody vines, made up of dead cells with thick, flexible walls. Cork insulates and protects the inner living tissues, and it is renewed by a cork cambium.

cross-pollination When pollen of one plant is transported to flowers or ovule cones of a different plant of the same species with resulting cross-fertilization.

cuticle Waxy film covering most leaf and young stem surfaces to reduce water loss by evaporation.

cycad Ancient group of cone-bearing seed plants with stout, unbranched or little-branched trunks, and large, divided, fern-like leaves.

dicotyledons (dicots) Largest subgroup of flowering plants, with embryos with two seed leaves, broad, net-veined leaves, and flowers with their parts mostly in fives or sometimes in fours.

dioecy (adjective, dioecious) Pattern in which some plants of a species have male flowers, producing only pollen, and other plants have female flowers, producing only ovules.

DNA See chromosomes.

domatia Flask- to pouch-like cavities on the undersides of leaves of some species, where the secondary veins meet the midrib and sometimes where higher-order veins meet as well.

drupe Fleshy fruit in which the innermost part of the ovary wall becomes hard, forming a stone, within which is a single seed or kernel.

egg Female sex cell that, when it fuses with a male sperm, develops into an embryo.

epicormic buds Dormant buds of some trees that are subjected to periodic fires. The buds are insulated in a layer of cork, but the heat of a fire breaks their dormancy, and they then replace the foliage killed by the fire.

epiphyte Herbaceous and woody plants whose seeds or spores germinate in tree crowns or on tree trunks. Some of the woody epiphytes, the hemi-epiphytes, eventually send roots down to the ground.

extrafloral nectaries Found on the leaves or twigs of some woody plants, diverting ants in particular from taking nectar from flowers that they are too small to pollinate. They also attract stinging ants that attack any animals that try to browse on the foliage of the host.

ferns Vascular plants reproducing by spores, with often large, much-divided leaves (fronds) that are spirally coiled when young.

flower Compact reproductive shoot of the flowering plants, with an outer circle of sepals, usually green, that protect the inner parts of the flower in the bud; within that a circle of often brightly colored petals to attract pollinators (when there is no obvious distinction between sepals and petals, they are collectively called tepals); then few to many stamens that produce pollen; and at the center, one or more carpels containing ovules.

follicle Dry fruit derived from a single carpel. The margins of the follicle, which met and fused during the development of the carpel, split apart again to release the seeds; generally considered to be the most primitive fruit.

gene Segment of a chromosome's DNA that controls a particular aspect of a cell's functions, alone or in combination with other genes.

geophytes Herbaceous plants whose aboveground parts die down during an unfavorable dry or cold season to underground water- and food-storage organs. During the favorable season, the latter sprout new leaves and flowers.

Gnetales Small and unusual group of cone-bearing seed plants that differ considerably from each other as well as from the conifers and cycads in a number of ways.

gynodioecy (adjective, gynodioecious) Pattern in which some plants of a species have female flowers and others have hermaphroditic flowers.

haustorium (plural, haustoria) Specialized outgrowth from a parasitic plant that draws water and nutrients from a host plant. Parasitic fungi also have small haustoria.

hemi-epiphyte See epiphyte.

hemiparasite Parasitic plant, such as a mistletoe, that has green leaves and is able to manufacture some of its own food by photosynthesis.

holoparasite Parasitic plant without chlorophyll, completely dependent on its host for food and water.

inflorescence A connected group of flowers.

invertebrates Insects and other groups of mostly small animals that do not have an internal skeleton.

juvenile form A sometimes prolonged state of young plants of some species in which the leaves and sometimes the stems differ markedly from those of the adult.

labellum Lowermost petal of an orchid flower that is modified as a landing stage for a pollinating insect. Similar petals can be found in other flowering plant families.

liane (also spelled liana) Woody vine, mostly of tropical forests.

lichens Organisms that are combinations of a fungus and many cells of a unicellular alga or blue-green bacterium.

lignotuber Large woody tuber at and below ground level formed by some trees of fire-prone habitats. If the trunks and branches of such trees are destroyed by fire, new growth develops from epicormic buds in the lignotubers.

liverworts Nonvascular plants reproducing by spores, with a body comprising flat sheets of cells, or stems with small leaves, and sporangia that open by longitudinal splitting.

mistletoes Parasitic plants of tree and shrub branches that have green leaves and so are able to provide some of their own food requirements.

monocotyledons (monocots) Smaller of the two subgroups of flowering plants, with embryos with one seed leaf, mostly long, narrow, parallel-veined leaves, and flowers with their parts in threes.

monoecy (adjective, monoecious) Pattern in which a species has male and female flowers or cones on the same plant.

mosses Nonvascular plants reproducing by spores, with stems and small leaves, and sporangia that open by terminal lids.

mycorrhiza (plural, mycorrhizas or mycorrhizae) Association between the roots of many plants and fungi. The fungi get sugars from the plants, and the plants get water and mineral nutrients from the fungi.

mycotroph (adjective, mycotrophic) Type of small plant parasite, generally growing in forest litter, that lacks chlorophyll and is connected to tree roots by fungal filaments. The mycotroph steals some of the sugars the fungus has obtained from the trees.

nectary Structure in a flower, and sometimes elsewhere (see extrafloral nectaries), that produces a sweet fluid known as nectar as an attractant to pollinators.

nitrogen-fixing bacteria Although they require nitrogen, plants are unable to utilize it directly from the air. It has to be combined with oxygen in a molecule known as nitrate. Some bacteria, including the blue-greens, are able to make nitrates, either where they live in the soil or within plant tissues, to the benefit of the plants.

oil bodies Appendages of some seeds that contain oil and are used as food by ants; also called elaiosomes.

parasitic plants Plants that are partly or completely dependent on other plants for their food and water.

petal See flower.

pheromones Odors produced by females of some insect species to attract males. The flowers of some plants produce similar odors, and the male insects attracted bring about pollination of the flowers when they attempt to copulate with them (pseudo-copulation).

phloem Conducting tissue that conveys sugars manufactured in the leaves by photosynthesis to all parts of the plant. Phloem cells are living at maturity, are vertically elongate, and joined end to end in continuous files. The transverse cross walls are perforated like a sieve, and strands of protoplasm pass through the perforations.

photosynthesis Process whereby the green parts of plants use the energy of sunlight trapped by chlorophyll to combine water from the roots with carbon dioxide from the air to make sugars, with oxygen as a by-product. There are several patterns of photosynthesis. The commonest is known as C_3 and is utilized by the majority of plants that grow where temperatures are moderate and rainfall is reliable. At high temperatures this method ceases to function and the relatively few plants that can survive under such conditions utilize the C$_4$ method. The CAM method is used by mostly succulent plants of arid habitats—the stomata are open at night to take in carbon dioxide when water loss by evaporation is at a minimum, and the carbon dioxide is used in photosynthesis during the heat of the day with the stomata firmly closed.

pollen Pollen grains of flowering and cone-bearing seed plants form pollen tubes to reach the ovules of the same or different plants of their species. The nucleus of each pollen grain divides to form two sperms that fuse with eggs in the ovules. The cell resulting from the fusion of a sperm and an egg is the first cell of a new plant.

pollination See cross- and self-pollination.

pollinia (singular, pollinium) Pollen grains that cohere in sticky clumps and are transported as a group. Orchids are best known for this, but it occurs in other families.

prickle Sharp-pointed outgrowths from the leaf and stem surfaces of some plants.

pseudobulb Swollen, water-storing bases of the leaves of some orchids.

pseudocopulation See under pheromones.

pseudotrunk Coalesced roots, connecting to the ground, of a tree that began life as an epiphyte on another tree.

respiration Reverse of the process of photosynthesis. Using oxygen, plants and animals break up sugar molecules to release the life-enabling energy captured by photosynthesis. The by-products are water and carbon dioxide.

resurrection plants Small plants of arid habitats that shrivel up during drought and quickly revive when it rains.

rhizome Stem growing parallel to the substrate, on the surface or often just below it.

saprophytes Some fungi and flowering plants that lack chlorophyll and gain their energy by breaking down organic compounds in dead plant litter on the forest floor. Some flowering plants formerly considered saprophytes are now classified as mycotrophs, that is, indirect parasites on tree roots via fungal filaments.

sclerophyll Type of leaf borne by many plants of arid habitats, usually small, thick, and tough in texture, with a thick cuticle and other modifications to reduce water loss.

seed Reproductive unit of the flowering and cone-bearing seed plants. A seed is multicellular and sometimes quite large, and develops from a fertilized ovule. The seed contains an embryonic plant and usually food reserves.

seed bank When seeds build up in the soil or in unopened dry fruits or cones, sometimes over a number of years. Often the seeds are in a state of dormancy, which is broken by the heat of fire or by a good rainfall in the case of desert plants. The dry fruits or cones generally open with high temperatures, particularly when there is a fire.

self-incompatibility Where the pollen of a plant is chemically inhibited from forming pollen tubes on the stigmas of the same plant.

self-pollination When pollen tubes of a plant reach the ovules of the same plant, resulting in self-fertilization.

sepal See flower.

serpentine soils Soils derived from alkaline ultramafic rocks which contain toxic metals such as nickel and chrome. Some plants have evolved that can tolerate the toxicity of such soils.

sperm See under egg.

spine Often long, hard, sharply pointed process, modified from entire leaves or from their marginal teeth.

sporangium (plural, sporangia) Rounded organs with hollow interiors containing spores.

spore Single-celled, microscopic, reproductive unit of nonseed plants.

stamen Appendage in flowers that consists of a stalk or filament, bearing at its tip an anther with cavities containing pollen grains.

stigma See carpel.

stolon Often arching stem above the ground that forms a new plant where it touches the ground and often gives rise to another stolon.

stomata Microscopic pores, mostly on the undersides of leaves, through which oxygen and carbon dioxide enter and water vapor is lost. The stomata (singular, stoma) are able to reduce in size or even close if water loss is excessive.

syconium (plural, syconia) Distinctive hollow inflorescence of the fig family (Moraceae) in which the hollow interior is lined with many small flowers.

tendril Slender, touch-sensitive structure, modified from various plant parts, that twines around slender supports.

tepal See flower.

thorn Short, sharply pointed, modified branchlet.

ultramafic rocks See serpentine soils.

vascular plants Plants with water-conducting xylem and sugar-conducting phloem.

velamen Outer layer of aerial roots of orchids that is made up of dead, water-absorbent cells.

vertebrates Mostly larger animals with internal skeletons.

vessel Dead, hard, narrow, water-conducting cells joined end to end. The end walls are perforated so the vessel acts like a pipe.

xylem Water-conducting tissue (see vessel) of vascular plants.

References

♦♦♦

Arnold, M. 1997. *Natural Hybridization and Evolution.* Oxford University Press.

Attenborough, D. 1995. *The Private Life of Plants.* BBC Books, London, and Princeton University Press.

Benzing, D. H. 1989. The evolution of epiphytes. Chapter 2 in U. Lüttge (editor), *Vascular Plants as Epiphytes: Evolution and Ecophysiology.* Springer-Verlag, Berlin.

Benzing, D. H. 1990. *Vascular Epiphytes: General Biology and Related Biota.* Cambridge University Press.

Bisset, K. A. 1970. *The Cytology and Life History of Bacteria.* 3rd ed. Livingstone, Edinburgh.

Bjorkman, E. 1960. *Monotropa hypopitys* L. An epiparasite on tree roots. *Physiologia Plantarum* 13: 308–327.

Bond, W. J., and B. W. van Wilgen. 1996. *Fire and Plants.* Chapman and Hall, London.

Brooks, R. R. 1987. *Serpentine and Its Vegetation.* Dioscorides Press, Portland, Oregon.

Carlile, M. J., and S. C. Watkinson. 1994. *The Fungi.* Academic Press, London.

Chapman, R. F. 1976. *A Biology of Locusts.* Edward Arnold, London.

Cole, M. M. 1986. *The Savannas: Biogeography and Geobotany.* Academic Press, London.

Crawley, M. J. 1983. *Herbivory: The Dynamics of Animal–Plant Interactions.* University of California Press, Berkeley.

Dallman, P. R. 1998. *Plant Life in the World's Mediterranean Climates.* Oxford University Press, and University of California Press, Berkeley.

Darrow, H. E., P. Bannister, and D. J. Burritt. 2002. Are juvenile forms of New Zealand heteroblastic trees more resistant to water loss than their mature counterparts? *New Zealand Journal of Botany* 40: 313–325.

Dawson, J. W. 1988. *Forest Vines to Snow Tussocks: The Story of New Zealand Plants.* Victoria University Press, Wellington.

Dawson, J. W., and R. Lucas. 1993. *Lifestyles of New Zealand Forest Plants.* Victoria University Press, Wellington.

Dawson, J. W., and R. Lucas. 1996. *New Zealand Coast and Mountain Plants—Their Communities and Lifestyles.* Victoria University Press, Wellington.

Dawson, J. W., and R. Lucas. 2000. *Nature Guide to the New Zealand Forest.* Random House New Zealand, Auckland.

Estrada, A., and T. H. Fleming (editors). 1986. *Frugivores and Seed Dispersal.* Junk, Dordrecht.

Evenari, M., I. Noy-Meir, and D. W. Goodall (editors). 1985–1986. *Ecosystems of the World 12A–B: Hot Deserts and Arid Shrublands.* Elsevier, Amsterdam.

Eyre, S. R. 1968. *Vegetation and Soils: A World Picture.* 2nd ed. Edward Arnold, London.

Friedmann, F., and T. Cadet. 1976. Observations sur l'heterophyllie sur les Iles Mascareignes. *Adansonia,* sér. 2, 15: 423–440.

Gill, A. M., R. H. Groves, and I. R. Noble (editors). 1981. *Fire and the Australian Biota.* Australian Academy of Science, Canberra.

Greenwood, R. M., and I. A. E. Atkinson. 1977. Evolution of the divaricating plants of New Zealand in relation to moa browsing. *Proceedings, New Zealand Ecological Society* 24: 21–33.

Hogarth, P. J. 1999. *The Biology of Mangroves.* Oxford University Press.

Howe, H. F., and L. C. Westley. 1988. *Ecological Relationships of Plants and Animals.* Oxford University Press.

Huxley, C. R., and D. F. Cutler (editors). 1991. *Ant–Plant Interactions.* Oxford University Press.

Jackson, M. H. 1985. *Galapagos: A Natural History Guide.* University of Calgary Press.

Jones, D. L. *Cycads of the World.* 1993. Reed, Chatswood, New South Wales, Australia.

Juniper, B. E., R. J. Robins, and D. M. Joel. 1989. *The Carnivorous Plants.* Academic Press, London.

Kopke, E., L. J. Musselman, and D. J. de Laubenfels. 1981. Studies on the anatomy of *Parasitaxus ustus* and its root connections. *Phytomorphology* 31: 85–92.

Kuijt, J. 1969. *The Biology of Parasitic Flowering Plants.* University of California Press, Berkeley.

Levine, A. J. 1992. *Viruses.* Scientific American Library, New York.

Lloyd, D. G., and C. J. Webb. 1986. The avoidance of interference between the presentation of pollen and stigmas in angiosperms. 1. Dichogamy. *New Zealand Journal of Botany* 24: 135–162.

Lucas, R. 1998. *What's That Pest?* 2nd ed. Open Polytechnic of New Zealand, Lower Hutt.

McGlone, M. S., and C. J. Webb. 1981. Selective forces influencing the evolution of divaricating plants. *New Zealand Journal of Ecology* 4: 20–28.

Macmillan, B. H. 1973. Biological flora of New Zealand 7. *Ripogonum scandens* J. R. et G. Forst. (Smilacaceae). Supplejack, kareao. *New Zealand Journal of Botany* 10: 641–672.

Nais, J. 2001. *Rafflesia of the World.* Sabah Parks, Kota Kinabalu, Sabah.

O'Dowd, D. J., and R. W. Pemberton. 1998. Leaf domatia and foliar mite abundance in broadleaf deciduous forest in north Asia. *American Journal of Botany* 85: 70–78.

Page, C. N., and P. J. Brownsey. 1986. Tree-fern skirts: A defense against climbers and large epiphytes. *Journal of Ecology* 74: 787–796.

Pemberton, R. W., and C. E. Turner. 1989. Occurrence of predatory and fungivorous mites in leaf domatia. *American Journal of Botany* 76: 105–112.

Prance, G. T., and T. F. Lovejoy (editors). 1985. *Key Environments: Amazonia.* Pergamon, New York.

Proctor, M., P. Yeo, and A. Lack. 1996. *The Natural History of Pollination.* HarperCollins, London, and Timber Press, Portland, Oregon.

Purvis, W. 2000. *Lichens.* Natural History Museum, London.

Putz, F. E., and H. A. Mooney (editors). 1991. *The Biology of Vines.* Cambridge University Press.

Rattenbury, J. A. 1962. Cyclic hybridisation as a survival mechanism in the New Zealand forest flora. *New Zealand Journal of Botany* 16: 348–363.

Rauh, W. 1986. The arid region of Madagascar. Chapter 9 in M. I. Evenari et al. (editors), *Ecosystems of the World 12B: Hot Deserts and Arid Shrublands.* Elsevier, Amsterdam.

Reimold, R. J., and W. H. Queen (editors). 1974. *Ecology of Halophytes.* Academic Press, New York.

Ridley, H. N. 1930. *The Dispersal of Plants Throughout the World.* L. Reeve and Co., Ashford, Kent, England.

Rundel, P. W., A. P. Smith, and F. C. Meinzer (editors). 1994. *Tropical Alpine Environments: Plant Form and Function.* Cambridge University Press.

Sculthorpe, C. D. 1967. *The Biology of Aquatic Vascular Plants.* Edward Arnold, London.

Sohmer, S. H., and R. Gustafson. 1987. *Plants and Flowers of Hawaii.* University of Hawaii Press, Honolulu.

Turner, I. M. 2001. *The Ecology of Trees in the Tropical Rain Forest.* Cambridge University Press.

van der Pijl, L. 1982. *Principles of Dispersal in Higher Plants.* 3rd ed. Springer-Verlag, Berlin.

van Steenis, C. G. G. J. 1981. *Rheophytes of the World.* Sijthoff & Noordhoff, Alphen aan den Rijn, Netherlands.

Wagstaff, S. J., M. J. Bayly, P. J. Garnock-Jones, and D. C. Albach. 2002. Classification, origin, and diversification of the New Zealand hebes (Scrophulariaceae). *Annals of the Missouri Botanical Garden* 89: 38–63.

Wardle, P. 1963. Evolution of the New Zealand flora as affected by Quaternary climates. *New Zealand Journal of Botany* 1: 3–17.

Werger, M. J. A. (editor). 1978. *Biogeography and Ecology of Southern Africa,* Volume 1. Junk, The Hague.

West, N. E. (editor). 1983. *Ecosystems of the World 5: Temperate Deserts and Semi-Deserts.* Elsevier, Amsterdam.

Whitaker, A. H. 1987. The role of lizards in New Zealand plant reproductive strategies. *New Zealand Journal of Botany* 25: 315–328.

Wielgolaski, F. E. (editor). 1997. *Ecosystems of the World 3: Polar and Alpine Tundra.* Elsevier, Amsterdam.

Wright, S. D., C. G. Yong, J. W. Dawson, D. J. Whittaker, and R. C. Gardner. 2000. Riding the Ice Age El Niño? Pacific biogeography and evolution of *Metrosideros* subg. *Metrosideros* (Myrtaceae) inferred from nuclear ribosomal DNA. *Proceedings of the National Academy of Sciences U.S.A.* 97: 4118–4123.

Zwinger, A. H., and B. E. Willard. 1972. *Land Above the Trees: A Guide to American Alpine Tundra.* University of Arizona Press, Tucson.

Index

♦♦♦

Caladenia flava, 117
Calamus muelleri, 18
Calceolaria, 113
Calceolariaceae, see Calceolaria
Callistemon, 116, 136, 285
Callitris, 117, 135
Calocedrus decurrens, 147
Calochortus kennedyi, 87
Caltha, 193
Caltha obtusa, see Psychrophila obtusa
Calycanthaceae, see Calycanthus
Calycanthus, 236
Calycoseris wrightii, 87
Calycotome villosa, 109
Campanulaceae, 287; see also Lobelia, Trematolobelia
Caprifoliaceae, see Lonicera
Carduus, 198
Carex, 196, 232, 254
Carex secta, 4–5
Carnegiea gigantea, 90, 242
carrot family, see Apiaceae
Caryophyllaceae, see Cerastium, Colobanthus, Silene
Cassytha, 59, 60
Cassytha filiformis, 59
Castilleja, 58, 59
Castilleja angustifolia, 58
Casuarina, 117
Casuarinaceae, 136, 148; see also Casuarina, Gymnostoma
Catalpa family, see Bignoniaceae
catclaw, see Acacia greggii
cat's-paws, see Anigozanthos
cattail, see Typha
Ceanothus, 110, 134
cedar, incense, see Calocedrus decurrens
cedar, Port Orford, see Chamaecyparis lawsoniana
cedar of Lebanon, see Cedrus libani
Cedrus libani, 109
Cerastium, 146
Ceratophyllaceae, see Ceratophyllum
Ceratophyllum, 162

Ceratopteris, 168
Cercidium, 84–85
Cercidium floridum, 86, 90
Chaenomeles japonica, 211
Chamaecyparis lawsoniana, 146
chamise, see Adenostoma fasciculatum
cheese bush, see Hymenoclea salsola
Cheilanthes parryi, 86
Chenopodiaceae, 106, 117, 151, 153; see also Salicornia, Sarcocornia
chestnut, water, see Trapa natans
chickweed, mouse-ear, see Cerastium
Chilopsis linearis, 85, 86
Chionochloa, 186–187
Chlamydophytum, 57
cholla, see Cylindropuntia
Christmas tree, see Nuytsia floribunda
Cistaceae, see Cistus
Cistus, 109, 134
citrus fruit family, see Rutaceae
cleavers, see Galium
Clematis, 15, 110, 257
club moss, see Lycopodium
Clusia, 46
Clusiaceae, see Clusia, Garcinia
Cobaea scandens, 242
coconut palm, see Cocos nucifera
Cocos nucifera, 258
Colensoa physaloides, see Lobelia physaloides
Collospermum, 33, 39–41
Collospermum hastatum, 32, 40, 41
Colobanthus quitensis, 198
columbine, see Aquilegia
Combretaceae, see Combretum, Terminalia
Combretum, 122
Compositae, see Asteraceae
Convolvulaceae, see Convolvulus, Cuscuta
Convolvulus, 15
Coprosma, 28, 46, 289
Coprosma grandifolia, 215
Cordyline, 127
Cordyline australis, 206–207
corpse flower, see Amorphophallus titanum, Monotropa uniflora

Eleocharis sphacelata, 4–5
elm, see *Ulmus*
Elodea, 160, 162
Elodea canadensis, 159
Encephalartos ferox, 218
Entada gigas, 259
Epacridaceae, see Ericaceae
Ephedra, 89, 94, 235
Epilobium, 183, 185, 257
Equisetum, 281, 282
Erica, 109, 114
Erica cerinthoides, 115
Erica sessiliflora, 136
Ericaceae, 46, 62, 114, 116, 132, 148, 183, 196, 197, 271; see also *Arbutus, Arctostaphylos, Dracophyllum, Erica, Monotropa, Rhododendron, Vaccinium*
Eriodendron anfractuosum, 257
Escallonia, 113
Escalloniaceae, see *Escallonia*
Eschscholzia californica, 88
Espeletia, 198, 201
Eucalyptus, 103, 116, 117, 123, 131, 132–133, 136, 208, 285
Eucalyptus macrocarpa, 2
Eucalyptus regnans, 127
Eugenia, 133
Eugenia dysenterica, 122
Eugenia inundata, 177
Euphorbia, 72, 97, 99, 105, 109, 122
Euphorbia dendroides, 109
Euphorbia ingens, 98
Euphorbia pulcherrima, 241
Euphorbiaceae, 98, 212; see also *Euphorbia, Hevea, Mabea*
Euphrasia, 58, 59
eyebright, see *Euphrasia*
Fabaceae, 17, 24, 116, 132, 134, 214, 245, 258, 275–276; see also *Abrus, Acacia, Astragalus, Bauhinia, Brachystegia, Caesalpinia, Calycotome, Cercidium, Cytisus, Entada, Genista, Isoberlinia, Julbernadia, Kennedia, Lupinus, Paraserianthes, Pisum, Prosopis, Ulex*

Fagaceae, see *Fagus, Quercus*
Fagraea, 46
Fagus, 113, 232, 248, 285
Falcatifolium taxoides, 60
fern, filmy, see *Hymenophyllum, Trichomanes*
fern, kidney, see *Trichomanes reniforme*
fern, king, see *Angiopteris, Marattia*
fern, staghorn, see *Platycerium*
fern, tree, see *Cyathea, Dicksonia, Todea*
ferns and fern allies, 41, 43–45, 54, 95, 97, 280–283, 284, 285; see also *Angiopteris, Asplenium, Azolla, Blechnum, Ceratopteris, Cheilanthes, Cyathea, Dicksonia, Drynaria, Equisetum, Hymenophyllum, Isoetes, Lycopodium, Lygodium, Marattia, Microsorum, Platycerium, Psilotum, Pyrrosia, Salvinia, Selaginella, Tmesipteris, Todea, Trichomanes*
Ficus, 46–48, 231–232
Ficus carica, 46
Ficus dammaropsis, 231
fig, see *Ficus*
fig family, see Moraceae
fir, see *Abies*
fir, Douglas, see *Pseudotsuga menziesii*
fireweed, see *Epilobium*
forget-me-not, see *Myosotis*
Fouquieriaceae, see *Fouquieria*
Fouquieria splendens, 85
Fragaria, 223
Freesia, 115
Freycinetia, 26
Fuchsia, 221, 245
fungi, 8–9, 60–62, 224–225, 267–271; see also *Peziza, Puccinia*
Furcraea foetida, 224
Gaiadendron punctatum, 64
Galium, 252
Garcinia mangostana, 251
Gastrodia, 61, 227
Gastrodia cunninghamii, 61, 227
Genista, 109
Gentiana, 183, 185
Gentianaceae, 62; see also *Fagraea, Gentiana*

Isoetes, 160
ivy, see *Hedera helix*
ivy family, see Araliaceae
Jacaranda brasiliana, 122
japonica, see *Chaenomeles japonica*
Jasminocereus, 286
Joshua tree, see *Yucca brevifolia*
Julbernadia, 121
Juncaceae, 158, 244; see also *Juncus*
Juncus, 171
Juncus maritimus, 152–153
juniper, see *Juniperus*
Juniperus, 89, 183
Justicia californica, 74
Kalanchoe, 102, 105
Kalanchoe fedtschenkoi, 223
kangaroo paws, see *Anigozanthos*
kapok, see *Eriodendron anfractuosum*
kelp, bladder, see *Macrocystis*
kelp, bull, see *Durvillea antarctica*
Kennedia coccinea, 140
Kingia, 131, 138
Kingia australis, 130, 139
Kniphofia, 115
Labiatae, see Lamiaceae
Lagarosiphon, 160
Lamiaceae, 109–110, 111; see also *Rosmarinus, Salvia, Thymus, Vitex*
larch, see *Larix*
Larix, 183, 205
Larrea tridentata, 80, 86, 89, 90
Lauraceae, see *Cassytha, Cryptocarya, Laurus, Umbellularia*
laurel, see *Laurus nobilis*
laurel, California, see *Umbellularia californica*
laurel family, see Lauraceae
Laurus nobilis, 110, 113
Lavandula, 109
lavender, see *Lavandula*
Lecythidaceae, see *Bertholletia*
legume family, see Fabaceae
Leguminosae, see Fabaceae
Lemaireocereus euphorbioides, see *Neobuxbaumia euphorbioides*

Lemna, 159, 169
Lemnaceae, see Araceae
Lentibulariaceae, see *Utricularia*
Leptinella, 185
Leptinella dendyi, 192
Leptospermum, 116, 136
lettuce, sea, see *Ulva*
Leucadendron, 114, 136, 138
Leucanthemum vulgare, 237
Leucospermum, 114
lichens, 30, 44–45, 87, 95, 188, 196, 197, 198, 201, 272–274; see also *Pseudocyphellaria, Sticta*
Lignocarpa carnosula, 192
lilac, California, see *Ceanothus*
Liliaceae, 98, 138, 235; see also *Calochortus, Tulipa*
lily, desert, see *Hesperocallis undulata*
lily, mariposa, see *Calochortus*
lily, water, see *Nymphaea*
lily family, see Liliaceae
Liquidambar styraciflua, 202
Lithops, 99
Lithraea caustica, 113
liverworts, 30, 281, 283, 285; see also *Monoclea*
Lobelia, 198, 201
Lobelia physaloides, 249
Lobeliaceae, see Campanulaceae
Loganiaceae, see *Fagraea*
Lonicera, 15, 110
Lophocereus, 90
Loranthaceae, 62, 64, 247; see also *Gaiadendron, Nuytsia, Peraxilla, Phrygilanthus*
lotus, see *Nelumbo*
lupin, see *Lupinus*
Lupinus, 198
Lycopodium, 41, 281
Lycopodium scariosum, 278–279
Lycopodium varium, 42
Lygodium, 21
Lythraceae, see *Trapa*
Mabea occidentalis, 244
Macrocystis, 158

Magnolia, 235

Magnoliaceae, 235, 236, 245; see also *Magnolia*

mallee, see *Eucalyptus*

Malus, 209

Malvaceae, see *Adansonia, Durio, Eriodendron, Gossypium, Pseudobombax*

Mangifera, 250

mango, see *Mangifera*

mangosteen, see *Garcinia mangostana*

mangrove, see *Rhizophora*

manzanita, see *Arctostaphylos*

maple, see *Acer*

Marattia, 284

marigold, desert, see *Baileya pauciradiata*

Martyniaceae, see Pedaliaceae

Medinilla, 46

Melaleuca, 116, 117, 132, 133, 285

Melanthiaceae, see *Trillium*

Melastomataceae, 46; see also *Blakea, Medinilla, Miconia*

Mesembryanthemum, 115, 151

mesquite, see *Prosopis*

Metrosideros, 46, 48, 287–288

Metrosideros excelsa, 288

Metrosideros fulgens, 21, 25

Metrosideros perforata, 16, 26

Metrosideros robusta, 32, 49, 50–51

Miconia, 46

Microsorum scandens, 25, 26

milfoil, water, see *Myriophyllum*

milk vetch, see *Astragalus*

milkweed family, see Apocynaceae

mint family, see Lamiaceae

mistletoes, see Loranthaceae, Santalaceae

Mitrastemon, 56

Monoclea forsteri, 283

Monotropa hypopitys, 61–62

Monotropa uniflora, 60–61

Monstera, 24, 26

Moraceae, 24; see also *Ficus*

morning glory, see *Convolvulus*

morning glory family, see Convolvulaceae

moss, peat, see *Sphagnum*

moss, Spanish, see *Tillandsia usneoides*

moss, spike, see *Selaginella*

mosses, 30, 44–45, 196, 197, 198, 281, 283, 285

mule-grab, see *Proboscidea fragrans*

mulga, see *Acacia aneura*

Musa, 242, 250

Musaceae, see *Musa*

mustard family, see Brassicaceae

Myosotis, 185, 254, 269

Myriophyllum, 160

Myrmecodia, 53

Myrsinaceae, see *Myrsine*

Myrsine divaricata, 27

Myrtaceae, 24, 114, 116, 117, 132, 136, 148, 285; see also *Arillastrum, Callistemon, Eucalyptus, Eugenia, Leptospermum, Melaleuca, Metrosideros, Syzygium, Tristaniopsis, Xanthostemon*

myrtle family, see Myrtaceae

Mystropetalon, 57

Narcissus, 109

nasturtium, see *Tropaeolum*

Nelumbo, 162, 166

Nelumbo nucifera, 164, 165, 166–167

Nelumbonaceae, see *Nelumbo*

Neobuxbaumia euphorbioides, 213

Nepenthaceae, see *Nepenthes*

Nepenthes, 254, 260–262

Nepenthes vieillardii, 261

Nerium, 109

nettle, see *Urtica*

nettle, giant, see *Urtica ferox*

nicker nut, see *Caesalpinia bonduc, Entada gigas*

Niemeyera acuminata, see *Sebertia acuminata*

Nostoc, 95

Nothofagaceae, 148; see also *Nothofagus*

Nothofagus, 71, 113, 150, 183

Nothofagus fusca, 180–181

Nothofagus menziesii, 63, 64, 180–181

Nothofagus solandri var. *cliffortioides*, 180–181

Notholaena parryi, see *Cheilanthes parryi*

Notothlaspi rosulatum, 192